A Law from Eden

Solving the Mystery of Original Sin

MARILYN TAPLIN

JordanRiver
PRESS

Mount Vernon, WA

JORDAN RIVER PRESS
P.O. Box 806
Mt. Vernon, WA 98273 USA

Printed in the United States of America.
Copyright © 2001 by Marilyn Taplin.

First Printing 2001

10 9 8 7 6 5 4 3 2 1

Publisher's Cataloging-in-Publications
(Provided by Quality Books, Inc.)

Taplin, Marilyn.
    A law from Eden : solving the mystery of original sin
/ Marilyn Taplin. -- 1 st ed.
    p. cm.
    Includes index.
    LCCN 00-192542
    ISBN 0-9705191-0-9
        1. Sin, Original--Biblical teaching. 2. Sex--
Religious aspects--Christianity.   I. Title.

    BT720.T37 2001   233'.4
                               QBI01-700019

Editors: Michael Barrett, Teddy Kempster
Cover and interior design by Lightbourne

Cover painting: by Benjamin West. Detail of *The Expulsion of Adam and Eve from
Paradise*, Avalon Fund and Patrons' Permanent Fund, © 2000 Board of Trustees,
National Gallery of Art, Washington, 1791, oil on canvas.

Scripture quotations are from the King James Bible, copyright 1945 by
J.D.W. Company, and the King James Bible, published by the World
Publishing Company.

Contents

SECTION FOUR
Spiritual Eyesight

Preface

ॐ

Have you ever asked yourself any of these questions?

What is sin?
Why hasn't Christianity saved the world by now?
Why can't Christians get along with each other?
Why does America seem more immoral now than in the 1950s?
What's gone wrong in America?
Why is there so much hurt and unhappiness?
Where does real happiness come from?
Where does hate originate?
What is love?
Does God love the sexually perverse?
What will really happen at the end of time?
How can I know I will go to heaven?
Where do we go when we die?

We all have the same questions, but have you noticed how varied and puzzling the answers are? Everyone seems to have a different opinion. If you choose to read one more set of answers in this book, expect some honest, straightforward reasoning. In the words of a favorite television series, I plan to "boldly go where no man has gone before." There will be moments when your mind refuses to believe what your eyes are reading. Moments of denial. Moments when you may feel anger.

Be angry! But do not be afraid of the journey. Investigate, probe, seek out, and do your own dissecting along the way. You will need logic, common sense, judgment, and wisdom. For this is an adventure of the mind, for renewal and rebirth, an encounter for persuasion.

On this voyage, banish fear. If it looms to block your vision, face and conquer it and keep on moving. As you work your way through many feelings, the end result will be cleansing and, I hope, enlightening. If at times you are overwhelmed by the depths of the darkness we are coming out of, and the brightness of the light approaching, take time to close your eyes and rest. Meditate. Relax. Sleep. Cry. Laugh. Temporary total shutdown is permissible for short periods. I needed to shut down, myself, during peak over-load. Once I took the outbound plane to Hawaii, leaving my thoughts in my computer, my notepad by my bedside. I relaxed surrounded by fragrant flowers, the blue Pacific Ocean, and warm sunlight until the time arrived to return to my thoughts. You must return also. Reactivate when you're ready. Proceed at your own speed. Don't be pushed.

Throw guilt to the wind. There is a place for everything, but there is no place for guilt when using mind power to probe the validity of truth. Consider this: when people do not know the truth, they can listen to lies and not know they are listening to lies. Truth must be recognized before lies can be identified. When you do not know the truth yourself, you are open game for predators who can manipulate and destroy you. If you already have a solid, profound grasp of truth, no one can prove you wrong. Do not feel guilty or be afraid to examine your own truth, or to compare it with someone else's. Guilt over thinking about truth is not allowed to stow away on this expedition. As you read, occasionally examine your "baggage" to see if guilt is hiding there. Don't let it hold you back.

Are you ready? Let's activate our reasoning power. The journey itself will not be painless, but in the distance beckons a land where tears are wiped away, sorrow and crying will be a thing of the past, and pain is banished. Our America is so far from being a land with no pain that we cannot fathom, even with our most liberated, free, far-reaching imaginations how we can become a land with no pain. We are far from the land God promised. Most of us have lost hope of ever arriving there. Yet, God keeps His promises, in His own time. He does not lie. He cannot lie. There will be a generation to reach the Promised Land.

I give you my understanding of the course we need to set if we want to arrive on that distant shore where we'll find "Peace on Earth." If you have a plan of your own, please present it for consideration!

If you have nothing to explore, if you already know all the answers, please exit to the left. Everyone else, welcome.

ॐ

This is uncharted territory.
Please, keep your mind's eye open.

Dedicated to all people.
Intended for the good of mankind
and written without malice
or discrimination.

The Mark of
the Beast

৯৫৹

New Eyes

Blind eyes cannot see the truth
we need to see
to find the road to peace on earth
prepared for you and me.
For darkness covers our grand earth
and hides the path to our new birth.

New eyes will see a truth so bright
the mind will wake from its great light.
And man will find the way of peace
we have pursued with our blind might.

To these new eyes the trek belongs.
A law is light.
The darkness gone.
With peace in sight,
the movements strong.

When we arrive on yonder shore,
our holy feet will stand no more
where they stood wrong so long, before.
No storms will blow.
No tears will flow.
For peace will settle o'er this globe.
When mortals dress in holy robe.

CHAPTER ONE

Repercussions from Original Sin

ॐ

One generation after another has asked the question: What is original sin? And yet a satisfactory answer has never been given. It is a question needing an answer so mankind can determine how to find again the tranquillity of the Garden of Eden. If we do not understand why we were expelled from the first paradise, how can we know what needs to be corrected so we may find the last perfect paradise of peace on earth?

Spiritually speaking, only three locations exist where the human race can live: in the Garden of Eden, in the wilderness of sin, or in the Promised Land of peace on earth. If you had to choose, where would you say we are living now? In the Garden, in the wilderness, or in peace? Logic tells us there is only one answer; we are currently in the wilderness of sin, and all our problems here stem from the same wrong Adam and Eve practiced. All three locations are earth itself, and we are presently standing in the place where the land of peace will someday be. It is to earth that peace has been promised.

Geographically speaking, we are there. The need to journey

over land mass or sea or space to arrive at our destination of peace on earth is not necessary. The problem is not where we are standing; it is how we are living. We need to adjust our vehicle of transport accordingly. The mode of transportation required to move forward from the wilderness is the power of our own mind. The fuel for power is a mixture of truth and logical thinking. The answer to the mystery of sin must be present in truth. This wisdom must also be present in logical thinking before the fuel has sufficient power to move us. We cannot succeed in our adventure without an answer to what put us in the wilderness in the first place. We should not start our journey without this knowledge, for it is illogical to do so, and all our efforts to complete the mission will end in failure.

In the Book of Joel we read, "The land is as the garden of eden before them, and behind them a desolate wilderness" (2:3). A land, just like the Garden, was in front of them and they left the wilderness behind. It is true man cannot return to the Garden; we cannot go back. It is impossible to go backward in time, but we can proceed forward to the same perfection in the Garden we once had, and leave this barren wilderness behind us. The missing element in the formula to accomplish peace on earth is the answer to the question: What is original sin?

But first, before I answer that question, let us investigate three good reasons why an answer to the sin question is needed:

1) **The first reason is sin causes backward thinking.** Eve, when imagining sin, considered it to be a wise action. "And when the woman saw that the tree was good for food, and that it was pleasant to the eyes, and a tree to be desired to make one wise, she took of the fruit thereof, and did eat, and gave also unto her husband with her; and he did eat" (Gen. 3:6). Eve saw sin as wisdom. She believed it would make her wise. She thought wrong. Seeing sin as wisdom is turning truth around. Backward thinking keeps us from moving forward. Forward is the direction we need to follow, for peace on earth is in front of us. The longer we continue to think

sin is wisdom, the farther from peace we travel. And the wilderness becomes more evil as more people are deceived and move backward, away from God.

Sinners are going in the wrong direction and will continue to walk farther away from peace as long as this reverse thinking continues. "But walked in the counsels and in the imagination of their evil heart, and went backward, and not forward" (Jer. 7:24). An evil heart proceeds backward. A change of direction is required before advancement is possible.

The straightforward truth? Original sin is actually foolishness. Psalm 36 is titled "The Estate of the Wicked," and verse 3 clearly states: "He [the wicked] hath left off to be wise, and to do good." Eve actually left wisdom. To leave wisdom is to become foolish. Foolishness was the route Eve and Adam took out of the Garden. This truth must be faced. Denial of the fact that sin is foolishness dooms the human race to remain in foolishness. Seeing this first offense as folly will reverse our thinking, and only then will we proceed forward.

When the eye of the mind sees clearly enough to make a different choice, and truth and wisdom are understood and sin is identified and seen as foolishness, then we will be able to travel from the wilderness to the Promised Land. This passage from one land to the other will begin in the mind. The journey can begin when we understand what foolishness (original sin) is. Returning to wisdom is an "about-face" (a change of direction) from backward to forward thinking. Forward is the direction we need to travel. We must restart/turn around and begin again.

Wisdom will produce a better world than foolishness has. Several years ago, I attended a one-hour class on problem solving. The primary emphasis was placed on the importance of identifying the root problem. I never realized how difficult that can be until our instructor read a lengthy story with a variety of perplexing circumstances all stemming from one wrongful situation hidden in the essence of the story. There were eight students, and I was eighth in line when the instructor asked us to identify the basic problem. I had chosen my answer but did not expect her to reach me, knowing the correct response would surely be given by someone else. Seven times I was surprised as I listened to a wrong answer. Everyone selected one of the troublesome situations that had developed solely, as in a domino effect, from the first one. Yet, we are doing this same thing with the wrongs of life on this earth. We can identify many social ills. Many are quite easy to recognize, but we have not reasoned out the one major, rudimentary evil from which all wrongs are born. Life's difficulties, hurts, and inequities all generate from original sin. With no explanation of this foolish, basic, root source, it is altogether impossible to solve the majority of the secondary problems created by its presence.

Most of us do not take the eating of the fruit (usually referred to as an apple) literally. If we did, then eating fruit (or apples) would be the root of all the ills in our society, and we could solve them by removing fruit trees from the earth. (The Scriptures do not identify the fruit.)

If we make the eating of the forbidden fruit a symbolic act of disobedience, if God were only testing Adam and Eve's willingness to obey, then disobedience is original sin and we could put an end to all of our problems if men and women would simply obey. But this is too vague. Obey what?

If we are born sinners as some believe, or born with a sinful nature, then in order to put an end to wrongdoing it would be necessary to put an end to childbirth. Sinning would go on as long as sinners are born. We could end sin by not reproducing. I do not accept this reasoning.

We need an explanation. Sin cannot be some vague, undefinable, mysterious something-or-other. That brings us back to the same question we began this chapter with: What is original sin?

What does God want us to obey? What must we put an end to?

What could a man and his wife have done to provoke God to take such severe action as to drive them from their perfect, peaceful environment? If at this point you were to say the Ten Commandments, I would question your answer because they were not written until Moses, several generations later. Most of the Ten Commandments, as we have been taught, would not apply to Adam and Eve. Since they are alone in their story, they could not have committed adultery, for there is no other person to commit adultery with, no one to murder, and no other human to steal from. The Ten Commandments were not needed at this time. Before sin was committed, life was perfect, and the laws that govern us here in the wilderness were not required.

If we are given a nonsensical, or illogical answer such as eating an apple, we will not find solutions. Would destroying all fruit trees from planet earth solve even one problem? No! If we are given a vague, something-or-other answer, such as "we must obey," this answer is not clearly defined enough for us to act upon, and we will not find our way out. If we are born sinners, or if we inherited Adam's sinful nature then let us give up the idea we will ever arrive in paradise, or that earth will ever have tranquillity. If we are given no explanation whatsoever, then we have not been given the knowledge we need to find the path out of the wilderness. With no reasonable explanation to what sin is, the human race will continue to wander blind and lost in this wasteland. We will be hopelessly doomed to remain here with sickness, war, crime, murder, divorce, famine, injustice, pain, and all the other social ills created by this first affront to God. With insufficient information, we cannot even plan an escape.

I believe, without God's intervention, mankind would be unable to find the way to peace. In time, the human race would either self-destruct, or, more probably, it would remain in its present condition of overpopulation, famine, poverty, war, crime, disease, political and social corruption, drugs and immorality, pollution of the earth and its waters, and racial and religious conflicts, all worsening until chaos alone exists, creating an everlasting hell on earth. And still the mystery of original sin goes unanswered. It has gone unanswered from the Garden until this present time.

2) **A second good reason why the human race needs an explanation of this first act of rebellion, and why it so imprisons us here is that sin changes a person's God, from God to the devil.** "He that committeth sin is of the devil" (1 John 3:8). This is a somber truth, but it is truth, and there is no exception to this reality. No one, absolutely no one, can commit the same act Adam and Eve chose and expect God to still be their God. When they were in the Garden, God was their God. After sin, the Divine Creator left them. He did not walk or talk with them any longer. And when they left Eden, they departed without God. Both of them had been deceived into choosing the devil for their god. Original sin will do the same to you and to me. This law from Eden determines who our God is, and without the knowledge of what this first defiant act was, it is absolutely impossible for me to know who my God is, and it is just as impossible for you to know who your God is.

Like Adam and Eve, you and I and the rest of the human race, as individuals, have only two choices: God or Satan. There is no other choice, and no neutral ground. Everyone stands with the one, true God. Or they stand with the other god, Satan, Lucifer, the prince of darkness. Everyone alive today can be placed in one of these two categories, those who commit original sin, and those who live in agreement with God and do not. Original sin marks the devil's people like a branding iron marks possession of a man's cattle. It is the common denominator of Satan's people, and his followers can be identified by this first misbehavior. At times this first sin is referred to as the mark of the beast.

Adam and Eve had one law and they committed one sin; as a result of doing that, their God changed. Throughout Scripture when "sin" is mentioned in the singular, it is almost always referring to the one "sin" of Adam and Eve. When the "law" is mentioned in the singular, it is referring to the one "law" given in the Garden. When "commandment" is used in the singular, it also pertains to the one "commandment" given to the only two persons in the story of Eden. Let's look a some examples:

"Whoso keepeth the law is a wise son" (Prov. 28:7). Keeping the law is wisdom, and a wise person does not commit sin. Disrespect for this first decree is foolishness. No matter what, and no matter how many people think so, sin will never be wisdom. A foolish person will break the law given in Eden, and when he does, he becomes a foolish follower of Satan.

"Blessed are the undefiled in the way, who walk in the law of the Lord" (Ps. 119:1). Those who walk in the law are blessed and undefiled. Those who walk contrary to this first religious rule are cursed and defiled. Adam and Eve were cursed. All who revolt are cursed and defiled.

"For the commandment is a lamp; and the law is light" (Prov. 6:23). Imagine yourself in a room with no windows and no source of light except a solitary light bulb hanging from the ceiling. If you were to break the light bulb, you would sit in the dark. Spiritually speaking, consider this one fundamental standard given in the first paradise to be spiritual light. When this law is broken, a person is in spiritual darkness, and when the majority of earth's people have disobeyed this order, the earth is covered with darkness. In this blackness the path to peace cannot be seen, because there is no light. When original sin is revealed, when this law of the Garden goes out, it will be a shining light giving us new knowledge and the information needed to see a pathway through the darkness, and show us the only way out of the wilderness of sin, and the entrance to peace.

"Whosoever committeth sin transgresseth also the law: for sin is the transgression of the law" (1 John 3:4). To transgress is to overstep, to cross over a line, to go too far. God set an everlasting standard for human behavior. He established an absolute no! This limit was pre-determined for all mankind, and sin is an act of crossing over God's line. Original sin exceeds what God will tolerate from His sons and daughters. When you commit sin, your Father says you have gone too far. It doesn't really matter what man says. We need to know what God says is "too far." He drew a line. Man didn't. When that line is crossed, the person crossing it steps from God's territory into Satan's territory. Mankind needs to know what that line was and still is.

In Hebrew, transgress means to revolt, or to rebel. Sin is rebellion against our Creator. God said "No," and Adam and Eve stomped their feet and said, "Yes." They declared war against God. Whatever they did, they became the enemies of the Creator, as all who sin have done. Sinners have overruled the Supreme Being, their Creator, and no longer place God in a position of authority over them. Man becomes his own authority. When departing from God to join Satan, you take a stand against God, for they (God and Satan) oppose each other.

3) **The third good reason why we need to know what original sin is, and why it powerfully holds the sinner immobile, is that it causes death—spiritual death.**

"But of the fruit of the tree which is in the midst of the garden, God hath said, Ye shall not eat of it, neither shall ye touch it, lest ye die" (Gen. 3:3). God warned Adam and Eve they would die if they were to eat the forbidden fruit. This death is a spiritual death. Sin separated them from God. Without God, they would be spiritually dead. The serpent countered this truth with another lie, and once again, Eve believed the devil. "And the serpent said unto the woman, Ye shall not surely die" (Gen. 3:4). Even though Satan, the prince of darkness, is the father of all lies, Adam and Eve believed Satan. Now they have believed two lies: 1) sin would make them wise, and 2) they would not die from having committed it. They were wrong in both cases. Sin is fool-ishness and does not make a person wise, and it causes spiritual death. Everyone who has bowed to evil has died a spiritual death, even if they, like Eve, do not believe they have. When Adam and Eve left Eden, they were both dead, and foolish. Here are a few examples, among many in the Scriptures, where death is spiritu-al, not physical:

"For the wages of sin is death" (Rom. 6:23). Most adults work for a wage. After a forty-hour work week, it is reasonable to expect payment for your work. Those who have been deceived in the same manner as the couple in the Garden were, now work for Satan and are paid a wage for their work. Without exceptions, it is the same wage for everyone. The payment for sin is spiritu-al death. This does not sound like an intelligent agreement to me. When you are convinced of what sin is, ask yourself the question, is it worth it?

"Present your bodies a living sacrifice, holy, acceptable unto God, which is your reasonable service" (Rom. 12:1). Everyone is alive before disobedience. Or how could you die from sin if you were not first alive? God wants us to present ourselves to him as a living person, not a dead person. The dead are not acceptable to the Almighty, as Adam and Eve were not. This is not an unreason-able request from our Creator.

"Then when lust hath conceived, it bringeth forth sin: and sin, when it is finished, bringeth forth death" (James 1:15). First, orig-inal sin is a thought in the mind. Then it is acted out. When this evil is acted out, it always causes the spiritual death of the person committing the act of sin. Eve was the first to commit original sin, and then Adam. They both died. They lusted, then acted out that lust, and died spiritually.

"I am the God of Abraham, and the God of Isaac, and the God of Jacob. God is not the God of the dead, but of the living" (Matt. 22:32). When God states He is not the God of the dead,

He is not speaking of the physically dead. If He were, then physical death would be the end of our relationship with God. Life on
earth would be all there is. There would be no eternity, no everlasting life, no Heaven. God is speaking of the spiritually dead,
those who commit original sin. He is not their God. Satan is the
god of the spiritually dead. The Almighty God is the God of the
living, those who have never overstepped this basic law of life,
and He gives Abraham, Isaac, and Jacob as examples of those
who never once engaged in original sin. They are the living.

At this time, if you were asked to place your name on one of
these two lists (and all of earth's population can be placed on one
list or the other) you would not have enough information to do so.

GOD'S PEOPLE	SATAN'S PEOPLE
Not deceived by Satan	Deceived by Satan
The wise	The foolish
The living	The dead
Abraham, Isaac, Jacob	Adam and Eve
Abel	Cain and Esau
Job	Job's wife
Jesus	All those who did commit
All those who did not	original sin
commit original sin	The mark of the beast

Are you a wise person or a foolish person? A knowledge of
original sin is required before an answer can be given. Are you
alive or dead? Again, without a definition of that first rebellious
act, you do not have enough information to answer that question.
Do you stand with God or with Satan? Original sin is what makes
the difference, and you do not know what it is. Are you marked
with the mark of the beast? At this time you do not know. It takes

knowledge of "what was, always has been, and still is original sin" before you can place your name on one list or the other.

ॐ

Yes! We do need a better answer to
what was and still is original sin.

CHAPTER TWO

Defining Original Sin

ༀ

A re you beginning to understand how valuable an answer to this question is? It is important to each of us as individuals. As a nation, we need this answer to solve our country's problems. Our planet needs an answer before the wrongful conditions of earth can be made right. Collectively, we are spending an enormous amount of energy, time, and money trying to solve the many complications resulting from this first basic transgression. Individuals, churches, local government agencies, state agencies, federal and now international task forces, United Nations councils and conferences all play a part in an effort to make life's problems go away or become less troublesome. A United Nations Global Summit Meeting was held in Copenhagen, Denmark. The 14,000 people in attendance represented 117 nations, all gathered to discuss the plight of those who live in poverty worldwide. Yet poverty is a secondary happening, caused by the presence of sin on earth. We should continue an effort to improve the quality of life for the poverty-stricken peoples of earth, but the situation will remain until we eliminate sin from our world, and then it will go away along with all the other wrongs.

Our seemingly endless social ills will not be solved, nor will the personal sorrows and hurts caused by sin be removed from our planet, until we first put an end to original sin, the source of all our pain. This knowledge is more valuable than all our gold and silver, rubies, and diamonds, and all the moneys of the world put together. It is more helpful then all our weapons of war. Money cannot buy peace. Weapons of war do not achieve peace. Only an answer to the sin question can begin an advancement toward an earth with no misery, hurts, or wars—a peaceful, safe, sinless, and gentle homeland.

When we look at the distressing conditions of our society, and I am sure you could add a few to the ones I have mentioned, we should be well aware we have not found the answer to what causes them. This means we do not know what original sin is, for if we did, we would already have the solution.

Satan was determined to deceive everyone. He will not succeed, but he will come close. For the prince of darkness to almost succeed in deceiving all people, it would mean most of the population has committed the original sin. For evil darkness to cover our globe, the majority of us will have been deceived. Today, almost everyone disobeys this first order. This makes sin universally acceptable in all cultures. Violating this first law given to man is considered quite a normal part of human life, and considered by many to be a wise way to live. Today, sin is still considered life, not death.

What is original sin? When the answer is given, do not be surprised at how commonplace it is in all civilizations. In the United States, this sin is as American as apple pie and baseball, and almost everyone has had a slice and played the game.

"My people are destroyed for lack of knowledge: . . . seeing that thou hast forgotten the law of thy God" (Hosea 4:6). Ignorance of the standard of living the Holy One established for all mortals in Eden will cause sin to increase. Sin destroys people, and when the law is forgotten, many people are destroyed. When those who commit original sin do so without knowing it is an offense to God, they still destroy themselves and others. They still become foolish. Death still occurs. Sin does not become less deadly simply because a person is not aware of what it is or what to name it. Sin retains its nature. It remains constant. It is always foolishness. Original sin is always from Satan. Sin is always fatal, even when done in ignorance.

Since the beginning, this "Garden Law" has been forgotten, possibly lost, deliberately removed from our hearing by those who break it, and just ignored, causing many to be deceived. Because this has gone on so long, right now, at the end, the fallen greatly outnumber the upright. The wicked far exceed the righteous. The dead have nearly removed the living, and the foolish have almost eliminated the wise, producing this dysfunctional world we now live in. Spiritual darkness covers our earth. The law has been cast aside by almost everyone, and Satan's foolish dead are in charge of the earth. The vast majority of the population have been deceived, just as Adam and Eve were. It was a man and wife who first committed original sin. There is no other person mentioned in this story of deception. This fact alone would eliminate the majority of sins, narrowing the possibilities.

In my sixty years of living, I have never heard an explanation of original sin. Therefore, it is difficult for me to see how anyone can know they have achieved deliverance from it when they do not know what they need to be delivered from? How can anyone say they have triumphed over sin, when they do not know what they need to conquer? How can an end be put to this misbehavior when it has not been identified? This mystery still plagues our generation, as it has all previous generations. When this mystery is solved, those claiming to have victory over sin may be surprised to find it has been an "acceptable" activity in their own lives. You will not stand alone. Because of the worldwide acceptance of sin, this embarrassing situation will involve nearly everyone.

At the end, the end of all things as we know them in this wilderness, there will be a generation of people who will see what no others have seen. All people will see what original sin is, and will end it. The removal of this first wrong will bring us to a Garden-like utopia as in the beginning. Sin will lose its power to imprison us here.

"Now to him that is of power to stablish you according to my gospel, and the preaching of Jesus Christ, according to the revelation of the mystery, which was kept secret since the world began" (Rom. 16:25). The world began in the Garden of Eden and a mystery has been kept secret ever since, and it will be revealed at the end of time. It will be unveiled to a generation, and that generation will see a light (the law is light), and the light will show them the way to peace on earth.

"But now is made manifest, and by the scriptures of the prophets, according to the commandment of the everlasting God, made known to all nations for the obedience of faith" (Rom. 16:26). This secret will be explained according to the commandment. Once again, the word "commandment" is used in the singular and refers to the one given in the Garden.

This rule of life, which has been hidden, will be made known to all nations. If peace on earth is to be a reality, every nation must see and believe the law. Original sin is exactly the same for every person and every nation on earth. God is no respecter of persons or nations, and salvation is to all people: every person, every race, every nation without exception. It is this Garden Commandment every nation needs to hear.

When we see this mystery being made public, when the evidence is before our eyes, we can know the ending of the wilderness is near. The law from the Garden is light, and it will remove the darkness. The keeping of this command will be the end of an age. Obedience will bring an end to sin, and will remove all that the sinners have created. It will change all things as we know them today. With this knowledge of original sin, the wilderness of sin can be put behind us, and the peoples of earth will begin a journey of healing and peace. This land of peace, the earth, with no war, crime, sickness, or sorrow, is a new frontier, never before explored by any generation since the first one. It should be the most thrilling adventure of a lifetime. If we are the generation to see the law, then we are the chosen generation.

"But ye are a chosen generation, a royal priesthood, an holy nation, a peculiar people; that ye should shew forth the praises of him who hath called you out of darkness into his marvellous light" (1 Peter 2:9). This is Peter speaking, one of the disciples of Christ. Peter identifies himself with that chosen generation, the one to see the law, the commandment; the last lost generation that will see what sin is and put an end to it. To believe Peter is part of the generation to see the end of all things is to put Peter on earth at the close of this present age. He will teach the law and begin a movement leading us out of the wilderness.

As you continue to read this book to the end, I will prove beyond all reasonable doubt what original sin is. My conviction about the disobedience of Adam and Eve is not an impulsive idea. More than thirty years of reasoning and Bible study have gone into my belief. It has been painstakingly researched, and can be proven beyond doubt with the King James Bible.

What is original sin? Adam and Eve both committed an act of oral sex, one to please the other. Eve first, and then Adam. This is sin for every person who commits it, without exception. It is sin for a man and his wife, sin for a man and a woman who are not married to each other, sin for two women, and sin for two men. It was, always has been, and still is original sin; the basic, root misconduct that is the source of all earth's problems. All the wrongs of the past, and all the social ills and sorrows we are experiencing on this earth today and will continue to experience, are a result of original sin—oral sex. A man and his wife who commit this first act of rebellion against God cannot say they do not stand in the foolish and spiritually dead cities of Sodom and Gomorrah along with the bisexual and the homosexual, for they most assuredly do.

"Therefore thou art inexcusable, O man, whosoever thou art that judgest: for wherein thou judgest another, thou condemnest thyself; for thou that judgest doest the same things" (Rom. 2:1). Any person who commits oral sex and then condemns another person for the same act is condemning himself. Yet, I have witnessed condemnation, and name-calling, from husbands and wives who commit the exact same acts as the bisexual and the homosexual.

Examples:

1) In my own church, I was informed, husbands and wives can commit oral sex and it is not wrong. However, the same person who told me this will not teach in a school where homosexuality is taught as an alternative lifestyle. She verbally and openly condemns the lifestyle of the gay community. How can she do this without condemning herself? It cannot be done. Can any minister of a church who believes husbands and wives can commit oral sex condemn a lesbian without condemning himself? No! The acts each commits are identical.

2) On a television talk show, a gay man was on stage openly discussing his lifestyle, when a married women in the audience stood and started quoting Scripture to him. He half stood, pointed a finger at her, and with some anger said, "Lady, when you get your act together, then you can tell me how to live." I stood in the middle of my living room and gave the man a standing ovation. For he is right. One person committing oral sex cannot condemn another person who does. How ridiculous.

3) I attended a public meeting between the Christian Coalition and gay-rights activists, where the married speaker for the Christian Coalition stated three times that a man and wife can do anything and it is not sin. Yet, he judged the young homosexual speaker to be ungodly. Why couldn't he also judge himself and his wife to be ungodly? He and his wife believe in committing the same sex acts as the homosexual. It was not two men and it was not two women who

were removed from the Garden of Eden. It was a man and his wife! Husbands and wives should take this into consideration. Adam and Eve had no one to commit sin with except each other.

If you honestly believe a marriage license legalizes oral and anal sex and makes it okay with God, then homosexuals should be allowed marriage licenses, also. Why shouldn't a man and wife want a gay or lesbian couple to have the same legal approval they claim? Why wouldn't they be fair enough to want them to have the approval of God and the church? Is it purely selfishness? Is it homophobia? Is it fear they, too, will become homosexual? No, I do not believe these excuses apply. It is blind self-righteousness in its purest state. Certainly it is blindness. They are blind to what is original sin.

On Judgment Day, a heterosexual married couple who engaged in oral and anal sex may stand before God beside a gay couple and a lesbian couple who committed the same acts. If God were to let the heterosexual married couple into heaven and refuse entrance to the gay and lesbian couple, that would be sex discrimination. The female partner of the heterosexual couple is performing the same act as the male partner of the gay couple. The male heterosexual partner is committing the same act as the lesbian partner. The truth is, all six of them are sinners. All will be found in error, guilty of original sin. For they have all exceeded what our heavenly Father will tolerate from his children. How can the heterosexual couple set themselves up as judges? Maybe it is time for the self-righteous to stop judging. It was a man and his wife who got removed from the Garden!

"Except the Lord of hosts had left unto us a very small remnant, we should have been as Sodom, and we should have been like unto Gomorrah" (Isa. 1:9). A remnant is left at the end, a small portion of the original. To look at life from beginning to end in a paragraph or two, I give you an oversimplified illustration: A large island is surrounded by deep water. All human life is standing on the island with God. Those who choose to practice original sin are removed from the island and placed on logs in the middle of the water. A man and wife consent first and are placed on a log with their backs toward shore. In front of them is placed a bisexual, and a homosexual is placed on the far end of the log.

Husbands and wives are not as far away from God as the bisexual, and homosexuals are the farthest away. They are the most unlike God. As time goes on, more people go sit on logs. By the end of time, only a few are left on the island. Those on the island are called a remnant (a small portion of the original left at the end). Those on the logs populate Sodom and Gomorrah. The remnant believe in God. Sodom and Gomorrah were deceived by Satan and are separated from God.

At the conclusion of our present age there will be only a remnant of people left who are not like Sodom and Gomorrah. No deliverance from this sin has yet been offered to Sodom and Gomorrah. When it is, it will be offered to all those guilty of breaking the Garden Law, including husbands and wives.

Below are the lists of some who did, and some who did not, commit original sin. You now have enough information to know if you are guilty of this same transgression and to place your name on one of these two lists.

THE REMNANT	SODOM AND GOMORRAH
God's people	Satan's people
Not deceived	Deceived by Satan
The wise	The foolish
The living	The dead
No oral sex	Oral sex
Abraham	Adam
Isaac	Eve
Jacob	Esau
Abel	Cain
Job	Job's wife
Jesus	Have the mark

If you can envision all civilizations having written their names on this list, then you can see the condition of our planet at this time. Only a few names will appear on the side of the remnant, and the vast majority on the side of Sodom and Gomorrah. If Adam and Eve were alive at the end of time, they could not with any honesty place their names on the side of the remnant. They left God, were deceived by Satan, and stand in Sodom and Gomorrah. They have no other list to write their names on.

Please remember, when evil darkness covers the earth, nearly everyone has broken the Garden Law. "For, behold, the darkness shall cover the earth, and gross darkness the people: but the Lord shall arise upon thee, and his glory shall be seen upon thee" (Isa. 60:2). Sin is an "acceptable" activity of almost everyone when the earth sits in darkness. Oral sex is considered normal behavior today in our society. At present, there are only a few, a remnant, who have not been deceived. It is this remnant who serve God. At this time, they are the only people on earth who presently do serve God. All the sexually perverse serve Satan, even if they stand in what we are presently calling God's house, the church.

Ask yourself the question: Who will Jesus be sent to? Obviously, the remnant do not need a Jesus. It is Sodom and Gomorrah who need a Jesus to bring them out of the darkness of sin. So when these questions are asked: Does God love the sexually perverse? Does God love Sodom and Gomorrah? Does God love the homosexual? your answers should be an obvious yes! They are the ones to whom God will send Jesus. He will reconcile them back to God, their Creator and their Father.

The Supreme Being gives Sodom and Gomorrah some advice in Isaiah when he says, "Hear the word of the Lord, ye rulers of Sodom; give ear unto the law of our God, ye people of Gomorrah" (1:10). Sodom and Gomorrah need to listen to the law. Law is once again in the singular and refers to the first decree given to Adam and Eve. Husbands and wives need to listen to the law given to

Adam and Eve. Oral sex is an absolute No! It was invented by man, and was the only thing God instructed Adam and Eve not to do. God knew if they did this, they would invent many other activities unacceptable to God, such as anal sex, sex with animals, sex with things, sex with relatives, and many others. God calls this first invention of man "sin," and rejects all who commit it, without exception. All are of the devil, deceived, dead, and foolish. They have received the mark of the beast.

When this first rule for living is obeyed among all nations, there will be no oral or anal sex on earth, and the darkness will pass over, wisdom will return to the foolish, life will return to the dead, and all the earth will return to serving God. Sin will end.

Forsaking original sin will begin the elimination of all earth's problems, and begin healing the hurts and sorrows. Abolishing sin will begin our progress toward peace on earth. This Garden Law is the light that will remove the darkness, educate the wicked in wisdom, and give life to the dead. It will begin the recovery of our beloved nation, the United States, and the light will spread to all countries.

Again, what is original sin? Oral sex is original sin. Does it shock you? While growing up in America in the fifties, I never saw those words in print, nor did I hear them spoken. In this society of the nineties, you can wait in a doctor's office or a beauty shop, or just buy groceries in the supermarket, and read an article on oral sex. You can turn on a television talk show, or listen to the news and hear it being openly discussed, or go to a bookstore and find a how-to book, diagrammed and illustrated, demonstrating the so-called art of evil. Today is quite different from the fifties.

I was nearly thirty years old, married for twelve years and the mother of two beautiful children, when I first heard the words "oral sex." I had trouble believing humans engaged in such activity. Immediately I asked myself two questions. The first was: "I wonder what God has to say about this?" I began a study to find the answer to that question.

My second question was: "Does this activity have anything to do with cancer?" Some years later, I wrote the following letter to the Fred Hutchinson Cancer Research Center in Seattle, Washington.

September 3, 1992

Fred Hutchinson Cancer Research Center
Attention: Dr. Day
1124 Columbia
Seattle, WA 98104

Dear Dr. Day,

For several years I have been wanting to ask these questions of you, but have been hesitant to do so. These questions stem from my own curiosity, from a belief not many people share.

To put it simply, I believe Adam and Eve each committed an act of oral sex, and oral sex is original sin. Before sin life was perfect; no sickness, no sorrow, no pain, no war.

My questions are these:
1) If the sperm was never intended to go through the digestive system, how much damage can it do to our bodies?
2) Do you have equipment powerful enough to see what a sperm is capable of doing on the way through the digestive system?
3) Has research already been performed in this area? If so, how may I acquire the results of that research?
4) Can a marriage or union of the sperm or any portion of the

sperm take place with any portion of a cell, or a gene that would produce a germ which would war against healthy cells?

5) And finally, knowing a sperm has the power to fertilize an egg, which is a cell, and cause it to grow, could there be any connection between a wandering sperm and cancer? Could a sperm, or any product created by its presence, fertilize a living cell or one in the process of dying, and cause it to grow?

I realize, as a rule, we could theorize, the sperm would pass through and out of the body like any other protein. However, sperms have life and are not like all other protein. I cannot help but ask these questions about the possibility of the few which might arrive at a perfect, given set of conditions which could cause harm.

I would appreciate any assistance you are able to offer concerning these questions.

Sincerely,
Marilyn Taplin

The Fred Hutchinson Cancer Research Center informed me they could find no documentation in their library indicating any research had been done in this area. They advised me to send the same letter to the National Cancer Institute at Bethesda, Maryland. I did forward the letter, for they appropriate funds for cancer research, but received no answer. I am still curious and would like answers to my questions.

These are only two of the many question I have asked myself since discovering oral sex is commonplace and considered to be a very normal part of life. I have listened to this majority from the spiritually dead cities of Sodom and Gomorrah, not for the purpose of learning how I should live and think, but rather to learn how they think and why they think as they do. I have read their books, for they have written most of the bestsellers. I have watched their movies, for they have written, starred in, and produced most of our films. I have listened to radio and television talk shows, for those who reside in Sodom and Gomorrah will now openly discuss many of these issues. I have asked people questions and have listened to their answers. I have observed this environment I live in and have seen a great amount of pain, sorrow, and tears. I see confusion. And I have heard few reasonable answers that will solve the confusion about how to live life. Mainly, I hear a lot of talking, and have listened to much loud arguing, even yelling, and I see a great deal of judging. I see the war between good and evil, but I also see a war among those who are evil.

For me, to believe their views of life would be absurd. Since I stand with the remnant, those who have not committed oral sex, it would be illogical for me to accept their answers. They are the ones who see backward and have turned the world upside down, who call good evil and evil good, who put bitter for sweet and sweet for bitter. They are the ones who have produced the hurts and sorrows of the world we now live in. They have ignored the Garden Law. They follow Satan. All those who live in these spiritually dark cities of Sodom and Gomorrah do not know truth. They have caused the darkness. They see sin as wisdom, and death as life. They see wrong. They think backward. All their answers are wrong.

When I could not accept their sin, I also rejected all their answers concerning life. I realized that in order to answer my own questions regarding life on planet earth, I would have to undertake a great study. I have done that, and will pass my answers on to you for your consideration. Like my answer to the question, "What was original sin, always has been sin, and still is sin?" my answers will be different from most you have heard before. I offer you some answers you may initially reject. They may make you angry, even frighten you. But they are not given out of anger or spite, simply out of seeing a need to know the root source of our problems. Our beloved country, and the rest of earth's nations, can become more peaceful and kindhearted, and the next generation can have fewer or no tears. To create a kinder America and a peaceful earth will require new answers. New solutions. New ideas. New thinking. New eyes to see life in a new way.

Changing the way we think and see will cause the darkness to pass over. "And God shall wipe away all tears from their eyes; and there shall be no more death, neither sorrow, nor crying, neither shall there be any more pain: for the former things are passed away. Behold, I make all things new" (Rev. 21:4-5).

God will make all things new at the end of time. Pain, sorrow, tears, and grief will disappear. At the finish of our present age, we can expect wonderful and marvelous changes. I believe every present-day religious belief will change giving us fresh truths and new beliefs. We will have a new and victorious church. All eyes will see all things differently. It is only through seeing that the mind changes.

ॐ

No deliverance from sin has been offered to man.
Not yet!

CHAPTER THREE

Sex and Sodom
and Gomorrah

৯৭

I s homosexuality sin? Many times I have heard ministers, laymen, and the unchurched alike, state that the Bible says very little about homosexuality, and yet, in the first chapters, we see the division between God's people and Satan's people, based solely on a choice of sexual activity: the choice of original sin—oral sex.

Once I watched a speaker demonstrate what she believed Jesus had said concerning homosexuality. She stood with her lips closed in silence until the crowd applauded. Many people would like to believe Jesus said nothing. But it is not true. The truth is, neither the Bible nor Jesus single out homosexuals as an individual group of evildoers, but identify all those who commit oral sex as evildoers, and the homosexual is included in this group.

We have looked at how this one sin marks the difference between the wise and the foolish, and between the living and the dead. But these are not the only words used to distinguish between the sexually perverse (Sodom and Gomorrah), and those who are not (the remnant). Some of the biblical words used to communicate the favorable state of the remnant are: righteous, upright, holy, good, clean, godly, blessed, lambs, and "they did right in the sight of God." Some of the biblical words that reveal the unfavorable condition of the people of Sodom and Gomorrah are: wicked, fallen, profane, unholy, evil, unclean, ungodly, cursed, goats, and "they did evil in the sight of God." I mention only the most commonly used words; there are many others. When you understand the biblical meaning of the words you are reading, the truth is you can open the Bible to virtually any page and find this subject of human sexuality. The reason is that: oral sex is the difference between good and evil, and the subject of good and evil is the basis of all Scripture.

If you expect to find the more modern words we have applied to human sexuality such as sex, oral sex, anal sex, genital activity, heterosexual, bisexual, homosexual, gay, and lesbian, you will not find them in the King James Bible. Most of these words did not exist when this Bible was translated. I choose not to change the King James Bible, but to understand what it is saying with the words it does use. The Bible must be understood before it is "updated." Otherwise, error is unavoidable, and the truth will, at times, be changed to untruth. I believe the individuals from Sodom and Gomorrah have done exactly that. They lack correct knowledge (wisdom). Their spiritual eyesight is impaired. Pride will not allow them to admit to being wrong, so in their delusions they create their own Bibles of partial untruths. I liken them to an electrician who cannot understand the manual on electricity, and so rewrites it to his own understanding. If you were building a new home and such an electrician came to wire your house, would you trust him? Your life might depend on his work.

Our spiritual lives depend on truth, so for our own good, let us be principled and ethical in seeking it. We must examine our motives. Mark Twain once said, "It is not what I don't understand about the Bible that bothers me, it is what I do understand." Almost everyone understands that once God destroyed Sodom and

Gomorrah. How many people who presently live in those two cities want that truth changed? Are the biblical "updates" motivated by a refusal to consider as true what they do understand?

Or is change motivated because the King James Bible is too difficult to understand? If that is the case, then there is no way of knowing if the newer translations are truth. Either reason is a wrong motive for changing the Scriptures. First, understand them. Second, believe them. Then you may or may not have the desire or see a need to change them. But wait until you understand the Law from Eden.

Before continuing our examination of biblical truth, let me offer an explanation to avoid misunderstanding. When I mention Sodom and Gomorrah, I am always speaking of all those who commit oral and anal sex, including husbands and wives. All are citizens of these two dark cities, which have grown to nearly cover the face of the earth.

The first word we will look at is the word "fornication." Most newer Bible translations have eliminated the word "fornication" altogether. This word should not have been tampered with, and will be the first we investigate. Noah Webster, born in 1758, published Webster's Dictionary, the first authority to emphasize American rather than British word usage. He included an incorrect definition for the word "fornication." America has never been given a correct definition of this word. The religious scholars of our day should have recognized and corrected this misinformation long ago. They chose not to. Instead, they wrote it out of Scripture and have chosen Biblical translations that have removed the word altogether. When people build a house and call it God's House, they should get their truth from the Bible. If they wish to use Noah Webster's truth, then they should call the house they build, the House of Webster.

Fornication:

1) **The sex of Sodom and Gomorrah.** "Even as Sodom and

Gomorrah, and the cities about them giving themselves over to fornication." [Fornication is what they gave themselves to.] "Woe into them! For they have gone in the way of Cain" (Jude: 7,11). Fornication is the description of the sexual activity of Sodom and Gomorrah. Cain is wicked in the sight of God and the above Scripture tell us Sodom and Gomorrah took the same path as Cain took, which makes Cain like Sodom and Gomorrah, and Sodom and Gomorrah like Cain. Cain also had a wife and children, evidence that bisexuals are also part of Sodom and Gomorrah.

2) **Our bodies were not made for fornication.** "Now the body is not for fornication, but for the Lord; and the Lord for the body" (1 Cor. 6:13). This is one of the verses that prompted my letter to the cancer research center. If the body is not made for fornication, then how much damage can it do to our bodies? A baseball bat is not made to be used as a hammer, and when it is misused as a hammer to drive nails into a wall, the baseball bat is damaged. Could this also be true when the body is used in a wrong way? Does damage occur to the body? We know fornication causes psychological damage, but does it also cause physical damage? Has it caused all the sickness, both mental and physical, mankind has experienced from the beginning of time? There was no sickness before sin.

When God made male and female, He created vaginal intercourse. Intercourse between a man and his wife is good and clean. It does not defile either the man or his wife. Before sin occurred, Adam and Eve were advised by God to multiply and replenish the earth. "Male and female created he them. And God blessed them, and God said unto them, Be fruitful, and multiply, and replenish the earth" (Gen. 1:27-28). No one can say the body is not made for intercourse. Nor can it be said intercourse was original sin. But to say the body is not made for fornication is saying the body was not made for the sex of Sodom and Gomorrah, oral and anal sex. God never intended the body to be used for fornication. When the body is misused in this manner, it is defiled. A lie has been embraced, and God (truth) is gone.

The body is for the Lord, a house for the Holy Spirit. But fornication defiles this house and makes it an unfit dwelling place for the Holy Spirit. The bodies of Adam and Eve were not made for fornication. Neither my body nor your body was made for fornication. God has left all those who practice fornication. They are without God

God has no favorites and will treat everyone alike. He leaves all people who commit oral sex. Everyone will be judged by what they have done with the law given to the couple in the Garden. This is an everlasting law, never to be forgotten or broken without the consequence of losing God.

3) **The fall of man.** "Neither let us commit fornication, as some of them committed, and fell in one day three and twenty thousand" (1 Cor. 10:8). The human race was not born fallen. Each one of us is born alive, good, and upright. If we fornicate, we fall. We fall out of grace with God in the same way as Adam, Eve, and Cain did. Adam and Eve fell, Cain fell, and all other fornicators have fallen. This fall does not happen collectively, but one at a time. The first time a person commits original sin he stumbles and falls. On our earth today, many people will violate this holy order for the first time. They will fall. They will change gods, from God to Satan. They will become foolish. They will die a spiritual death. God will leave them. From this first act onwards, having lost God, they become bent toward, obsessed with, repeating sin. They become slaves to this act. Today, would the number be more than 23,000 fallen? On this battlefield in the war between good and evil, could we keep a daily count of the dead? Yes! God does.

It has taken time for the human race to fall. When summer is over and before the dead of winter, the leaves will drop from the trees. We call this season fall. When we see the leaves begin to cover the ground, we know they will not all tumble downward at once, for it will take weeks for them all to separate from the trees. This is how the fall of man has been. It began in the Garden of Eden; and men, women, boys, and girls are still dropping from this sin of fornication, one by one, until the earth today lies in the dead of winter. Nearly everyone on earth has fallen. It has taken a long time from the Garden of Eden until this present age for the earth to sink into the condition of evil we now experience. Spiritual darkness is the result of so many separating and falling away from God. The darkness will be appalling at the end of time

Before sin, a person is upright. This is true of every person. Job is an example of an upright person who did not fall. "There was a man in the land of Uz, whose name was Job; and that man was perfect and upright, and one that feared God, and eschewed evil" (Job 1:1). We are all born the same as Job: upright, perfect, holy. If we had all remained upright, we would still be living in Eden. If men and women would stand upright again, we could advance to another perfect environment, peace on earth, the same tranquility of a paradise.

David is another example of an upright person "I was also upright before him, and I kept myself from mine iniquity" (Ps. 18:23). Neither Job nor David committed fornication; neither of them was sexually perverse, therefore, neither of them fell. If Job and David were alive at the end of time, both would stand with the remnant. They would not be citizens of Sodom and Gomorrah.

It is not possible to be upright and fallen at the same time. Try it! Stand and fall at the same time. Either a person is upright or fallen.

4) Blaspheming the Holy Ghost. "Flee fornication. Every sin a man doeth is without the body; but he that committed fornication sinneth against his own body. What? Know ye not that your body is the temple of the Holy Ghost which is in you, which ye have of God" (1 Cor. 6:18-19). Do you not know that your body (your mind) is a house for the Holy Ghost/truth? And have you ever wondered what sin makes the Holy Ghost/truth leave a person? How do you blaspheme the Holy Spirit? Fornication, the sex of Sodom and Gomorrah, is the answer to that question. Original sin is sin against yourself, it fills your mind with lies, therefore, truth is gone; The Holy Spirit is gone.

Original sin is an activity everyone should flee. To flee is to run for your life. A man from Cambodia once described how he and his wife had had to flee their country. He explained how they left early in the morning, leaving the door unlocked, so if anyone came to visit, they would think the two were out for a walk. Taking only the clothes they were wearing and some money, they ran and walked. Trying to hide and look normal at the same time, they finally crossed the border into another country. It took courage to flee, but they knew if they stayed in Cambodia, they would be killed. They were running for their lives. Flee fornication! It is deadly, as Adam and Eve learned. Run from it as if your spiritual life depends upon it, because it does. Fornication is detrimental to your mind.

NOT AGAINST THE BODY	AGAINST THE BODY
Lying Stealing Envy Adultery (David) Killing (abortion)	Fornication

The sin of fornication stands alone, and is why the word "sin" is so often used in the singular. This wrongful act is more serious in the eyes of God than any other act, and is the only one to cause a person to become profane/unholy/unlike God. Those who engage in this offense are said to have gone whoring after another god.

5) Whoring. "Thou hast also committed fornication with the Egyptians thy neighbours, great of flesh; and hast increased thy whoredoms, to provoke me to anger" (Eze. 16:26). Fornication is whoring. The word "fornication" is interchangeable with the word "whoring." When a person goes whoring, they always leave God to serve another god. And Satan is the only other power man has to serve. Both men and women who commit oral sex are biblically called whores. Adam and Eve both went whoring after another god, Satan. They are called whores, but they were not prostitutes. Prostitution and whoring are not interchangeable words, for not all whores are prostitutes. Fornication/whoring angers God, and it is foolish to anger God.

Once again my home dictionary (Webster) gives me misinformation when it identifies whores as female prostitutes, or any woman who engages in promiscuous sexual intercourse, as though a male cannot be a whore. And it leaves out all sex except intercourse. On the internet, the Merriam-Webster Dictionary defines a whore as a male or female who engages in sexual acts for money. This also is incorrect. A biblical definition of "whore" is anyone, male or female, who commits the sex of Sodom and Gomorrah. Money may or may not be part of the agreement to sin. It is that simple, and it is a choice.

Nevertheless, God will never take our freedom of choice away from us. Man will always have the freedom to choose good or evil. To take this freedom away from us would be to make us slaves. God will never make slaves out of us. Obedience to God will come only from a person's desire to love and serve God, not from any kind of force, deceit, or slavery. It will be a willing desire, based on love of God and sound reason. The human race will decide to please God and end the whoring of our own free will. We will see obedience as sane, logical, intelligent, and reasonable.

When presented with truth, man will see the unfathomed benefits of wisdom. I believe God is putting His trust entirely in the reasoning power He gave to His children, and rightfully so. God knows us better than we know ourselves. He knows He made the mind for truth and reasoning. The human mind is made for logical thinking. Whoring cannot be reasoned to result in a logical, happy conclusion. Sin will eventually destroy all that is good. Deep down in our subconscious we know that. Godliness can be reasoned out to a logical and happy conclusion. Godliness will create everlasting happiness.

6) **Grounds for divorce.** "Whosoever shall put away his wife, except it be for fornication, and shall marry another, committeth adultery: and whoso marrieth her which is put away doth commit adultery" (Matt. 19:9). Jesus will change the grounds for divorce from adultery to fornication. To the remnant, those who serve God, this is logical and welcoming news. When an individual from the remnant marries somebody from Sodom and Gomorrah that individual is unequally yoked together with a non-believer. God does give the righteous person permission to leave the marriage. Fornication should have been the only grounds for divorce from the beginning. (This will be discussed further in Chapter Eighteen.)

7) **Drunkenness.** "With whom the kings of the earth have committed fornication, and the inhabitants of the earth have been made drunk with the wine of her fornication" (Rev. 17:2). The leaders of the nations have committed fornication and all the peoples of the earth are drunk from this wine. Sexual perverseness causes spiritual drunkenness.

Many biblical passages referring to wine are about fornication, the devil's wine of fornication. Few, if any, of the Scriptures speak of man-made wine. Spiritually speaking, the wine of fornication has the same effects on a person as man-made wine has on a person physically. We can look at the intoxicating drink man makes from grapes to see a spiritual comparison to the wine of fornication.

MAN-MADE WINE	WINE OF FORNICATION
Impairs vision	Impairs vision
Impairs judgment	Impairs judgment
Impairs your walk	Impairs your walk
Puts you to sleep	Puts you to sleep
Causes disease	Causes disease
Causes raging	Causes raging
Causes death	Causes death

"Wine is a mocker, strong drink is raging: and whosoever is deceived thereby is not wise" (Prov. 20:1). The drinkers of the wine of fornication have been deceived and are not wise. Their thinking has been impaired. They rage. I have heard it said that this generation of young people is more angry than any previous generation. This will happen when fornication runs wild. Whoring creates anger. There is always rage behind violence, driving it onward. "For they eat the bread of wickedness, and drink the wine of violence" (Prov. 4:17). The wine of fornication is the wine of violence. Wickedness and violence are Siamese twins. They cannot be separated. In the days of Noah, the earth was filled with abusive behavior just as our day is, and for the same reason. We live in a crooked and perverse generation, as both Moses and Noah did. Today, simply looking at the dramatic increase in all areas of violence: crime, drugs, gangs, corruption, and rage confirms fornication has increased in America since the 1950s.

In the Books of Revelations and Jeremiah we learn more about wine when we examine Babylon. "MYSTERY, BABYLON THE GREAT, THE MOTHER OF HARLOTS AND ABOMINATIONS OF THE EARTH" (Rev: 17:5). "Babylon . . . that made all the earth drunken: the nations have drunken of her wine; therefore the nations are mad" (Jer: 51:7).

Babylon is called the mother of fornication, and her fall is predicted. However, before her fall, all nations will follow her drunk-
en ways, which will cause a madness on earth. This prediction of
the fall of the mother of fornication also predicts the fall of Sodom
and Gomorrah (the same prophecy, only worded differently).
"Thus saith the Lord; Behold, I will raise up against Babylon . . . of
them that raise up against me, a destroying wind" (Jer: 51:1). The
Scriptures repeat, in various ways and with different stories, that
there will be a day when Sodom and Gomorrah, Babylon, Satan's
world will cover our earth, and then Lucifer's kingdom will fall. We
are approaching the day when Satan's kingdom will be over-
thrown. This is good news!

I am sure you could make a list of activities you would call madness. My partial list includes: bombs (all of them); the bombings in
New York City, Oklahoma City, London, and Jerusalem; war,
murder, and mass murder. Living in a homeland plagued with
drive-by shootings, school shootings, gangs, drug trafficking, car-
jacking, rape, child molesting, and spousal abuse. Allowing acid
rain to destroy our rain forests where much of our oxygen is produced. We pay our farmers not to grow food, then sit in our easy
chairs and watch thousands die from starvation.

We have invented a society where criminals are manufactured,
and then we imprison them in an intensified environment that produced them in the first place—"schools for criminals." We have
wicked, wealthy, powerful political leaders who have only their
own self-interest at heart. Many of us love money more than goodness. The Mafia. If all of you could add your partial lists to mine,
they would fill volumes. Fornication has caused this madness.

"Awake, ye drunkards, and weep; and howl, all ye drinkers of
wine" (Joel 1:5). These drinkers of wine need to wake up. They
need to feel sorrow over their disobedience to God, their Father,
the God who created them. God did not have to create us. If it
were not for The Almighty, we would not be! Yet, the creation is

saying to the Creator, we think we're smarter then You are. We can override what You say. In Scripture that is repeated many times this way: "And they exalted themselves above God." Mortals have invented their own truth and have declared that it supersedes the truth of the Master of the universe.

"But the end of all things is at hand: be ye therefore sober, and watch unto prayer" (1 Peter 4:7). When the end of all things as we know them is at hand (and that will come at the conclusion of this present age), this is when Sodom and Gomorrah will sober up. The elimination of fornication in the lives of everyone will end all things as we know them. Soberness is the end of the drunken madness caused from the wine of fornication presently covering our earth. Abstinence (the absence of original sin) will end the madness.

In the Book of Acts, Paul preaches soberness, "I am not mad, most noble Festus; but speak forth the words of truth and soberness" (26:25). Paul will preach the end of fornication. People will think he is mad. When sin covers the earth, can you see how difficult opposing original sin would be at first? When darkness nearly covers the entire planet, truth cannot be found; and when truth is first spoken in this gloomy blackness, it will sound radical. Jesus, Peter, and Paul will begin a church that will teach truth and a new strange doctrine: abstain from fornication, be sober. A church that does not preach spiritual soberness is not from God.

Sodom and Gomorrah, the drinkers of wine, will oppose this wineless church at first. They are the gates of hell. They will express and act out strong opposition, but they will not prevail, or be victorious in their efforts to defeat this sober church. We will have a sinless church at the conclusion of this age. The end of original sin will be preached, and sanity will return to the church and then to the earth.

"But they also have erred through wine, and through strong drink are out of the way; the priest and prophet have erred through strong drink, they are swallowed up of wine, they are out of the way through strong drink; they err in vision, they stumble in judgment" (Isa. 28:7). When ministers and pastors err through wine, the wine of fornication, they are out of the way. They do not walk in the ways of God. When this happens, those pastors err in vision, and cannot see the spiritually correct path. They stumble in judgment. They are not able to judge good from evil. They stumble and fall. These are signs of spiritual drunkenness resulting from fornication. When a church supports the gay-rights amendment, as so many have, it is because there are so many Adams and Eves (husbands and wives who believe in oral sex), bisexuals, incest victims, and open and closet homosexuals already in the church. The church is already in error, as it combines error with more error. This is a visual demonstration of backward thinking. The church has already strayed from God, and now it wanders farther (and farther) from God. It is traveling in the wrong direction. Today's church, going backward, will never arrive at peace on earth.

8) **Fornication is learned.** "Sexual orientation" is a new buzz phrase. A small study was conducted on a few people, and a theory was put forth that homosexuals are born that way. Almost overnight, this theory has been construed as fact. It is not true; for the Bible proves that theory to be wrong. "Notwithstanding I have a few things against thee, because thou sufferest that woman Jezebel, which calleth herself a prophetess, to teach and to seduce my servants to commit fornication, and to eat things sacrificed unto idols" (Rev. 2:20). Fornication is always taught, many times by force or by deceit and seduction, but always taught. We are actually born with the inward common sense that oral sex is not right. And that is the reason behind so much guilt, self-loathing, denial, hiding, and all the lies. Why hid and lie if you do not know it is wrong?

The examination of the word "fornication" uncovers some of the biblical words used to describe the sexually perverse. When you read the Bible, you will see these words or phrases as verbal descriptions of Sodom and Gomorrah: fornicators, harlots, blasphemers, whores, whoredoms, whoremongers, whoring, drunkards, drinkers of wine, crooked and perverse, out of the way, and erring in vision. Other words such as awake, be sober, make straight paths, listen to the law are words of guidance given to Sodom and Gomorrah. As we travel onward, you will be introduced to other biblical words used to paint a picture of Sodom and Gomorrah, and you will hear more of God's advice for them.

CHAPTER FOUR

The War between Good and Evil

ॐ

Just means to be: lawful, right, proper, righteous, and upright

Unjust means to be: unlawful, wrong, not proper, unright-eous, and fallen (per Noah Webster)

The Bible has much to say concerning the just and the unjust, and it repeatedly supports Noah Webster's definition of these two words. It is a theme carried throughout the Scriptures from Genesis to Revelations. In Genesis we look at two just men, Noah and Lot.

Noah was just. "Noah was a just man and perfect in his gener-ations, and Noah walked with God" (Gen. 6:9). The just walk with God. If Noah was just, then he was right, proper, righteous, upright, and, as the above verse says, perfect. He was good, not evil. Noah lived in the middle of a crooked and perverse genera-tion, but he was not part of the evil. If he were, he would have been in the water and not in the ark, and he would have been an unjust person. Here again, nearly everyone on earth (an entire generation) was lost. Only eight just persons were in the ark, and the unjust were in the water. Everyone on earth was divided into two groups, the just and the unjust, those who served God and those who bowed to Satan.

"And the Lord said unto Noah, Come thou and all thy house into the ark; for thee have I seen righteous before me in this generation" (Gen. 7:1). Noah and his family represent the only righteous people on earth at that time. A few were in the ark, the masses were in the water. This same ratio between the righteous/just and the unrighteous/unjust will once again be the condition of the lost but chosen generation at the end of time.

A generation can be everyone on earth at a given time. This is how God describes the last generation. "But as the days of Noe [Noah] were, so shall also the coming of the Son of man be" (Matt. 24:37). In the last days, when Jesus comes to earth, there will be a few good, just, upright, righteous people on earth, and the masses will have fallen from original sin, becoming unjust (evil) from being sexually perverse.

We are all born in a righteous state, and have been given the choice to remain just or to become unjust. Noah was righteous because he kept the Garden Law. Unlike Adam and Eve, Noah believed he would die if he broke this law, so he did not bow to Satan. He was wise. The righteous are righteous because they have not fallen by fornication. The wicked are wicked because they have fallen by fornication, oral and anal sex, the sex of Sodom and Gomorrah.

Lot was just. "And turning the cities of Sodom and Gomorrah into ashes condemned them with an overthrow, making them an ensample unto those that after should live ungodly; And delivered just Lot, vexed with the filthy conversation of the wicked" (2 Peter 2:6-7). Lot lived in Sodom and Gomorrah, but he was not part of it. He did not participate in the sexual activity of Gomorrah. Lot was just. Here again, the people of Sodom and Gomorrah are the unjust, the ungodly. If Lot were unjust, he would have been part of Sodom and Gomorrah, and if other just people lived in Sodom and Gomorrah, they would have been delivered with Lot. A neutral position is not an option, for one does not exist.

In the last days, the remnant are the just and Sodom and Gomorrah are the unjust. And again, the difference is between those who did and those who did not transgress the Garden Law. The Holy One condemned them (these two cities) with an overthrow. At the boundary line between sin and peace, God will once again overthrow Sodom and Gomorrah. The Almighty will overpower them with sound reasoning. They will actually see the foolishness of their ways. This is good news.

Whenever these two words, *just* and *unjust*, are used in Scripture, the meaning is almost always the same: the just are not like the inhabitants of Sodom and Gomorrah, and the unjust are the people of Sodom and Gomorrah.

Characteristics of the just. The Scriptures give the human race excellent and valuable advice when we understand the difference between the just and the unjust:

"The God of Israel said . . . He that ruleth over men must be just, ruling in the fear of God" (2 Sam. 23:3). The God of creation tells us that just men fear God. God-fearing men are haters of evil. The God of the earth says, only the just should rule over us. We, as a nation, should vote into office only men and women who are just. This is true at all levels of government: local, state, and federal. The mayor of our town should be a just person. The governor of our state should be a just person, and the President of the United States of America should be a just person. All the nations of earth should choose just people to rule over them. This is God's advice to the human race, and it is intelligent advice. We have ignored this wise advice from the good God of creation.

The same is true for the church; only just people should rule over the church. Only a person like Noah and Lot, should stand behind the pulpit. Adam should not be a minister, nor should Eve play the church organ, for Satan is their god. Only the just should lead the musical department, or be in charge of the Sunday school department, or head a church committee. Just people should be denominational leaders at the state, national, and international level.

The truth is, only just people should build a church. The unjust, Sodom and Gomorrah, should not build God's house. They belong to Satan. If you do build a church to worship your god in, be honest and call it the House of Satan. If Adam and Eve were to build a church to worship their god in, and if they were honest, they would call it Satan's house. Confusion is created when the wicked call the church they build the House of God. Today, there is massive confusion regarding truth. Why? Because the blind, foolish, dead have built our organized religions. They do not want those who serve God in their house of worship. They only want other blind, foolish, dead people who agree with them to join the church they have built. This is backwardness. Neither we as a nation nor the earth as a whole have followed this sensible biblical advice from the wise God—leaders must be just.

"But the path of the just is as the shining light, that shineth more and more unto the perfect day" (Prov. 4:18). To find a perfect day, a day when life on earth is as it should be, we must follow the path of the just. The just walk in the light, meaning they walk in the law, for the law is light. This light shines toward a more perfect day, telling us the just know the way to peace.

"The tongue of the just is as choice silver: the heart of the wicked is little worth" (Prov. 10:20). Silver is precious and valuable, and so are choice words of wisdom. And the just speak valuable wisdom. But the mind of the wicked is worth little.

"The just man walketh in his integrity" (Prov. 20:7). This word integrity in the King James Bible describes a "man of character," or

a man who fears God. Integrity is what makes a person depend-
able, honest, trustworthy, kind, and basically a good person. Just
people have integrity. They have an inner goodness. This is
because they are holy and still have the Holy Spirit. They have
God. If we were to put just people into political office, they would
have integrity. This integrity would eliminate corruption.
Corruption comes from the people who have lost their integrity,
inner goodness, the Holy Spirit, God.

"If a ruler hearken to lies, all his servants are wicked" (Prov.
29:12). This is to say, "As a leader is, so are the people under him."
Sometimes when I look at the followers of a leader I can tell if the
leader is wicked, unjust. It works both ways. In the church, an evil
congregation wants a wicked minister. They would have it no
other way. And an evil minister gathers a wicked congregation.

In all areas of political service, church leadership, and business
management, leaders will choose like people to serve under them.
If a man is just and has integrity, he will want those who work under
him to be just and have integrity; and those who do not have
integrity and are unjust will choose other unjust people, those without integrity, to work for them. When evil is everywhere, the just
person may have difficulty finding and maintaining employment.

Many church members today would ask a just pastor to leave,
for the congregation is unjust and they want a leader who is also
unjust. I have seen an unjust pastor run out of town because he
started to believe in being just.

"Who is wise . . . the ways of the Lord are right, and the just
shall walk in them: but the transgressors shall fall therein" (Hosea
14:9). God's ways are right. The just walk in them. Our world
would be wiser, our earth would be godly, and our lives would be
happy, if only just people lived on earth. Even if there were no
hereafter, no heaven, and no eternity to consider, the earth would
be better place to live, if only just people ruled· "When the righteous are in authority, the people rejoice: but when the wicked

beareth rule, the people mourn" (Prov. 29:2). When the righteous, just, and holy people of integrity rule, there will be rejoicing on earth. But when the unjust rule, people mourn. Life is always saddened when sin runs wild. I am speaking of the circumstances of life that make us happy and not of the economy. For unjust rulers will at times provide a growing economy.

When I search the earth by way of books, travel, movies, television, radio, newspapers, or magazines, it becomes clear to me that the unjust are ruling. Sodom and Gomorrah rule the earth today. This condition will not last forever, and we can thank the goodness of God for that. There is hope for a better, brighter tomorrow. Rejoicing will come. Mourning will end.

John the Baptist is just. "For Herod feared John, knowing that he was a just man and holy" (Mark 6:20). The just are also holy. Why? Because they have not sinned the trespass that blasphemes against the Holy Spirit by committing fornication.

Jesus is just. "Have thou nothing to do with that just man? I am innocent of the blood of this just person" (Matt. 27:19,24). Pilot is speaking of Jesus and calling Him a just man. Jesus is not like Sodom and Gomorrah. On Judgment Day, He will judge these two cities of immorality. He stands in opposition to them, and the unjust stand in opposition to a just Son of God.

If you are an unjust person, place yourself alone in a room with a just Jesus. Christ would be against you. And you would be against Christ. You are His enemy. You would be the antichrist (against Christ). Some scholars declare that "anti" also means "in place of." Now imagine putting all the unjust persons on earth together in that room. Collectively, you make up the body of the antichrist and stand against Jesus with an agenda to overthrow Him. You want to rule in place of God.

Your desire is to populate the earth with the unjust. This opposes the desire of Jesus to replenish the earth with just people. Your plan is to replace, or to be "instead of Jesus." Your strategy is the desire of Satan, but the desire of Jesus is of God. The unjust would entirely expose the earth to evil, creating an ever-worsening hell on earth. Jesus would cover the earth with good, just people, making a heaven on earth. Your own reasoning power should tell you not to oppose Jesus when He begins to put an end to Sodom and Gomorrah. Don't continue to try to replace His agenda with your own agenda. You would be better off if you were to change gods again and return to the One who loves you, and can give you true happiness.

When you who are unjust claim to be like Christ and call yourselves Christians, which means "like Christ," I hope you are beginning to understand what a slanderous lie that is. I believe that when you meet Jesus, He will not hesitate to identify you as a liar, a blasphemer, a hypocrite, and a slanderer.

Some of the characteristics of the unjust. "An unjust man is an abomination to the just: and he that is upright in the way is abomination to the wicked" (Prov. 29:27). The just and the unjust are an abomination to each other. One is good and the other is evil. There is a war going on between good and evil: both God and Satan want to rule the earth and have all the peoples of the earth serve them. When Jesus wins the war, we will have heaven on earth. If Sodom and Gomorrah were to win this war in the battle between good and evil, we would have this present and ever-worsening hell on earth forever.

GOD	SATAN
Just	Unjust
Good	Evil
Christ	Antichrist
The remnant	Sodom and Gomorrah
Heaven on earth	Hell on earth

It would be to the advantage of every person on earth if all those who dwell in Sodom and Gomorrah would wave the white flag of surrender, voluntarily give up, relinquish control, believe truth, abstain from sin, turn from wickedness, and return to the God who loves you. Leave the god who cares nothing about you.

"O deliver me from the deceitful and unjust man" (Ps. 43:1). This is David speaking. Remember, he was upright, just, godly, and would stand with the remnant if alive at the end of time. The unjust are deceitful. It is difficult for those who are honest to live with those who are deceitful. It would be more enjoyable if the just could be separated from the unjust and live on the left side of earth, while all the unjust live together on the other side. But this is not the case; we all live together, and the just suffer at the hands of the unjust.

I am reminded of a woman who spoke at a local community college concerning AIDS. She had been married to the same husband for seventeen years and did not know he was bisexual. He contracted the AIDS virus and had passed it on to his wife before he was aware he was infected. Since she spoke, both have died. How deceitful this husband was. Can you imagine now many lies he told? And what a farce their marriage was. If his wife were a just person and had never broken the Garden Law, she surely suffered at the hands of an unjust, deceitful husband. I am also reminded of how many spouses and children are verbally, physically, emotionally, and sexually abused at the hands of the unjust.

"The just upright man is laughed to scorn" (Job 12:4). The law breakers laugh at and ridicule the law keepers, the upright. The people of Sodom and Gomorrah are cruel people and delight in tearing down all of mankind to their level of living. The devil destroys. He knocks the upright down. He laughs at the righteous. Satan is evil, cruel, and hurtful.

God is good. He will not hurt you. God creates and builds. He will pick the fallen up and stand them upright again. He will wash them off and clothe them with white robes of righteousness. He will forgive and have mercy on them when they return to Him.

"But the wicked shall be filled with mischief" (Prov. 12:21). The unjust are filled with mischief. Up to no good, you could say. They bring no goodness to earth.

"The way of the wicked is as darkness: they know not at what they stumble" (Prov. 4:19). We saw where the just walk on a lighted path. The opposite is true for the unjust. Their pathway is in the darkness.

The portion of this Scripture or the words, *they know not at what they stumble*, may be the reason why so many people are honestly asking, "What's gone wrong in America?" "Where is the violence coming from?" "Why is there so much hurt and unhappiness?" "Why hasn't Christianity saved the world by now?" Can the solution be so simple that by simply recognizing the law they are stumbling over and should not have broken, they will have the knowledge they need to answer their own questions?

Understanding the difference between the just and the unjust once again gives us a good picture of God's people and Satan's followers. It is at the end of the world that these two groups of people will be separated. Until then, we all live together.

"So it shall be at the end of the world: the angels shall come forth, and sever the wicked [unjust] from among the just" (Matt. 13:49). The wicked will rule until the end, and then their reign on earth will be over. We will all thank the goodness of God when this becomes a reality.

The evil doers will see a lighted path back to God making it possible to leave the wilderness and to return to God. Light (the law) will flood the earth once again. Sin will end and the harsh wasteland will be in the past. We will have heaven on earth precisely on time—God's timing.

CHAPTER FIVE

The Wise and The Foolish

ॐ

Although we have looked briefly at the wise and the foolish, the Scriptures have much more to say on this subject. Don't make the mistake of thinking wisdom or foolishness is determined by a person's IQ. Intelligence has nothing to do with wisdom or foolishness. The wise keep the Garden Law and the foolish break it. Foolish people can attend colleges, gain volumes of knowledge, realize high positions in society, but have no wisdom whatsoever. Most degrees would not be needed if all people were wise. For instance, if all were wise, we would not have war. None of the knowledge associated with war would be necessary. There would be no sickness, and the degrees granted to the medical profession would not be required. The Church would settle all disputes, eliminating the need for the law profession. I could go on. Your own imagination can carry you on to the removal of most positions men and women hold to earn their living.

We would certainly use our intelligence in a different fashion if only Adam and Eve, and no one else, had sinned. To what degree, and in what direction our minds would take us, is a mystery. Sin, going backward from God, negative thinking, living with hate, and destructive attitudes create a narrow vision of life centering around self. Self-protection, a mind focused on lust, reverse thinking, and the absence of truth are probably some of the reasons why we use only a small portion (I've heard as little as eight to ten percent) of our brain power. Sin diminishes our ability to reason. Original sin demands we use our mind on all the curses it creates. Without sin and the complexities of life it produces, what would it be like to use one hundred percent of our brain power? I do not know. It is a golden avenue I'd like to travel on, and some day we may all do so.

Let us begin with the fools. God does not water down truth. At times you could say He uses "tough love" and is verbally ruthless on the wicked. He says what He means and means what He says, a characteristic of God you can always count on.

A wise son keeps the Garden Law. A fool does not. The sexually perverse (the citizens of Sodom and Gomorrah) are the fools of the Bible. The following are some short phrases about the fools:

"Professing themselves to be wise, they became fools" (Rom. 1:22). They profess to be wise. If you listen to what they say, you may be deceived into believing they are wise. So do not believe their words. Look at what they became; fools. The wisdom they claim to have is not reality. The fool they became is a reality. However painful it may be for the fools, reality must be faced before correction of foolishness can take place. Denial of reality imprisons the fool to remain a fool. Facing truth will open the prison doors of the mind, and wisdom will flood in. Every fool has the potential of becoming wise. Foolishness begins at sin. And wisdom will begin again when sin ends.

"But the fool rageth" (Prov. 14:16). On the "sea of life," fools are angry. If there were no fools, life itself would be calm, free from anger and madness. Peaceful.

"The foolish people have blasphemed thy name" (Ps. 74:18). Once again they are the ones who blaspheme the name of God. Not by words, but by a lifestyle that makes God look bad. They have blasphemed the God of truth, and have replaced His truth with lies.

"In the mouth of the foolish is a rod of pride" (Prov. 14:3). Pride will not permit the fools to admit they are wrong. They need to humble themselves. Pride is your most warlike defense and your own worst enemy.

"Fools die for want of wisdom" (Prov. 10:21). The death of the fool came to pass when he left off being wise, which took place at the moment of sin. Spiritual death occurs when wisdom is gone. The fools are dead, but wisdom will revive them.

"The way of the fool is right in his own eyes" (Prov. 12:15). If a fool looks through his own eyes, he will see himself as being right. This dooms the sexually perverse to remain in foolishness unless he is willing to look, temporarily, through the eyes of someone wise, until his own vision is corrected. It is this truth that lets a man and his wife, while committing sin, look at themselves and see no wrong. They are right in their own eyes. They can see others to be wrong, but cannot see themselves.

The wise. A wise son keeps the Garden Law. A foolish son breaks the Garden Law. This is Bible 101, very basic Bible.

"Then I saw that wisdom excelleth folly, as far as light excelleth darkness" (Ecc. 2:13). Probably no one could express the truth of how far light exceeds darkness better than a person who was born with perfect eyesight and enjoyed all the sights and beauty of life and nature, then because of illness or an accident lost the ability to see, and now is in total darkness. Such persons would have difficulty finding adequate words to express how far light excels darkness. They have experienced both. They know the difference, and could tell us if words were available to express their inner feelings.

Spiritually speaking, wisdom will surpass foolishness to the same degree as light is superior to darkness. We have not experienced a wise earth, so we cannot compare, yet. We can only imagine the wonders that await us on a wise planet. When the human race lives in wisdom, then we will be able to look back at the insanity and see the great benefits of wisdom.

"The law of the wise is a fountain of life, to depart from the snares of death" (Prov. 13:14). The law the wise person keeps, the Garden Law, is a fountain of life. When the disobedient keep this first mandate, they can escape from death. A foolish person can become both wise and alive again by simply keeping the law given to Adam and Eve.

Paul relates this truth to us; that in Jesus there are hidden treasures of wisdom. "In whom are hid all the treasures of wisdom and knowledge" (Col. 2:3). Wisdom holds great treasures. When a treasure chest is found and opened, a person may be surprised at what is inside. Wisdom and knowledge may amaze us when we see the future it holds for each one of us, our nation, and the earth. Jesus is a just person, and these hidden treasures are found in Him. Secret riches are found in righteousness. The surprises will all be good, because they come from the good God.

"For the price of wisdom is above rubies" (Job 28:18). There is nothing more valuable than wisdom.

"For the wisdom of this world is foolishness with God" (1 Cor. 3:19). "The world" means the world Adam and Eve walked into, Satan's world. Everyone who has committed oral sex has walked into Satan's world. Oral sex is the entrance into "the world." God considers what "the world" calls wisdom to be foolishness. What Eve saw as wisdom, God sees as foolishness. Adam and Eve (mankind) had and still have a disagreement with God on what is wisdom.

"Through desire a man, having separated himself, seeketh and intermeddleth with all wisdom" (Prov. 18:1). Through sexual desire, a person can separate themselves from God. By doing so, they meddle with wisdom.

I lived close enough to Indianapolis for a few years to become a lifetime fan of the "Indy 500" auto race. When I sat in the stands and watched the race cars lined up waiting for the words, "Gentlemen, start your engines, please," I could feel the hopes and anticipation of not only the drivers, but all those who played a part in the planning and preparation of that perfectly tuned race car. It had been prepared to perfection. If someone were to meddle with the timing, the wing alignment, the fuel, the engine, or even the tires, the car could not perform well enough to be competitive, and possibly could not begin the race.

Spiritually speaking, the fools have meddled with life itself. Foolishness meddles with the perfect tuning of the mind, interferes with right thinking, and sends the mind into reverse. It generates confusion and a sick mind. We say we live in a sick society. Foolishness is what makes our society sick. This sickness seems to be everywhere.

It is illogical to think you can win the "Indy" with your race car in reverse, and even more illogical to think you will reach the promised land while living in foolishness.

I have read and heard about some of the atrocities that happened within the walls of these two dark cities of Sodom and Gomorrah. I read the book *When Rabbit Howls*, a true story of a small child who suffered continual sexual abuse from her stepfather. When reading the details of what she remembered going through, I had to leave the book open, face down on my dresser for several weeks, before I could make myself pick it up and finish it. It was just too painful to read. I listened to a young man in his thirties tell about when he was fifteen and riding his bicycle home on a country road. A man in a pickup truck stopped, asked directions to the school, and convinced the young man to throw his bicycle in the back of his truck and personally direct him. After arriving at the school, he drove around to the back, out of sight, and at knife-point demanded oral sex from the boy. I watched the trial of the Menendez brothers on television, and listened to the story of sexual abuse by a father who demanded sex from his own sons.

In Canada, a support group organized for men who had been abused by their fathers aired a program on television. I listen to a man in his sixties tell how at the age of six his father would pull him around by the hair on his head and force him to commit oral sex. When he finished speaking, he put his face in his hands and wept. The pain was still there after all these years had gone by. These horrors seem to be very common in our society today.

Personally, I would not follow a Jesus who would say nothing about this type of cruelty. I would not follow a God who would say nothing about sexual perverseness, about Sodom and Gomorrah, or about the sex they yield to.

Those of you who think He will be silent with respect to oral and anal sex have never met Him. Nor do you understand the Scriptures. The Bible clearly states the purpose of Jesus in coming to earth. "He that committeth sin is of the devil . . . For this purpose the Son of God was manifested, that he might destroy the works of the devil" (1 John 3:8). The devil's "first work" was on a man and his wife. Jesus comes to destroy that work. He will remove original sin (oral sex) from the earth. Foolishness will end.

To put it bluntly, Jesus comes to earth to destroy Sodom and Gomorrah—that is His purpose. And those two cities are populated by all who commit oral sex.

Jesus will not fail! You can count on this. This is guaranteed good news; for His assignment is authorized and endorsed by God. Wisdom will return to this planet.

The End of Satan's World

In preparing this book, I have occasionally used cross-references. They have been taken from the King James Bible, Viking Press, copyright 1945 by J.C.W. Company, and the King James Bible, published by The World Publishing Company.

A cross-reference is given to shed further light on a portion of the verse first read. Example: "In the beginning 'God created the heaven and the earth" (Gen. 1:1). The cross-reference indicated by the (') refers the reader to Revelations for further reading and will shed more light on the original portion, "God created." It reads, "Thou art worthy, O Lord, to receive glory and honour and power: for thou hast created all things, and for thy pleasure they are and were created" ('4:11). This verse gives more information about the God who created all things.

I begin using cross-references starting with this chapter. I hope you comprehend their importance and see their value. Make a habit of using them in your own study of the Bible.

CHAPTER SIX

The Last Days

⁂

A covenant or testament is a solemn agreement between two or more people that involves promises on the part of each to the other. God made two arrangements with the human race, and is the reason the Bible is composed of two Testaments, the Old and the New.

The old covenant was quite simple. In the beginning, God gave a law to all mankind and expected us to obey it. When we abide by the law, we remain holy and acceptable to God. But if we are disobedient and commit original sin, we become profane, unholy, God leaves and gives us over to Satan.

We are blessed with intelligence and reasoning power so we can make our own choices and believe truth or lies, granting us the freedom to choose God or Satan. God becomes angry with disobedience, but He will respect our decisions. "Woe unto you" means God will let us live with the miseries of life that are directly related to how numerous our sins are. This concludes the original arrangement. It is this old covenant we have been exploring up until now. The constant and intensifying confusion America is experiencing directly correlates with the breaking of this first covenant.

Here in the wilderness we all live with our decisions, for in this original contract no provision is made for those who followed Satan to change their minds and return to God.

This old covenant is in effect from the Garden until the Son of God comes. Jesus' plan of redemption, the new covenant, is unveiled in the New Testament and will be offered to man in the last days. The New Testament was written before the coming of Jesus so that when He does come we can recognize Him, His plan, and His followers. We can expect Him at the end, in the last days.

Before Jesus comes with the plan of salvation, almost everyone will have broken the old covenant. Over time, belief in God has almost disappeared from the earth, and darkness is everywhere. And this is why, at the end of time, mankind can be divided into just two groups: the remnant and Sodom and Gomorrah. The remnant are the few left who believe in God and have not committed oral sex. And the majority are Sodom and Gomorrah; those who have committed oral sex. They have no belief in God and live in spiritual darkness. Under the old agreement we are condemned to remain here in sin forever.

These two groups, the remnant and Sodom and Gomorrah, are not the only evidence I have uncovered in my exploration of Scripture that would place Jesus at the conclusion of all things as we know them, for neither of these family portraits is a portrait of a Christian. In this present age there are no Christians yet. For as God has stated, He will conclude the world in "unbelief." And the spiritual darkness of unbelief will encompass the Christianity of the last days. The earth is presently in spiritual darkness. Today, our planet is in the same condition as it was in the days of Noah: a few good people and a countless number of wicked people.

Many Bible passages reveal that Jesus will stand with the last, lost generation at the end of time. Therefore, He has not come yet. When I began to study this, in my mind's eye I placed a scale on the table and began to weigh the evidence. I piled verse after verse on one side or the other until the scale dropped to the table with a thud on the one side; He has not come to earth yet. You will want to weigh the evidence yourself. Do not put your soul into the hands of someone else. Do your own thinking. Prove it one way or the other to yourself.

The following are a few of the many Scriptures I have weighed. They have proved to my own satisfaction this truth: Jesus did not come to earth 2,000 years ago. The generation now living is the generation to which God has elected to offer deliverance from sin, thus giving mankind the end we hoped for from God. Peace on earth. We can expect Jesus at the entrance to the Promised Land. It is the light from the law that will make the Promised Land a reality.

"For God hath concluded them all in unbelief, that he might have mercy upon all" (Rom. 11:32). To conclude is to bring to an end. Unbelief is no belief in God. This is a picture of our earth in the last days. The masses having no belief in God. And mercy is promised to everyone at the conclusion of this age. Not before.

God has concluded, meaning God has allowed this total unbelief at the end to happen. Then He will have mercy on all mankind. Everyone! All those who do evil, all those who have broken the law given to Adam and Eve, will be offered mercy as a gift from God at the closing of time. "Mercy to all" is a loving and generous gift from the good God of love to such a stubborn, sinful, rebellious, and now shameless generation as this one.

Mercy is: kindness in excess of what is expected. What should the population of Sodom and Gomorrah expect? Not to be killed, stoned, or burned alive in a fire, as some have been told and believe; nor should you expect to be accepted as you are, sinful. You could count on being forever separated from God: dead, foolish, and in bondage to sin. To live forever under the old covenant that provided no way out of the wilderness of sin. But instead of what you deserve, you will receive kindness from God.

Mercy is: compassion—sorrow for another person's plight combined with the desire to help. Your lifestyle brings grief to God. Grief is sorrow. God not only feels sorrow because you have left Him, but also for the hopeless situation you have put yourself in. God understands the hopelessness of sin. He will offer you help.

Mercy is: refraining from harming or punishing—no harm and no punishment; hard to believe, but true. God brings you no harm. Just mercy. Help. You have fallen. Your heavenly Father will help you stand up again. No punishment, but a full pardon. God will forgive and forget your sin when it is ended. He gives to you a second chance to please Him, a chance to begin again. To start over. To be holy and acceptable again.

Mercy is: pity—feeling sorry for another person. People say they do not want pity. But in the predicament the people of Sodom and Gomorrah find themselves in, I feel it is most appropriate. You are dead and think you are alive. You are blind and think you can see. You are lost and you do not know it. You are fools and think you are wise. You are wrong and think you are right. You are walking backward, thinking you are progressing. You have problems, but do not know where they come from or how to solve them. The probability you will find a better way, or locate peace on earth, or realize happiness on your own, is zero. God has left you. Your condition is hopeless.

Under the old covenant, it is impossible for you to find your way back to God. Unless God sends you help, you have no hope. If I were you, when God offers His pity, I would welcome it. The only wise teaching you will receive will come from God your Father, in the form of Jesus, who will come with truth, a law, and a new covenant, giving life to God's lifeless children.

Jesus and the new covenant are God's expression of His loving pity to fallen man. The truth is: God never stopped loving you. You stopped loving God.

At the end, The Creator will have compassion on Sodom and Gomorrah. He will show kindness and will withhold punishment, and in the place of deserved banishment from His presence forever, He will give the gift of salvation and reconciliation. He will offer you His helping hand, deliver you from the bondage of sin, and give you back your holiness without which no man can see God. He will give you a new beginning, reverse the direction in which you are moving (away from Him) and offer to you a chance to begin again (back with Him). Because of our ability to reason, to know truth when it is spoken, and to return to God, the new covenant provides an exit from sin and persuades us, of our own free will, to move forward into the promised land. The new covenant is better than the old one.

Once again "mercy to all" conjures, in our minds, visions of an earth we have never seen before. Coming out of the darkness by totally removing sin, we enter into clean and spotless living. It is a new environment, unknown as yet. We can only speculate what "mercy to all" will bring to earth. The end of sin. Forgiveness. Kindness to each other. Healing. Life. Joy. Amazement. Peace of mind. Wonderment. Love. Good surprises. Unexpected treasures. Hope for tomorrow. The end of "dysfunctional" and broken relationships. Peace between man and wife. Peace between all humans. Peace between man and God. Peace on earth.

Considering the energy, determination, and boldness of the wicked as we near the end of time, God's mercy is amazing news. We can all see the unyielding persistence of the bisexual and the homosexual in the open gay-rights agenda, and also the firm stance married couples have taken when declaring their own belief in original sin. God's compassion at the end-time, despite this public arrogance and shamelessness, only verifies the Scripture. God has concluded, and He understands, and He has permitted this situation we are witnessing. God has allowed even this blatant show of disobedience. He has permitted sin to cover the earth until the

multitudes are no longer afraid to stand up for sin. God is sover-
eign, meaning He is over all the earth, even this end-time display
of wickedness we are witnessing.

There is strength and a feeling of safety in numbers. The
wicked have become bold. They are standing up and defending
the god they believe in. The remnant have the same right, the
right to stand and defend their God, and the right to voice their
opinion. God stands with the remnant, which gives them a powerful advantage. This, too, will work toward the good of everyone.

This out-in-the-openness can be used to everyone's advantage.
Almost everyone is willing to discuss these issues now, which has
initiated a fierce and open debate. Standing up for one's god,
whether it be God or Satan, brings to the surface a person's position and the reasoning by which he or she defends that position.
A battle between two opposite beliefs cannot be fought when one
side remains silent. This book is my contribution to the ongoing
arguments I have been silently witnessing. In the 1950s, there was
no open dialogue. I did not see Sodom and Gomorrah, for they
were totally hidden from my eyes. No one talked about oral sex. I
did not know people committed it. I could not have written this
book in the 50s. Actually, it could not have been written until this
decade of open communication.

The sinners are now revealed. And I wonder, do any of you
see the remnant?

"Little children, it is the last time: and as ye have heard that
antichrist shall come, even now are there many antichrists; whereby we know that it is the last time" (1 John 2:18). Gay, open, out-
of-the-closet daring, and movements such as the Christian
Coalition incorrectly but loudly voicing God's approval of husbands and wives committing sin allows us to see the many
antichrists. The citizens of Sodom and Gomorrah make up the
body of the antichrist, and God is allowing them to go on parade
before our eyes. In the 1990s God is openly showing us how many

antichrists there are on earth; they are numerous. We can see for ourselves that it is the end-time.

"Hearken unto me, O Jacob and Israel, my called; I am he; I am the first, I also am the last" (Isa. 48:12). "I am Alpha and Omega, the beginning and the end, the first and the last" (Rev. 22:13). Jesus will be the last Jesus and the only true Jesus. He will walk on earth in the beginning and at the end. Not in the middle. Many false Jesuses will come before the real one. Sometimes we think of Charles Manson, Jim Jones, David Koresh, and other "gurus" as being these false Christs, but those men did not deceive many people over all the earth, very few, in fact.

Martin Luther came to earth and said he knew truth. Many people followed him. If he were alive today, he would be only a little over 500 years old. If Jesus came to earth 2,000 years ago with the truth, what happened to this truth that came to earth almost 1,500 years before Luther? Why would Martin Luther need to reform the truth of Jesus, which should have been well established by the birth of Martin Luther? John Calvin, another Protestant reformer, espoused the doctrine that became Calvinism, and several denominations have followed his beliefs. He is said to be the father of Presbyterianism. Many Baptist, and Congregational, churches consider themselves Calvinist in theory. John Calvin was born some 480 years ago. He also claimed to be truth in the flesh, and many have followed him. John Wesley, the founder of the Methodist church, would be nearly 300 years old if alive today. What was wrong with the truth Jesus supposedly brought to earth nearly 1,700 years before John Wesley? Many people have followed John Wesley. If we want to identify false Christs, men who say they are truth in the flesh and built a church, we should look at some of the men who have claimed to be "truth made flesh." Most church denominations are not 2,000 years old and cannot trace their origin back to Jesus, but only back to a man who said he knew truth and assembled a church. These men are false Christs, and there are many when you consider the number of churches began by an individual.

The Jesus of the Catholics and the Jesus of the Protestants cannot be the same person. Neither the Catholics nor the Protestants want their children to marry the other. The Jesus of Arminianism (humans have a free will) and the Jesus of Calvinism (all humans are predestined to go to heaven or hell) cannot be the same man. Even the Jews have two Jesuses, one who has been here, and one who has not. These groups have different perceptions of truth. If Jesus, the last Jesus, came to earth and stood up for all of them, Jesus would not be a credible person. How could He have been here and not have been here? How could He be a Catholic and a Protestant? How could He believe in both Calvinism and Arminianism? One person with all of these opposing beliefs would not be believable. Today's Christianity, when looked at on a broad scale, as a whole unit, is itself not believable.

The Messiah is one person. He will have one belief and that belief will be the same in all churches. At the end, with no sin and one unified belief, Christianity will become convincing, authentic. It will ring true in the ears of everyone.

"And it shall come to pass in the last days, that the mountain of the Lord's house shall be established in the top of the mountains. And many people shall go and say, Come ye, and let us go up to the mountain of the Lord, to the house of the God of Jacob; and he will teach us of his ways, and we will walk in his paths: for out of Zion shall go forth the law, and the word of the Lord from Jerusalem" (Isa. 2:2- 3). What does the Bible really say about the last days? Let me list from these two verses a few promises about the end of time.

- The Lord's house will be established. God will build a church with people who believe in God—not people who believe in Satan. This will happen in the last days, not before.
- The God of Jacob will build it. The God of Jacob is the true

and only God. This is not the god of Sodom and Gomorrah. Not the god of Adam and Eve. Not the god of Cain. And not the god of Esau. This is the God of Abraham, Isaac, and Jacob, the God of the living and the God of the remnant. Remember how Jacob would stand with the remnant? The God of the remnant will proclaim from this "mountain top" church: oral sex is sin. It causes death. It is foolishness and the source of all unhappiness. Jacob's God will build a church in the last days. There will be no sin in it.

- God's house will teach God's ways. In this new Christianity everyone will learn the ways of God. The lifestyle of Satan will no longer be tolerated. There will be no husbands and wives who commit sin and then judge others who perform the same act. There will be no bisexuals and no homosexuals in this church. No child molesting. No one will practice original sin. No one will believe in the god of Adam and Eve, Cain, and Esau, for their god is Lucifer, the prince of darkness, Satan. The ways of the God of Jacob will be taught.

- The law (Garden Law) will go forth in the last days. Law is in the singular. This first order from Eden presently is not being taught and will not be taught until the last days. For the first time in many generations, the Garden Law will go forth from the church. When you hear this law beginning to go out, you will be witnessing one of the signs of the last days.

- The word of God will also go forth. The truth will be published for all to read. From this time forth, truth will be the same for everyone. Every knee will bow to Jesus' truth. The day will come when no one will bow a knee to Mohammed, Buddha, Joseph Smith, or any of the many false gods of today's Christianity (Martin Luther, John Wesley, John Calvin, etc.), or any other self-proclaimed prophet dead or alive.

- All of Christianity will believe the same truth. There will be one united, sinless Christianity for all the earth. From this new church in the last days, Jesus will accomplish His purpose—to put away sin.

In this new house of worship built by the God of Jacob, Christianity will be all we ever expected it to be, and more. Righteous Christianity will not disappoint us. This new church will look like, be like, act like, and accomplish everything the Bible has promised to all of us.

Under the old covenant, when there was no deliverance from sin, both the righteous and the wicked had to cope as best they could. In today's culture, individuals read such books as *The Power of Positive Thinking* and try to live with a positive attitude. Some people develop a fatalistic approach to life, whatever will be will be, and accept life as it comes. Others become atheists and refuse to believe in a "God" of so many hurts. Many live as best they can. A few live as wickedly as they can and take advantage of everyone. Most live with tremendous guilt over sin, and some of those drown this guilt in liquor or drugs. A number live for money only. The wicked lust for the flesh (fornication), and learn to lie and hide it well. Many evil people desire to be accepted by God and have built churches to try and make themselves righteous, but they have failed.

"For they being ignorant of God's righteousness, and going about to establish their own righteousness, have not submitted themselves unto the righteousness of God" (Rom. 10:3). Today's Christianity is one of those man-made, made-up religions in which many have tried to make themselves holy but did not succeed. True righteousness is still a mystery for them, for they do not know what God calls righteousness. A church that is not righteous is wicked, and the wicked have believed lies. They tell us untruths because of their backward thinking and spiritual blindness. So when the authentic Christ comes in the last days, He will find a Christianity with no righteousness in it, and many

masterful persuaders of wrong thinking. He will find the hypocrites and the Pharisees, the self-righteous. They will be spreading the rumor that the Messiah came to earth before He really
comes. Their own self-righteousness is based on their make-
believe Jesus who came and gave them permission to sin. God calls
them wolves who are masquerading as lambs. Wolves in costumes
who sit in the dark, telling stories about fiery hells and ghosts coming out of graveyards, frightening themselves and others. Even
their god is in costume, Lucifer, the devil himself, masquerading as
an angel of light. They remind me of Halloween.

"Who concerning the truth have erred, saying that the resurrection is past already; and overthrow the faith of some" (2 Tim.
2:18). At the coming of Christ, some will say his resurrection is in
the past. It has already happened. He has already come. Upon this
belief will be based a Christianity fostering the woes of the hypocrites. This belief in the coming of our Savior before it really happens will also give birth to a generation who think they have
already been made clean. "There is a generation that are pure in
their own eyes, and yet is not washed from their filthiness" (Prov.
30:12). In our present generation are the ones who think they are
washed when they are not. This could only mean "washed in the
blood of the Lamb," washed by a Jesus who they say has already
come. When the Savoir does come, they will have to face the reality of their own uncleanness and begin again. The reality is, they
still sit in the filthiness of sin. No washing has taken place yet.
Washing away original sin and the filthiness of original sin will
make a person clean, the church clean, our nation clean, and eventually our earth clean, which is the requirement for peace on earth.

Actually, today's Christianity has been helping to spread the
lifestyle of Satan everywhere. Instead of putting an end to this
wrong the church members have been committing sin, counseling,
and encouraging others to follow their lead. All the woes of the
hypocrites recorded in the Word can be read to those professing

to be Christians today. They have tried to reach the Promised Land of peace on earth without the law in their possession, and all their efforts have failed.

"Woe unto you, scribes and Pharisees, hypocrites! for ye pay tithe . . . and have omitted the weightier matters of the law, judgment, mercy, and faith" (Matt. 23:23). You have omitted everything Christianity should be. You omitted the law. Once again law is in the singular and is referring to the instruction given in the Garden of Eden. Notice that this command is weightier; it carries more importance with God. To transgress this ruling is a greater offense than disobeying one of the Ten Commandments the church does teach. Judgment is omitted. (You cannot call sin, sin.) Mercy, that all-important "mercy for all," is also missing. Mercy would offer a helping hand to the sinner and stand the fallen upright. But the fallen remain fallen in the church of today. You omit faith. Faith in God is absent from this present Christianity. Wow! What? How? Because without a belief in obeying the law, you are not followers of God. Breaking this standard for living given in the Garden and omitting it from your doctrine makes you a follower of Satan.

If you commit oral sex, you serve Satan, regardless of the words you speak. The meaning of the word hypocrite is to pretend, to put on an act, or to claim to be something you are not. No unjust person is the likeness of a just Jesus. The unjust should not pretend nor declare they are like Christ. This causes confusion, great confusion regarding God. No one can look at you and see what God is like. Words do not make a Christian; a lifestyle makes a Christian. You either worship God by the way you live, or you worship Satan by the way you live. Church attendance or self-proclamation has very little to do with proving you belong to God. In fact, in my experience the person who does not believe in oral sex (the remnant, the Godly), is not welcome in most churches. The righteous are not welcome, only the sinners.

I attended a local Baptist Church for one service and was visited in my home by two women of the church. I had two teenage children at the time. I asked these women if I were to attend their church, and if one of my children were to marry one of their church's children, would this Baptist spouse expect my child to commit oral sex? They did not say, "No." They repeated several times that, "All you have to do is believe in Jesus." They left and never came back, nor was I invited to their church again.

A church I recently attended for five years offered a Wednesday morning women's Bible study. I joined, and when the lessons included discussions of sin, I voiced my views on oral sex. I was informed that oral sex is not sin for husbands and wives. The minister's wife used a book written by a man to prove the passages I read from the Bible to be wrong. This earth does not need a church whose only interest is to prove the Word of God to be wrong. I was removed from the class by the pastor. I have been silenced in my church. They stop up their ears against the truth, and want no part of knowing what sin is. Why? Because they believe in committing original sin. I see their wickedness and no longer believe their pretense.

I have scrutinized many churchgoers to see what they stand up for. God tell us to do this, "Beloved, believe not every spirit, but try the spirits whether they are of God: because many false prophets are gone out into the world" (1 John 4:1). Test people to see if they are of God or of the devil. Everyone should do this! How do you know whom to believe if you cannot tell who belongs to God and who does not? If you cannot recognize Satan's people, you can be fooled into believing anything. Once, I also believed in the organized religion of today, but that was thirty years ago, before I knew church members practiced original sin.

The churches of today leave the most important law out of their religion. When this happens, those who break the law are at ease in the house they built, for the law is never preached. I liken them to a house infested with ants and cockroaches. When the pesticide is only potent enough to kill the ants, without the strength to kill the cockroaches, the cockroaches will remain in the house until stronger methods are applied. The Ten Commandments will remove the lesser sinners from the church, the ants, if you will. But when the law is not preached, this will leave the worst sinners in the house of God, the cockroaches. It takes the holy standard from Eden to remove these greatest offenders. Without the law in the church, we find the most evil sinners behind the pulpit, playing the piano, singing in the choir, and sitting in the pews.

"Ye blind guides, which strain at a gnat, and swallow a camel" (Matt. 23:24). This is another indication that all sin is not equal. A camel is much larger than a gnat. The hypocrites commit a camel-sized wrong while they preach about the transgressions the size of a gnat. This size differential is even larger than that of an ant and a cockroach. The advice given to them is to first remove the camel (the greater sin) from their own life, and then they will see how to remove this greatest sin and also the lesser wrongs from our land.

"Ye hypocrites, ye can discern the face of the sky and of the earth; but how is it that ye do not discern 'this time?" (Luke 12:56). "This time," the time they did not know, is the time of Jesus' birth, as the cross-reference indicates. "But when the fullness of the time was come, God sent forth his Son, made of a woman, made under the law" ('Gal. 4:4).

To see the value of a cross-reference put the two verses together to understand better just what the religious leaders could not understand—the timing of the birth of Christ.

Today the religious leaders can tell what the weather will be like, they can discern the social climate, and can adjust to the present cultural demands made of them by sinful man, but they cannot comprehend what time it is spiritually. Their timing is off. Their birthday of Jesus is wrong. They place the birth of Jesus

2,000 years before he was born. Put the last days (the end of all things) at the close of this age, and the Word of God will become more understandable. First, put the deliverer on the boundary line dividing the wilderness of sin from the Promised Land, where sin will end. Next, make the Christians of today the hypocrites and Pharisees, the blind leaders of the blind. Now, you can answer every question you have ever asked regarding what is wrong with today's Christianity.

Although it may not seem like it to those presenting them-selves as Christians, this is also good news. God has no special people. You are not a singled out, favored bunch who will "make it" while you tell others they will burn. The news of the only gen-uine "followers of God" (the remnant) at the completion of our age gives hope to all, even to the hypocrites. For it tells of a perfect day coming, and a powerful authentic Christianity in the last days.

New vision will embrace this church that has failed, for you will be included in "mercy for all" and will make yourselves just again. Then you can truly claim to be justified. When you are holy, The Holy One will stand with you.

To look at this present earth and believe that all hope offered to man has come and gone, this is it, is to be in utter despair. If true, then Jesus is a failure, for He surely failed to defeat sin. The fact that the genuine Jesus Christ will be at the end bringing deliverance from sin, salvation, and a promise of mercy to all, brings hope to our present generation. It also brings good news to the church for the church will be made holy and have the power to bring us out of the moral confusion we are experiencing. I see a Christianity that is disillusioned with its own failures, for I've heard this disillusionment expressed by many ministers. The church is even wondering, "What is wrong with the church?" Three major news magazines had Jesus on their cover over Easter 1996. All three asked such questions as, "Did the Resurrection really happen?" "In search of Jesus; who was He?" "What are

Christians to believe?" After declaring that we have had two thousand years of truth, why are such questions being asked? Church,
why are the answers you give so unconvincing to so many?

Many people have lost faith in the church. I have heard the
phrase, "the post-Christian era" mentioned several times lately as
though Christianity has had its day, and it has failed. It's time to
move on. If you ever did have the truth, where on earth has it
gone? Where did you lose it? The truth is, you never had it. Light
is promised at the end. Hope for mankind is in front of us. We can
all use some hope for this planet in chaos.

"It is time for thee, Lord, to work: for they have made void
thy law" (Ps. 119:126). Void means having no effect or result. To
void a check you have written and do not want anyone to cash
you write "void" in large letters across it. The check will be as
though it had never been written. This is what the antichrists
have accomplished with this Law from Eden they defy. They
wrote "void" across it and have made this order nonexistent, as
though it had never been written. They have worked to eliminate
it from the church and from the earth, and have been extremely
successful. The Garden Law is nowhere to be found. The lawbreakers are undefeated in their efforts to fulfill their desire to
remove the law from our hearing. Score a major victory on the
battle field in the war between good and evil, a major victory for
evil. At the moment, it appears evil will win the war. But there is
one final battle left. Following this questionable victory, the lawbreakers will meet God, the God whose command they have
voided. God has allowed them this victory. Their work is finished. Now God will begin His work. The final battle is the battle of Armageddon, and the weapon used to defeat evildoers will
be the truth, all the truth, and nothing but the truth. It will be
fought with the law that the lawbreakers have made void. This
last battle is the final battle in the war between the just and the
unjust, between good and evil. The just will win the war. Good

news! Let them! Stand up and surrender. Follow them! For they know the way to the Promised Land.

Void: the total absence of something normally present. The Garden Law is an absolute, a spiritual order to be reckoned with. It should be present in every generation, and I think you will agree that it has been removed from the pages of Christianity and from the society in which we live. The commandment is totally gone and made ineffective.

The absence of this holy order is one of the signs of the end of time. God will soon go to work, not only to put the law back where it belongs (in the minds of his children and in the church) but also to remove evildoers from His house and from this earth. The Bible calls this Judgment Day. Perhaps you did not know you were going to be judged by the holy standard you have voided— or perhaps you did. Sodom and Gomorrah, did you really believe you could overthrow God? That is foolish.

ॐ

Yes, it will be at the end of
this age we can expect the deliverer.

CHAPTER SEVEN

Judgment Day

৵

Judge: A person qualified to settle controversy; to declare the law; having the power to set things right. (per Noah Webster)

Jesus comes to judge. "The Father judgeth no man, but hath committed all judgment unto the Son" (John 5:22). God and Jesus are like union men, for one union man will not do the work of another union man. God does all the condemning, but no judging. Jesus does the judging and no condemning. Under the old covenant, a person who breaks the law dies when sin is committed and is condemned. He has been sentenced to spiritual death by God the Father. At that point, the sinner is blind and so far removed from the thinking of his Creator he cannot be reached from heaven, and no program of deliverance is offered. Sight for the blind will come only from Jesus when he comes with the law (light).

Eventually God will send the Messiah (Jesus) to earth with a plan of deliverance. Jesus will find everyone condemned to hell and spiritually blind and dead when He arrives. Therefore, He will not condemn, for that has already been done, but He will judge everyone. In other words, He will explain the law to you and tell you why you have been doomed to death. He is qualified to end the argument between the sinner and God. His judgments, His wisdom, His truth will stand.

"Jesus said, For judgment I am come into this world, that they which see not might see; and they that see might be made blind" (John 9:39). Judgment has a two-fold purpose. Original sin causes a spiritual blindness, and those who are blind cannot see to judge themselves wrong, so someone must do this for them. The wisdom Jesus brings will prove the transgressors wrong and replace their blindness with sight. Looking at yourself through the eyes of God is not a pleasant experience, but it is necessary. Judgment will show you what God is seeing when He looks at you. He sees a dead animal. He sees an unclean, false image of Himself. Seeing yourself as God sees you is the key to change.

Simply telling people they are sinners, blind, dead, condemned, unclean, and abandoned by God is not enough. They must feel it, know it, understand why and how it happened, and express deep remorse from within. It must be proven to them. Then they know. This is only logical. A reality of this magnitude demands proof, and you should demand proof! Truth can only be found in the word of God; it can only be proven by Scripture. The intent of this book is to prove to you what original sin is, and what needs to be done by the sinners to return to God. I will show you a holy God, and then you will understand what The Divine Creator sees when He looks at you. When you see God, then it will be time to decide what you want to do about your own condition. And if you want to please your heavenly Father, you will take the necessary actions required to correct your own situation.

Judgment is also for the purpose of showing those who think they see, how blind they are. The blind leaders of the blind need to see their blindness. When wicked people follow wicked people, they all sit in the dark.

"For he [the Lord] cometh, for he cometh to judge the earth: he shall judge the world with righteousness, and the people with his truth" (Ps. 96:13). Everyone will be judged by truth, by the law given to Adam and Eve. Did you keep it, or did you break it? You will be measured by this righteous standard of God. Stand righteousness up, then stand beside it. How do you measure up?

"Arise, O God, judge the earth: for thou shalt inherit all nations" (Ps. 82:8). When our planet has been judged and made righteous, then all nations will belong to Jesus. They are His inheritance. Every knee will bow to Jesus. Seeing will cause this to happen. Judgment comes first, and then seeing. Seeing God, becoming aware of sin, perceiving righteousness, and understanding holiness are the benefits of judgment. Judgment brings deliverance, and only after Judgment Day will we experience a respectable and righteous Christianity.

And Jesus said, "Now is the judgment of this world: now shall the prince of this world be cast out" (John 12:31). The prince of this world is Satan, Lucifer, the serpent. Sodom and Gomorrah make up Satan's world. They are "the world," and the end of "the world" is the end of Sodom and Gomorrah. Jesus will defeat Satan, the Prince of Darkness. Truth is more believable than lies, especially when the devastation of lies and sin is so visible and the hurt so deeply felt.

"Fear God, and give glory to him; for the hour of his judgment is come: and worship him that made heaven, and earth, and sea" (Rev. 14:7). To "fear God" is to hate evil. "The fear of the Lord is to hate evil" (Prov. 8:13). Obey the law (hate evil), for that is what a God-fearing person does. To worship God is to depart from evil. This hour of judgment has been planned by our Creator and set by His timing. His hour will come, and will bring glory to the Master of the universe, and the end to sinners. Judgment will show God's goodness.

"For he hath judged the great whore, which did corrupt the earth with her fornication" (Rev. 19:2). This verse reveals and identifies exactly who will be judged: the fornicators, the great whore, Babylon, the mothers of fornicators. Babylon, "The world," Sodom and Gomorrah are names given to Satan's world of fornication, and it is this world that will be judged at the end of time. Judgment Day will begin the end of "the world," which Satan began in the Garden of Eden when he first deceived Adam and Eve. Oral sex is the entrance into "the world." Ending original sin is the way out of "the world."

This first act of defiance is also the mark of the beast, the one identifiable symbol that brands Satan's people. All those who have taken this mark live in "the world." Therefore, the end of "the world" is the end of Sodom and Gomorrah. The most overused and misunderstood passage in all the Bible is "For God so loved the world, that he gave his only begotten Son, that whosoever believeth in him should not perish, but have everlasting life" (John 3:16). A promise of deliverance to Sodom and Gomorrah whose inhabitants make up "the world." This verse could be stated like this: For God so loved Sodom and Gomorrah that he sent Jesus to them, and all those who believe His truth will not perish, but will have everlasting life. This promise of sending a deliverer is a genuine demonstration of love from God to Sodom and Gomorrah, and to the earth, for that matter, as these two cities have enlarged their borders of death to encompass the earth.

An understanding of this term, "the world," helps in clarifying the following verses:

- "But now once in the end of the world hath he appeared to put away sin by the sacrifice of himself" (Heb. 9:26). Jesus will be the one to end "the world." The one to remove original sin and all other sins from the earth. He will do it once.
- "The harvest is the end of the world" (Matt. 13:39).

When the earth is harvested, sin will end. Satan's world will fall. Harvesting has not begun yet, or "the world" would be diminishing and not increasing as it presently is.

- John the Baptist will say, "Behold the Lamb of God, which taketh away the sin of the world" (John 1:29). Sin is in the singular, meaning the sin of "the world," sexual perversion. Christians are people who follow a just Jesus and have returned to being just. True Christianity will end the lifestyle of the unjust.

- "For the bread of God is he which cometh down from heaven and giveth life unto the world" (John 6:33). God will come down from heaven. He will give bread, meaning truth, spiritual food, which will give life to "the world." He will do this in person. Real Christianity will bring life to the dead, and wisdom to the foolish. When you have put an end to sin in your life, you can then say you have been raised from the dead. This is the only resurrection of the dead I can find in the Word of God.

- "Then spake Jesus again unto them, saying, I am the light of the world: he that followeth me shall not walk in darkness, but shall have the light of life" (John 8:12). Earlier we learned the law is light. The Garden Law is light. To follow Jesus, one must walk in the law, for it is the light of life. For those in "the world," to follow Jesus you must come out of the darkness. You entered Satan's world by this practice of original sin, and you leave his kingdom behind when you stop. Following a just Jesus is an about-face, a change in direction. You will then be called the justified for now you are made just again, as you were before you first committed this insult to God and self. Forward motion begins.

- "I came not to judge the world, but to save the world" (John 12:47). The purpose of judging is to save. Jesus came to save Sodom and Gomorrah. "Fear not" is often repeated in reference to the new covenant. There is nothing to fear.

- "My kingdom is not of this world" (John 18:36). The kingdom Jesus will bring to earth is not like "the world." "The world" is Satan's kingdom. In the Kingdom of God there will be no original sin, which is the root of all injustice.

- "Love not the world, neither the things that are in the world. If any man love the world, the love of the Father is not in him. For all that is in the world, the lust of the flesh, and the lust of the eyes, and the pride of life, is not of the Father, but is of the world" (1 John 2:15-16). No one should love the world, Satan's world of fornication. If you do love original sin, love for God, yourself, and your fellow humans is not in you. Without love, you are without God, for God is love.

Oral sex is of Satan, making this unnatural act an act of hate. The person requesting the act is behaving in a manner which states, "I don't care if you go to hell." "I don't love you." "I hate you." Satan is hate.

God has always been honest with you. He repeated over and over again His disapproval of the lifestyle of Sodom and Gomorrah. He expressed it in Genesis when He removed Adam and Eve from the Garden, and emphasized it when He said, "But the men of Sodom were wicked and sinners before the Lord exceedingly" (Gen. 13:13). This means you are extremely sinful in the eyes of God and have gone beyond what God will tolerate. In Romans 1:24,26,28, God gives you up to uncleanness, over to vile affections, and a reprobate mind. And in Revelations He tells of the fall of Babylon, the mother of fornication. God did not change His mind somewhere in the middle, between the beginning and the end. He has always stood against Sodom and Gomorrah. Judgment Day should not come as a surprise to any one of you.

Jesus comes to judge Sodom and Gomorrah. The Scriptures have plainly stated this day will come. But remember, you have already been condemned by the God in heaven. Condemned to death forever under the old covenant. Judgment is not for the purpose of condemning, but is for the purpose of seeing. Seeing will bring deliverance. Freedom.

Sodom and Gomorrah, do you realize The Almighty is all powerful? The Son of God will come to earth and stand alone and be more powerful than all of you put together. Expect Jesus at the close of this age. He will come and build a new church. From this Holy House of God He will defeat you and the kingdom you established by original sin. This is good news. Exciting news for the entire earth.

Judgment Day is also called the Day of the Lord, and the Day of the Lord is also the Battle of Armageddon. Christ will come to fight this final battle in the war between Good and Evil. Good will win the war. Isn't Good supposed to? Don't we all believe Good should be victorious over Evil? Jesus should defeat Lucifer's kingdom. This final battle will put the wilderness of sin behind us, and peace on earth in front of us, and make a perfect day attainable.

Do you see the Promised Land yet? Can you see an earth without original sin, and with no one breaking the Ten Commandments? Then you see our destination—the Promised Land of peace on earth. It is a long, long way off. A lot of healing needs to take place. Seeing the highway we all must travel makes it achievable.

"Behold, the day of the Lord cometh . . . to lay the land desolate: and he shall destroy the sinners thereof out of it" (Isa. 13:9). God will remove the offenders. This first commandment from Eden will slay the sinner. God never had any other plan for the destruction of the wicked except to destroy them with truth, or you could say, to stone them to death with this first law from a past paradise. You must admit it will be less painful than fire, earthquakes, or nuclear bombs, and much more rewarding. You will still be physically alive and also spiritually alive to enjoy life on a safe and peaceful homeland, earth.

Once again, Noah Webster gives us an incorrect definition when he defines Judgment Day as: the end of the world; *doomsday*. Interpreted to mean the end of the earth. Just the opposite is true. Judgment day will bring a revival, rejoicing, and a peacefulness like we have never seen before. There is no salvation until the day of judgment.

"O Lord, correct me, but with judgment; not in thine anger, lest thou bring me to nothing" (Jer. 10:24). Lord, counsel us, we need it, but with mercy, wisdom, and truth; show us and teach us right living.

ॐ

To put salvation before Judgment Day is backward.
First Judgment Day. Then seeing.
Salvation comes after seeing.

CHAPTER EIGHT

The New Covenant

The new covenant is the new agreement God will make with His wayward children, presented to us through Jesus of the New Testament. It reads like this: "For I will be merciful to their unrighteousness, and their sins and their iniquities will I remember no more. A new covenant, he hath made the first old. Now that which decayeth and waxeth old is ready to vanish away" (Heb. 8:12-13). God is the one who will decide when this new agreement goes into effect, for He is the one who will have mercy, He is the one who will forgive the sins of His children, and He is the one who will no longer remember our wrongdoing. We have no control whatsoever over the timing of the new covenant. Man will live in sin in the wilderness, until it is offered. The war between good and evil will not end until the Lamb of God comes and the final battle has been fought.

The timing of the birth of the Jesus is in God's hands. The Son of God is a gift from our heavenly Father. A gift is given from the willingness of the giver, and not upon the demand of the receiver. A gift is also given to show friendship, affection, and support. God is showing His affection and love for His children by sending the gift of truth to earth.

Without the gift of Jesus, man is doomed. The day before the day of salvation is a day of no salvation, a day of darkness. Satan had a day. If man could have saved himself during this day, the day before the day of salvation, then a Redeemer would not need to come to earth.

Jeremiah, one of the major prophets of the Old Testament, prophesied a new covenant would some day be offered to man. He said it his way: "But this shall be the covenant . . . I will put my law in their inwards parts, and write it in their hearts; and will be their God, and they shall be my people. And they shall teach no more every man his neighbour and every man his brother, saying, Know the Lord: for they shall all know me, from the least of them unto the greatest of them, saith the Lord: for I will forgive their iniquity, and I will remember their sin no more" (Jer. 31:33-34).

The new covenant will put the law you have made void back into the church, back into your minds, and back into your hearts. "Written on your heart" is to know the law like you know the ABCs. You can recite the ABCs from memory and they are always with you, and when the new covenant is established, that generation will know the Law from Eden by heart. It will be a part of them. Everyone will be taught to comply with this holy standard and not to rebel. Then we will have a generation that does not need to teach everyone to know God, for all people will know The Almighty, from the least to the greatest.

When looking at the present condition of America, I have wondered what the future holds for my children and grandchildren. No more. The promises contained in the new covenant should end all the suffering parents are presently feeling regarding the future of their children and grandchildren. The future looks bright.

Reading the new covenant agreement reassures us God is good, and all His promises and desires for His children are good and kind. Some of the promises the Scriptures convey when speaking of the new covenant are these: The law will return, I will give them a heart to know me, I will set mine eyes upon them for good, I will be their God, I will turn their mourning into joy, I will bring health and cure and reveal peace and truth, I will cleanse them, I will pardon all their iniquities and remember them no more. These are only some of the many promises from God to Sodom and Gomorrah under this new covenant.

One condition must be met: Return to God. Stand up. Turn around and come back. Only then can we all move forward out of this confusion.

Under this new covenant, everyone on earth will know God. This theme is repeated over and over again and must occur before peace on earth is a reality. Here are a few passages that literally say all the earth will be saved:

- "All the ends of the world shall remember and turn unto the Lord: and all the kindreds of the nations shall worship before thee" (Ps. 22:27).
- "All the earth shall worship thee, and shall sing unto thee; they shall sing to thy name" (Ps. 66:4).
- "For thou shalt judge the people righteously, and govern the nations upon the earth" (Ps. 67:4).
- "God shall bless us; and all the ends of the earth shall fear him" (Ps. 67:7). To fear God is to hate evil. A day is coming when all the people on earth will hate evil.
- "Ask of me, and I shall give thee the heathen for thine inheritance, and the uttermost parts of the earth for thy possession" (Ps. 2:8). A promise from God the Father to His Son.
- "Yea, all kings shall fall down before him: all nations shall serve him" (Ps. 72:11). All government leaders and all nations will serve God at this time.
- And then we have the old, familiar Christmas story when the angel says, "Fear not: for behold, I bring you good tiding of great joy 'which shall be to all people" (Luke 2:10). The

cross-reference tells us this joy for all people will come in the last days. "And it shall come to pass in the last days . . . the Lord's house shall be established . . . and all nations shall flow unto it" ('Isa. 2:2).

To believe Jesus came two thousand years ago is to say "great joy to all people" has been in effect for the last two thousand years. Has it? No! We have not been in the last days for all these many years. Don't believe it. Great joy is coming in the last days, and it will come from the Lord's house, the house built by the God of Jacob. Then true Christianity will spread to all nations until peace comes to earth.

- "And all flesh shall see the salvation of God" (Luke 3:6).
- "He shall have dominion also from sea to sea, and from the river unto the ends of the earth" (Ps. 72:8).
- Some comforting words: "They shall not hurt nor destroy in all my holy mountain: for the earth shall be full of the knowledge of the Lord, as the waters cover the sea" (Isa. 11:9). When people understand God, no one will hurt or abuse or destroy another.

CHAPTER NINE

The Old Jerusalem

⤳

M ove true Christianity to the end of this age and stop making
excuses for why today's Christianity has not saved "the
world," nor delivered us from sin, or why it doesn't look like or act
like the Christianity of the Bible. Then believe that we can look
forward to all the wonderful, last-day promises.

Clergy and members of the congregation, you began to build
the house of God but have not finished it. You set out to save the
earth. But after all these many years, the earth is still not saved.
Many people feel you should be much closer than you are, and
cannot understand why you are farther from that goal than when
you began. America is more ungodly now than when we stepped
off the *Mayflower* with our Christian principles. Something is
wrong. Your efforts are failing.

You started toward peace on earth, but the distance between us
and peace is increasing every day. There is more and more confusion regarding truth. What is right and what is wrong? When the
church begins to put homosexuals in the pews and behind the pulpit (and some have performed wedding ceremonies to celebrate
same-sex marriages) most clear-thinking people know within their
hearts something is drastically wrong with the church.

And now you are complaining that people are persecuting the church, but the reality is spelled out in Luke 14, where a story is told of building a house and not being able to finish it. "For which of you, intending to build a tower, sitteth not down first, and counteth the cost, whether he have sufficient to finish it? Lest haply, after he hath laid the foundation, and is not able to finish it, all that behold it begin to mock him" (Luke 14:28-29). Do you have sufficient power to save the world? Can you bring peace to earth? Can you accomplish what you have started? No! And the time has arrived when all who behold it (the church) have begun to mock it. Church, you are not being persecuted. But you are being mocked! Laughed at. Ridiculed. And rightfully so. Adams and Eves, bisexuals, and homosexuals, when you built God's house you assembled it without the Supreme Being, for you are without God. You began a journey to the promised land of peace on earth without God or the Garden Law in your possession, and all your efforts have been a waste.

"Except the Lord build the house, they labour in vain that build it" (Ps. 127:1). When God's house is constructed by Satan's followers, it is built in vain. Vain means having no real value, worthless, without effect.

This present-day Christianity will soon become the old Christianity, and is biblically called the old Jerusalem. The fall of the old Jerusalem has been predicted to be so complete, not one stone will be left upon another stone, meaning not one false belief from this old Christianity will be left standing. It will be torn down so completely that even the foundation will be gone.

Henry Ford is responsible for the end of the days of the horse and buggy, but he put none of his time or energy into destroying horses or buggies. His labor went into building a mode of transportation all the world would prefer over the equine animal and a wooden buggy. Thus, everyone willingly gave up their horse-drawn carriages. And so it will be with the building of a new

Christianity. No energy needs to go into the destruction of the old Christianity. All efforts must be applied to building the new, and the old will simply disappear. No one will want it any longer.

The sixteenth chapter of Ezekiel gives us a good look at the old Jerusalem (today's Christianity), and we will look at this passage verse by verse. Ezekiel 16:2-5:

Verse 2: "Cause Jerusalem to know her abominations." Tell the church members about their uncleanness.

Verse 3: "Thus saith the Lord unto Jerusalem; Thy birth and thy nativity is of the land of Canaan; thy father was an Amorite, and thy mother an Hittite." Liken the birth of the church to a birth of a child. The birthplace of today's Christianity was in Canaan. Canaan (symbol of wickedness) is where the wicked Canaanites lived. From this symbolic land of sin, your father was an Amorite, a wicked person. Your mother was a Hittite, also a wicked person. Today's Christianity was birthed in sin by wicked people. Birthed by those who live in the cities of Sodom and Gomorrah.

Verse 4: "And as for thy nativity, in the day thou wast born thy navel was not cut, neither wast thou washed in water to supple thee; thou wast not salted at all, nor swaddled at all." At birth, an infant is separated from its mother when the umbilical cord is cut; then it is washed and tightly wrapped in a blanket. At the birth of this church, the umbilical cord was not cut. You did not cut yourself away from the sin of a Hittite and an Amorite, you did not separate yourself from Sodom and Gomorrah. You still sinned, and did not wash yourself clean. There is no salt in you. Salt is truth, and from the beginning, you have had no truth in you. You were not swaddled. When the blanket is tightly wrapped around an infant, even the arms are placed under this wrap, restricting movement. But this church did not restrict itself at all. Organized Christianity has believed in original sin from its beginning.

Verse 5: "But thou wast cast out in the open field, to the loathing of thy person, in the day that thou wast born." From the day you were born you have been a thing of loathing, a thing to hate, speaking of the church. A sinning church does great harm. The Bible states that one sinner destroys much good. Think of how much harm such a large assortment of sinners accomplish.

In Matthew, Jesus asks the hypocrites from this old Jerusalem, "Why do ye also transgress the commandment of God by your traditions?" (15:3). Why do you break the law and pass this great sin on to the next generation? The church has completely reversed its true purpose. The purpose of a church is to end sin (oral sex) and not to practice it and pass it from one generation to the next. Such visual evidence of backward thinking will happen when those who ignore the law build God's house. Today's Christianity is so sinful and so backward in its beliefs that none of its blind, literal explanations of truth will stand up under a spiritual clarification of truth.

Church members, when you see the remnant and encounter godly people, when you can distinguish between the holy and the profane (God and Satan), and when you understand the just, then you will know within your own hearts that God is justified in your destruction. You are mocking God. By calling yourselves Christians, you are saying you are like Christ, and Christ is like you. If that were true, then Jesus would be sexually perverse. But, Jesus stands with the just, meaning he is not part of Sodom and Gomorrah and does not believe in their shameful sin. You are telling a lie about Jesus. He will take strong exception to this perverse image of Him you are projecting to everyone.

I once believed in today's Christianity myself, until I saw the sexually disobedient behind the pulpit and in the pews. I left my church for twenty years. During that time I did not commit original sin, but I was aware of the world around me, as if walking through a strange land. Recently, I went back to the church. I sat in the old Jerusalem for five years, listening and watching, studying, and writing. I'll pass some of my observations on to you. In this age when people are beginning to really want usable, workable answers, none is given from this old Jerusalem.

When I hear the phrase, "All you have to do is believe in Jesus," I'll ask, "What did Jesus believe in?" There is usually silence, then a quickly thought-up answer such as, "the Bible." When I hear that phrase, "All you have to do is believe in Jesus," I see a brainless Jesus. To simply believe He existed means nothing. What was His doctrine? Did He believe anything that would make a significant difference? What? What did He teach?

I believe in Lenin, Engels, and Marx. I believe they existed. But more is required of me if I were to believe in socialism or communism. I would then have to believe in their doctrine of socialism, and the *Communist Manifesto*. Wouldn't the same be true if you were going to call yourself a Christian, a follower of Christ? Believing He existed is not Christianity. Pretending He comes into your heart is make-believe in the land of let's pretend. Believing in His doctrine is required of us before we can call ourselves followers of Christ.

Church doctrine is not the same as the doctrine of Christ. Church doctrine is what your church believes, based upon your founder's truth. It is different in every denomination, and is the reason why we have separate churches, and separate church schools and universities. The hypocrites teach their own beliefs for doctrine. They have many different beliefs, resulting in many churches.

I asked a minister if he knew the law of the new covenant, "I will write my law upon your heart." Everyone, especially a minister, should know this law from memory. He did not answer.

I asked two retired pastors if they knew the difference between the God of Jacob and the god of Esau. One said he did not know. That means he does not know the difference between God and Satan. He spent his entire professional life preaching the Gospel without knowing the difference between good and evil. Pitiful.

The other minister, caught off guard, gave a quick, flip answer: "They had the same God, didn't they?" Tragic! The world doesn't need ministers who do not know the difference between God and Satan. When the hypocrite reigns, the people are ensnared, for the hypocrite will pass their own confusion on to others. That is pitiful and tragic.

I've asked many, "What is the difference between the just and the unjust?" and have never been given a correct answer.

"What does glory mean?" I asked this in a seventeen-member group of experienced Bible students. No one attempted an answer. They only said, "That is hard to explain." Moses asked God to show him His glory "And he [Moses] said, I beseech thee, shew me thy glory" (Exod. 33:18). In verse 19, God answered, "I will make all my goodness pass before thee." In response to Moses' question, God showed Moses His goodness. Therefore, God Himself considers His goodness to be His glory.

"What is holy?" "Who is holy?" Various answers are given to these questions. None was based on knowing what sin makes a person unholy. Without an understanding of the word "fornication" and the difference between God and Satan, a correct answer cannot be given. God is holy. Satan is profane. One minister presented an entire sermon on holiness without defining holy.

I remember a time when I felt pity within me. The pastor had asked the congregation to come forward toward the pulpit and pray. They all held hands or placed their hand on the back of the person next to them and bowed their heads and prayed. I sat and watched. Satan's people are praying to God. Why? How sad! God wasn't listening. The following verse came to mind. "Behold, the Lord's hand is not shortened, that it cannot save; neither his ear heavy, that it cannot hear: But your iniquities have separated between you and your God, and your sins have hid his face from you, that he will not hear" (Isa. 59:1-2). When the Garden Law is disobeyed, those who have transgressed it do not serve God. God can hear you, but He will not hear you when you pray to Him. It is illogical to pray to a God you do not serve. Ask Satan for help. Why do you serve Satan and then ask God for what you want? Those who violate the law should first pray to the God of Jacob for forgiveness. Then, when forgiveness has been granted and your life is lived in accordance with the laws of the Supreme Being, you can ask God for what you want. The God who created the heavens and the earth, the only true God, will hear you then.

I did feel sorry for these blind people. Sin had separated them from God, and this separation is so wide, taking them so far from their Creator, He will not hear them when they pray. Yet they stood praying, believing God was listening.

I've listened to many stories of murder and death. Our society has been asking, "Where is all the violence and killing coming from?" We are blaming the television, from the cartoons to the evening news, accusing our movies, and condemning computer games. Have you ever considered the killing stories being told to children and adults alike from the Sunday School classroom and from behind the pulpit? The bloody story of the Crucifixion? The flood where God kills almost everyone: men and women, children, toddlers, the elderly, the crippled, the sick? God ordered all the first-born slaughtered. He kills babies. The most famous of all biblical characters after Jesus, Moses, killed a man and God never noticed. He stood up to applaud David for killing Goliath as if to say, "Good job, David, you kill well."

When my son was six years old and tucked into bed with a promise of a bedtime story, I picked up a newly purchased book of Bible stories and began to read about David and Goliath. I stopped short and re-placed it on the bookshelf, and never read it again. Instead, I picked up a Golden Book. Why put a happy, good child to bed with a story of murder?

This old, blind, literal Christianity will have to take its share of the blame for the violence. Passing on hate disguised as love and portraying such a killing God to mankind will only increase violence. This God of yours does not set a good example. Are we supposed to be better than God? For we are commanded not to kill. It sounds like, "Don't do as I do, do as I say." We tell parents this is bad parenting.

Insight into the spiritual meaning of the Scriptures will establish this truth: the God who wrote the commandment, "Thou shalt not kill," does not kill! He would not tell a person to kill, nor would He stand up in defense of anyone who does.

Church leaders, teachers, laymen, you need to put definitions to the words you use. You need to comprehend what you are saying. Knowing the difference between God and Satan is fundamental to Christianity. Serve God. Define holy. Identify sin. Name it, call it what it is, so it can be dealt with the way God tells us to deal with it. Then put sin out of the church. You need spiritual eyesight. Literal interpretation of Scripture is proof of spiritual blindness.

"The prophets prophesy falsely, and the priests bear rule by their means; and my people love to have it so: and what will ye do in the end thereof?" (Jer. 5:31). In the last days, the pastor/priest/rabbi will be wicked, and evil church members will love it. The people want to hear, "I'm okay, you're okay." The wicked shut their ears to those who would tell them the truth. They want lies. Some of these lies come in the form of fables. But the time will come when all the lies and fables will be no more, for they will be replaced by truth.

When God removes the false prophets from His house, what will they do? What will the people who love their teachings do then? Will they change? Will they believe truth? For all the earth to be saved, the answer is yes.

The Bible is full of parables, but what is a fable? In parable, an object or subject we understand and are familiar with is used in story form to convey to us a spiritual truth. For example, the story of the Prodigal Son is a parable. It is a literal story that communicates to us a spiritual truth. A youth leaves his father, home, and family to pursue his own sinful, selfish ways. And when he comes to his senses, he decides life at home with father and family was better than anything he had found elsewhere. The spiritual lesson to be learned is that when a person leaves God to pursue sin, they, too, will come to their senses and will understand that life with God is better than anything they found when they were away from God. They will return home to God. Our heavenly Father will welcome back with joy all those who left Him, the same as the father in the story of the prodigal.

A fable is just the opposite of a parable. A fable is when the spiritual is used to tell us a literal story. Fables will always mislead us. For they are false tales. For example, the word "fire," like the word "wine," has a spiritual meaning. Just as most of the Scriptures regarding wine have nothing to do with man-made wine, the word "fire" is also seldom used in a literal way. The Bible states: "The Lord will come with fire, . . . to render his anger with fury, and his rebuke with flames of fire" (Isa. 66:15). When the word fire is taken literally, like the fire that raged through much of Yellowstone Park, we will hear stories about how the earth will someday burn in a literal fire. That story is a fable, or a false tale, a falsehood. It is a spiritual truth taught as literal truth. Reality: God will come with fire, for the law is a fire, and He will rebuke (sharply reprimand) his children with this first fiery law given in the Garden.

"And they shall turn away their ears from the truth, and shall be turned unto fables" (2 Tim. 4:4). The same people, who will not listen to the truth or hear the Garden Law and want this truth removed from earth, will turn the truth of God into fables. The truth will be turned into lies by these fables. The stories come from their blindness, as they sit in the dark. Satan's people cannot comprehend the spiritual, because they are spiritually blinded by sin and lies. Since they believe lies they cannot know truth, and therefore, do not have the mind of God. The result: an inability to understand what God is saying. Blind religious leaders tell us many story that are not true.

When the many pastors who violate this first basic rule of conduct see what this law reveals, and compare it to their own explanation of Scripture, they will recognize many of their own narration of biblical truths to be falsehoods.

In the following chapters, each commandment will be clearly defined. I will explain how just one act of original sin breaks each commandment; and I will also show how original sin breaks all ten of the Ten Commandments at once. The unveiling of this unexpected new mandate will shine bright enough to clarify the true spiritual importance of the Bible.

ॐ

God speaks His own language. He shows us His own thinking and lets us see through His eyes as we look at the first fundamental law for living. An assessment of the law explaining original sin will reveal many new truths about God, and love, and goodness. We will see God's character.

❧

The Orthodox Jew
is
correct
in
waiting
for
the Messiah.

❧

The Doctrine of Jesus

৯৯

God commands us not to do
only that which will destroy us,
our home, and our nation.

A Deep Change

"Travel is more than the seeing
of the sight; it is a change that
goes on, deep and permanent,
in the ideas of living."

—Miriam Beard
B. 1901
American writer

CHAPTER TEN

The Law Giver

❦

We have been journeying deep into the darkness, proceeding carefully and cautiously while investigating how we arrived here, calculating the catastrophic devastation caused by original sin, viewing the dead, and acknowledging the madness. The human journey from the Garden of Eden to the Promised Land of peace on earth has been spent entirely in the wilderness of sin. The darkness becomes more and more dense with time, until at the end it will be the darkest before the dawn. We are presently in the dark before the dawn of the next age. As we follow the light from the law, we can venture onward. And because we are no longer blind to what imprisons us here in the wilderness, we are no longer lost here, unable to find our way out. Moving forward toward the outer edge of this wilderness, we will arrive at a crossing where we can enter the Promised Land. But first we must look more closely at the teachings that will make the crossing possible, the doctrine of Jesus.

Doctrine: something taught, a belief, teachings, the foundation a belief is built on.

"They questioned among themselves, saying, What thing is this? what new doctrine is this?" (Mark 1:27). According to Scripture,

Jesus taught a revolutionary new doctrine. It was a new belief for the whole earth. But what new belief was it?

The New Testament was written before the coming of Christ so that we may recognize Him when He comes. The words of Jesus: "I have not spoken of myself; but the Father which sent me, He [God] gave me a commandment, what I should say, and what I should speak. And I know that his commandment is life everlasting . . . so I speak" (John 12:49-50). "Commandment" is once again in the singular, because it is the law presented to Adam and Eve when there was just one. God gave Jesus this commandment, and that "commandment" is what He will teach. It is the foundation of His belief. Jesus will not take credit for this commandment, as the above verse states. At times, He will declare: "My doctrine is not mine, but his that sent me" (John 7:16). Jesus knew this information was given to Him by God. He also knew that this first basic standard for living embraces life (raises the dead), and so He will speak and teach the law. The Garden Law is the doctrine of Jesus. This holy standard is the law of the new covenant and will some day be written in everyone's memory. Conforming our thoughts and our lives to this ordinance is how we exit the wilderness. Submission to this first rule given to mankind is a new moral code and the gateway into the Promised Land. All the peoples of the earth will conform to a higher standard of morality than we have experienced while living here in the wilderness.

In the beginning of time the law was a dividing line. When broken, it separated the Garden from the wilderness. A line was crossed into disobedience; and at the end of time, when we obey this virtuous standard, it will separate the wilderness of sin from the Promised Land. And a line will be crossed into obedience.

We have already studied the Garden Law enough to know it is both life and death. When kept, it is life; when broken, it is the opposite of life—death. This commandment is the dividing line between many opposites, and has already enabled us to understand the following forces opposing each other.

WHEN THE LAW IS KEPT	WHEN THE LAW IS BROKEN
God	Satan
Good	Evil
Life	Death
Love	Hate
Wisdom	Foolishness
Light	Darkness
Just	Unjust
Heaven	Hell
The remnant	Sodom and Gomorrah

A few characteristics of this law speak for themselves and need no additional research:

- **The law is old.** "Brethren, I write no new commandment unto you, but an old commandment which ye had from the beginning" (1 John 2:7). From the beginning of time, this law has been in existence. It is not new. Although it was removed from our hearing, all the ramifications from breaking the command were never made void. The consequences of sin have continually been realized, and the earth is covered with the spiritually dead who live in the dark at this present time.

- **The law is new.** "Again, a new commandment I write unto you . . . and the true light now shineth" (1 John 2:8). Even though this commandment is as old as the beginning of man, it is new for this present generation, for they have never heard it. And the law is light. True light. Truth that shines. It will shine in this darkness, guiding us onward through the entrance leading into the Promised Land.

- **The law is love.** "We know that we have passed from death unto life, because we love the brethren. He that loveth not his brother abideth in death" (1 John 3:14). God is love. Satan is hate. Therefore, since the sin of Eden is of Satan, it is an act of hate. This line between love and hate is new to this last generation. Those who commit the act of original sin act out that they hate God. When they ask another person to commit this base act, they express hate toward their brethren.

Jesus was asked, what is the greatest commandment? He answered with, love God first and your brother as yourself. Translated: Do not commit sin yourself. Do not ask any other person to commit oral sex. Then you will know you love God, and you will know you love your brothers and sisters. Only then will you love yourself.

All who hate their brethren abide in death. Thus, if you stop hating, you know you are alive, and not dead, raised from the dead. "And this is love, that we walk after his commandments, this is the commandment, That, as ye have heard from the beginning, that ye should walk in it" (2 John 6). Here love is defined—keep the law! Obey the order given at the beginning of time in Eden.

- **The law gives peace.** "Great peace have they which love thy law: and nothing shall offend them" (Ps. 119:165). Peace of mind, reconciliation between you and God (peace), respect and love between the races (peace), and peace to all nations will come from supporting this first rule of conduct. Peace on earth. All wars, big and small, individual, political, and physical (germs warring against a healthy body), have basically come from this lewd conduct that reduces a person to being profane, ungodly, and unethical. Great peace is promised when living in agreement with God's first command.

- **The law converts and makes you wise.** "The law of the Lord is perfect, converting the soul: the testimony of the Lord is sure, making wise the simple" (Ps. 19:7). The law converts. Convert means to change. The law from Eden will convert (change) you. When you return to God, you have changed your mind about sin, and that will change the way you live. When you agree with the Creator, then you can say you have been converted. This sincere willing determination to obey God will make the foolish wise again.

No longer will you be running away from God. But now you will be walking with the Father and moving in a forward direction. As more people become transformed, change the direction in which they are traveling, and are made wise, the closer we will be to accomplishing peace, solving our social ills, and healing all of our wounds.

- **Think on the law.** "O how I love thy law! It is my meditation all the day" (Ps. 119:97). Since I have understood this first command, it has been on my mind always. I relate most of what I see and hear to this rule of action. If you were to practice viewing the entire earth from this light as I have, you would see life as it presently is. And you would begin to see life on earth as it should be.

Other matters of the law are a little more complex, and we will explore some more deeply for the remainder of this chapter.

- **The law is a fire.** Fire is a major topic in Scripture and is seldom used literally. Let us look at this concept of a fiery law more closely. As we did with the word "wine," look for a moment at the literal qualities of "fire" to better comprehend its spiritual meaning.

LITERAL FIRE	SPIRITUAL FIRE
Destroys	Destroys
Consumes	Consumes
Creates smoke	Creates smoke
Devours	Devours
Purges	Purges
Refines	Refines

The law God gave Adam and Eve is a fire. The law God gave
to Moses (one of the two tablets of stone) is a fire. The Garden
Law of the new covenant that Jesus brings to earth will kindle a
fire. They are one and the same. Think of this law as being a fire.
Visualize the Garden Law as having the same capabilities as literal
fire, only in a spiritual way.

In the hands of Satan, original sin is a blaze that will consume
and destroy the righteous, causing decay, wickedness, and spiritual death. When an upright person breaks the law, he or she dies in
a fire. The holy person is destroyed, and a profane person is created. Here are a few biblical passages that speak of the inferno
caused by committing this first act of defiance. If you have died in
the flames of original sin, you will identify with the meaning of
these passages:

"For every abomination to the Lord, which he hateth, have
they done unto their gods; for even their sons and their daughters
they have burnt in the fire to their gods" (Deut. 12:31). Many who
serve Satan will teach their children to practice evil. Child abuse
of this nature is rampant in America. Many youngsters have died
in the flames. The blaze comes from breaking the law, is sparked
by Satan, and can be called hell fire. These children live in a hell.

When this scandalous, cruel behavior is mentioned in God's
Word, this report sometimes follows: "Neither came it into my
mind" (Jer. 19:5). God didn't think you would do this. Humans
have fallen far below what God expected of them.

"For wickedness burneth as the fire" (Isa. 9:18). When the
masses are overtaken by sin, we can say the earth is in flames,
devouring and consuming all that is good, holy, and right—estab-
lishing an ever-advancing hell on earth, a wild fire.

"And others save with fear, pulling them out of the fire; hating
even the garment spotted by the flesh" (Jude 23). Jude is a one-
chapter book of the Bible and is exclusively devoted to describing
Sodom and Gomorrah. All who dwell in these two cites must be

pulled out of the flames; for everyone of them has died in a blaze Satan prepared. They are separated from God, tormented by sin, dead, in a grave, and in a fire. This sounds like hell to me! This may be the only hell God makes reference to. When the whole earth knows God (and that will come), there is no hell, neither is there a need for one, nor a place for one.

When building a fire, the fuel can be wood, oil, gas, or coal, among other things. When more fuel is added, the flames becomes hotter and more widespread. The same is true of the blaze sin ignites, except the fuel is holy, innocent, good, and alive people of God. After going through the fire of violating the first command, God's children are unholy, defiled, evil, and dead. Satan's fire destroys a holy person. It wrecks our homes. And it is spreading across our land bringing havoc to our nation.

Most of the biblical references to fire are pertaining to this Garden Law. This fiery commandment can both destroy and refine. In the hands of God, this same law will be a purifying fire and will create righteous people as it consumes and annihilates all who are wicked. The fuel for this burning is also people—the unclean. All who come through the flames will be purified. Obedience to this burning revelation slays the wicked, and they also die in the blaze. The evil person is destroyed (burned in a fire), and a righteous person emerges from the flames, purified, refined, clean, and holy again.

The following are a few examples of the law as it purifies, purges, destroys, and consumes the wicked:
- **Jesus comes to build a fire.** The Son of God announces in Luke "I am come to send fire on the earth; and what will I, if it be already kindled?" (Luke 12:49). If the fire has already been ignited, the Messiah need not come. But it has not. Jesus Christ will kindle the fire that will burn up the wicked with the law given to Him by God. Once kindled, no one will put the blaze out.

"But the chaff he will burn with fire unquenchable" (Luke 3:17). Once the flame has been lit, it will be unstoppable. Good news! Hell fire will not triumph over Godly fire. The wicked will burn like dry stubble.

Even though those who reside in Sodom and Gomorrah have been threatened with a fiery end, literally, the stories of earth being destroyed by literal flames are not true. They have been prepared and delivered to you from the blind eyes of others who sit in the same sin as you do, and have no spiritual eyesight. So they see the Scriptures incorrectly and tell you this fable. God never has had and never will have a plan to drop nuclear bombs or any other forms of fire on anyone. He does, however, have a plan to show mercy. A plan "B." A new covenant. A new agreement by which to deliver man from his own evil inventions. God, in his timing, has a process and a way to end immorality by a revelation of this first fiery law. This command is the only fire God ever planned on using to burn up the wicked. It causes no physical harm.

Yes, Sodom and Gomorrah, God does have a plan to reduce you to ashes. I expect this law to reduce the wicked to ashes as it purges sin and purifies you until you are once again holy. When you are gone, we will all have heaven on earth. And you, in your changed, purified state, will be included. Many who presently reside in wickedness here in the wilderness will be the same people who will enjoy righteousness in the Kingdom of God, the Promised Land, after all the blind can see and have been converted. Good news, not only for the generation chosen for deliverance, but also for their children and grandchildren.

- **Moses led the people with fire and smoke.** "The Lord came from Sinai . . . and he came with ten thousands of saints: from his right hand went a fiery law for them" (Deut. 33:2). It was a fiery law God gave Moses, and Jesus will be given the same flaming table of stone. Jesus will also come with thousands of saints. These saints are others who were not deceived by Satan and have not committed original sin. They will be called virgins, meaning untouched by Satan. They are the remnant we discussed in the first chapters, who are not like Sodom and Gomorrah.

Moses was given stones of fire, and as we approach the end of this age of sin, God tells us we can look to Moses for advice on how to move from the wilderness to the Promised Land. "Now all these things happened unto them for ensamples: and they are written for our admonition, upon whom the ends of the world are come" (1 Cor. 10:11). These events are written so we can learn from Moses how to end "the world" (Satan's world of sexual perversion). Knowing what Moses said and did to ready his people to leave the wilderness of sin will enable us to prepare ourselves to leave the wilderness and enter our own Promised Land of peace on earth.

Moses gave the law to the people. He was and still is called a law-giver. He came down from the top of Mount Sinai with two tables of stone—not one. "And he [God] gave unto Moses, when he had made an end of the communing with him upon mount Sinai, two tables of testimony, tables of stone, written with the finger of God" (Exod. 31:18). One set is the law given to Adam and Eve. The second set of commandments is the list we are most familiar with, those we call the Ten Commandments. "And the Lord said unto Moses, Come up to me into the mount, and be there: and I will give thee tables of stone, and a law, and commandments which I have written; that thou mayest teach them" (Exod. 24:12). On one table is the Garden Law. Sin, meaning original sin (sin in the singular), breaks the law (law in the singular). Sin breaks the law. Original sin breaks all Ten Commandments written on one of the tables. On the other table are the Ten Commandments as we have been taught them. Each table contains the same Ten Commandments. They were written twice for a good reason.

Ordered by God, Moses was to teach these two sets of commandments to the people. Teach the law and teach the commandments. He organized a number of fellow believers to help him do this, and they taught the people all the commands the Divine Creator had given to Moses. Submission to these holy orders was considered the foremost requirement for entering the Promised Land. Today, obedience to both set of commandments is still God's mandate for dwelling in the Promised Land of peace on earth. Keeping the law and the Ten Commandments will end all wrongdoing, thus ending the wilderness of sin.

Most of us are quite knowledgeable concerning the Ten Commandments being taught today in the house called God's house and once upon a time in our schools. And when we do not keep one of these commandments, most of us know we have disobeyed an order from God. We know it because we know the commandments. You could say we know them by heart. Commandments can be broken one at a time. For example, if I were to embezzle money from a fund placed in my charge, I would be breaking the commandment, "Thou shalt not steal." Because I know the commandment not to steal, if I do steal, I am aware I have broken that Godly rule. The intent of the new covenant is to write the Garden Law in your memory so you will know it as well as you know "thou shalt not steal." You will know it by heart.

However, the set concerning the law, which instructs us not to commit original sin (oral sex), has not been taught to this generation. Therefore, it has not yet been written on the hearts of this lost generation. No one knows it like we know the Ten Commandments. Not yet! "For by the law is the knowledge of sin" (Rom. 3:20). The law needs to be taught today so all will have the knowledge of what sin is. Once this information goes out, then you cannot consent to sin without knowing you are breaking a law from God.

The one set, referring to the law given in the beginning of time to Adam and Eve, cannot be broken one at a time. One act of original sin breaks all ten commandments at once.

The law is also weightier. If you were in the business of tearing down old buildings, and you did it the old-fashioned way with a wrecking ball and a crane, as you struck a building over and over again with a 500-pound wrecking ball, each blow at the point of impact would deliver a destructive force and cause the building to begin to crumble down. Now increase the size of the wrecking ball to 1,000 pounds. This would double the destructive force and demolish the building in even quicker time. The more weight, the more destruction. The first table of stone with the Garden Law written on it is the weightiest (greatest) sin. Original sin is extremely injurious. More spiritual, mental damage occurs to a person than when one of the commands from the second set is broken.

Remember how the Pharisees leave out the weightier matters of the law? "Woe to you, scribes and Pharisees, hypocrites! . . . [you] have omitted the weightier matters of the law" (Matt. 23:23). And when Jesus is asked what is the greatest commandment, he states, to love God first and your brother as yourself. To love God you must not commit original sin. If you love your neighbor, you will not ask a neighbor to commit this gross act of insulting God and self. If you love your spouse, you will not ask your spouse to consent to disobeying this first commandment. If you love your children, you will not teach your children sin. When you love yourself you will remove this act of disobedience from your life. This is the greatest, weightiest commandment. The most damage occurs to an individual, to a marriage, to a family, and to a nation when this commandment is broken.

Original sin is the most negative, the most damaging, and the most hurtful behavior of all. It knocks a person down, and he or she cannot recover from it. All our criminals are produced from this one most harmful and hurtful act. All the madness is caused by original sin. This greatest transgression is the root of everything that is wrong on earth today.

The hypocrites and religious leaders are guilty of committing the greatest offense. They spend their time trying to remove the lesser wrongs from those who will listen. God will instruct them to remove the bigger evil from their own lives. And then they will be able to see how to remove not only the greatest evil from earth, but also the lesser wrongs. In the book of Matthew that is said this way, "Or how wilt thou say to thy brother, Let me pull out the mote out of thine eye; and, behold, a beam is in thine own eye? Thou hypocrite, first cast out the beam out of thine own eye; and then shalt thou see clearly to cast out the mote out of thy brother's eye" (Matt. 7:4-5). A mote is a small particle, like a speck of sawdust, while a beam is a much larger piece of wood, usually the largest used in the construction of a home. First things must come first. Ministers must remove the beam from their own lives before trying to remove the lesser transgressions from the lives of others. The church must begin saving the earth by first removing original sin from the leaders of the church.

The law is the greatest commandment. God is love, but Satan is hate. Sin, oral sex, is an act of hate. Do not sin. If you do, you will hate yourself. Self-loathing and low self-esteem are a monumental problem in America today. Do not ask another person to commit oral sex. If you do, you hate them. Sin is hate acted out. You act these words out even if you do not say them: "I don't care about you!" "Go to hell!" "I don't love you!" "I'm selfish!" "I'll use you!" "I'll kill you!"

Understand the law—it is your friend. It should convert you. In this present-day Christianity (also called the old Jerusalem), no one has yet been converted. For when the law is left out, conversion does not occur.

The doctrine of Jesus is the law. Again, in the following chapters you will want to consider and explore the evidence yourself. Learn not to put your soul into the hands of someone else. Think for yourself, and master the art of believing what God says—not man. Do not believe without "King James" proof.

One act of original sin breaks all ten commandments written on the one table of stone. So in the following chapters we will

investigate each individual command to see how this one transgression breaks that commandment. The Bible will teach us.

ॐ

"Open thou mine eyes, that I may behold
wondrous things out of thy law."
Psalm 119:18

CHAPTER ELEVEN

Commandment 1

❧

Thou shalt have no other
gods before me.
Exodus 20:3

From the first chapters of this book you should already have an understanding of how Adam and Eve ignored this commandment. They chose Satan over God. All those who have committed original sin have chosen to serve Satan and not to serve God.

But the Word of God repeatedly speak of other gods as though there are many. It sounds as though Satan is not the only other god, yet we know we only have those two choices, God or Satan. There are only two powers, good and evil. Everyone on earth can be divided into just two groups: the just and the unjust, or the lambs and the goats, or the remnant and Sodom and Gomorrah, or those in the Ark and those in the water, as in the days of Noah. So how are so many other gods possible?

First we must understand that there is only one true God. He is the One who created the heavens and the earth and all that is. He is the master builder of all truth. Jesus is the truth made flesh, and He stated more than once He was repeating the same truth of His Father. They both maintain that any lifestyle that includes the practice of oral sex is idolatry. Any person changing this truth manufactures a lie and becomes a false god.

All lies come from Satan, and they are numerous and varied. The falsehood Adam and Eve believed, that husbands and wives can commit oral sex and it is not sin, is not the same lie the homosexual believes, that two men or two women can commit this first immoral sex act and it is not sin. The bisexual believes yet another variation of this same lie. The pedophile, the prostitute (male and female), the sexually promiscuous, and others whose lifestyles include this first sin all believe in various ways of breaking this fundamental standard. They all basically believe the same lie Lucifer told in the Garden, that oral sex is not sin. The serpent's lie constructs an assortment of lifestyles, and is why the Scriptures say, "Strait is the gate, and narrow is the way which leadeth unto life, and few there be that find it. Wide is the gate, and broad is the way, that leads to destruction, and many there be which go in thereat" (Matt. 7:13-14). There is one highway to heaven and many paths to hell.

Believing oral sex is not sin changes truth and makes you a fool. The book of Romans speaks of the sexually perverse: "Professing themselves to be wise, they became fools. Who changed the truth of God into a lie, and worshipped and served the creature more than the Creator" (Rom. 1:22,25). When you change the truth of God, you place yourself above God. This makes you a god. Not the one true God, not the God of truth, but a false god. A god (person) who tells lies.

People are false gods, people-gods, who tell falsehoods. Today, with so many people violating the law and exalting themselves above God, there are many lying gods. In Scripture they are referred to as false gods, strange gods, molten gods, and gods of the people around about you. These false gods are called idols.

Serving these idols is called idolatry, for you serve the creature (humans, the false gods) more than you serve God.

Adam and Eve became gods. "For God doth know that in the day ye eat thereof, then your eyes shall be opened, and ye shall be as gods, knowing good and evil" (Gen. 3:5).

"Ye shall be as gods." When people exalt themselves above God they become gods who tell lies, for they follow the author of lies, Satan, and become masters of deceit.

These gods, because of pride, are too proud to admit they are wrong, and continue on through life believing they know more about life than God does. They will many times convince, even force, others to serve them. Then they continue to insist they have done no wrong. I believe the reason for this persistence stems from the fact that sin is so foolish it is hard to admit to being that foolish.

The Bible is filled with examples of other gods, and the serving of other gods always involves breaking the Garden Law. "Then shalt thou say unto them, Because your fathers have forsaken me, saith the Lord, and have walked after other gods, and have served them, and have worshipped them, and have forsaken me, and have not kept my law" (Jer. 16:11). Any time the law is not kept, that person has forsaken God, has become a god, and then will serve others who have also broken the law. When sin is asked for, he or she will comply. In our present age, we believe consenting adults can commit original sin and it is okay. Yet Adam and Eve were consenting adults.

"Then Jacob said unto his household, and to all that were with him, Put away the strange gods that are among you, and be clean, and change your garments" (Gen. 35:2). Being a false god is always filthiness, for sin is filthiness. Putting away strange gods from among you will make you clean. Stop believing in lifestyles man invented and start believing in the lifestyle God does sanction and bless.

"Lest thou make a covenant with the inhabitants of the land,

and they go a whoring after their gods, and do sacrifice unto their gods, and one call thee, and thou eat of his sacrifice" (Ex. 34:15). Whoring is always sexual perverseness, and the sexually perverse are serving gods who demand them to go whoring and eat of their sin. Some husbands expect this "duty" from their wives. Some wives expect this service from their husbands. Those who believe in oral sex need a partner to perform the act of sin. That partner is serving a false god.

God always gives to us good advice. He states in Proverbs, "My son, if sinners entice thee, consent thou not" (1:10). Do not serve sinners. Neither a marriage license nor an "agreement of consent" puts God's stamp of approval on original sin.

Many times our worst enemies are those in our own family. "If thy brother, the son of thy mother, or thy son, or thy daughter, or the wife of thy bosom, or thy friend, which is as thine own soul, entice thee secretly, saying, Let us go and serve other gods, which thou hast not known, thou, nor thy fathers. Thou shalt not consent unto him, nor hearken unto him . . . neither shalt thou spare, neither shalt thou conceal him" (Deut. 13:6,8). Do not consent and do not conceal the wicked. Covering up and hiding such detestable behavior only supports it. Sin will not end if it is concealed and allowed to go unchallenged. Instead, it will spread like a plague. Adam and Eve hid. Some people hide in their own homes and practice wickedness with family members.

Many of you may have promised someone that you would never tell. You promised to keep it a secret forever. Maybe this promise was made to your father, mother, or another relative. If that is the case, you need to understand that you must break that promise. How can you repent, come clean, and be healed without breaking it? How can you face reality and deal with the hurt and anger you feel? It cannot be done. And this is why you are told you will need to love God more than your parents. "He that loveth father or mother more than me is not worthy of me" (Matt. 10:37).

And so we add one more biblical word to the many describing the sexually perverse: idol, idolatry, idolater. These are woven throughout the Scriptures, from beginning to end, and without exception describe the sexually perverse.

- **Idols.** "For all the gods of the nations are idols" (Ps. 96:5). All those who are sexually perverse are idols.

"For it is the land of graven images, and they are mad upon their idols" (Jer. 50:38). Fornication is whoring; whoring is idolatry, and worshipping idols is the reasoning behind the madness we are experiencing on earth today.

- **Idolatry.** "For the time past of our life . . . when we walked in lasciviousness, lusts, excess of wine, revellings, banquetings, and abominable idolatries" (1 Peter 4:3). Peter is saying there was a time when we lived in base immorality, and there will be a time when we do not. The generation chosen to see peace on earth will someday say, "Remember when we lived in abominably idolatry? That was a long time ago."

To state this commandment in a positive way: Thou shalt serve the Lord God with all thy mind and with all thy strength and with all thy soul. For God is above all gods. Serve only the God of truth. "And they put away the strange gods from among them, and served the Lord" (Judges 10:16). They stopped serving strange gods—humans who serve Satan. This is a positive, forward movement and will be required of all before entrance into the Promised Land.

As the population of earth today can be divided into a remnant and Sodom and Gomorrah (only two groups of people) so can all the biblical characters, leaving the Bible with a great deal to say about those who are like Sodom and Gomorrah and those who are not. When you read the Bible, identify those who serve God and those who serve idols, for it will open up your understanding of Scripture

Did you notice that all these commandments are written in

stone? The Garden Law is a fire, and stones on fire are called brimstones, hot rocks. God does plan to drop fire and brimstone on Sodom and Gomorrah. These stones with commandments written on them are the only hot rocks God ever planned to rain on Sodom and Gomorrah. Some of them are exceptionally powerful. And when one or more of these burning, fiery stones are used to kill a wicked person, aim between the eyes where the brain is located. Truth is for the mind, and we are promised by God: truth will slay the wicked. Truth should bring about your death as it did when David killed Goliath with just three of the five stones he prepared. David first practiced on a lion and a bear (people who are false images of God, which will be explained in the next chapter) before tackling a military giant. He tested these stones, and he knew they did work.

ॐ

This first commandment demands that we do not serve these false gods who believed the same lie that Eve did. The generation willing to bow their knee to a just Jesus will end original sin. This action of bowing is not literal, but rather a mental exercise of agreeing with God, and will require all people (every knee shall bow to Jesus) to humble themselves in submission to the one true God.

Humble means: To lower your rank. Place yourself under God's authority, for the sinner has reversed this position and has exalted himself above God. Humility will correct this inappropriate placement. God is not being unreasonable when He requires of you to lower your rank.

CHAPTER TWELVE

Commandment 2

༄

Thou shalt not make unto thee any graven image,
or any likeness of any thing that is in heaven above,
or that is in the earth beneath, or that is in
the water under the earth.
Exodus 20:4

God is at times harsh, passionate in His disapproval, and vividly graphic in some of His descriptions of the wicked. "A naughty person, a wicked man, walketh with a forward mouth. He winketh with his eyes, he speaketh with his feet, he teacheth with his fingers" (Prov. 6:12-13). Naughty is one expressive illustration, but in that picture I can feel the tenderness and warmth of a loving parent concerned about the stubborn rebellion of a child. The wicked are God's naughty children, and He loves them the same way any parent loves a wayward child, with a hurt for the hurt of the child.

However, tenderness it difficult to find in this second commandment. It is strong, graphic, illuminating. God displays His mind, uncovers His face to show to us His basic character, and communicates to us how deeply original sin insults Him. To see

God is to see His mind, the way He thinks, and the way He would live if He were human. And He made us like Him, to think like Him and to live like Him.

Our heavenly Father tells us we are created in His image. God is invisible, so we are not speaking of our physical appearance, but how we think and act. "And God said, Let us make man in our image, after our likeness" (Gen. 1:26). If God were to stand in front of you or me and look at us, He should see Himself. We are an image. We are either the image of God or we have changed to what is not like God. Either way, we are an image: a true likeness of God or a false likeness of God, a false god.

When you look into a mirror, you see an image. The image looking back at you looks like you physically, and you physically look like the image. Now, you be the mirror. Put God in front of the mirror. You are the image God is looking at. You should be like God, and God should be like you, in a spiritual likeness, in the way you think and live.

Now look at this second commandment and compare it to the first chapter of Romans describing Sodom and Gomorrah. "Professing themselves to be wise, they became fools, And changed the glory of the uncorruptible God into an image made like to corruptible man, and to birds, and four-footed beasts, and creeping things" (Rom. 1:22-23). These sinners changed the image. Who is the image? They are! They changed themselves. They become images of birds, beasts, and creeping things, making themselves a false image of God. Now they no longer think or live like God. They changed their goodness to evil.

Sodom and Gomorrah, stand up. Let God stand facing you. Allow God to look at you. Listen to what He tells you He sees. The Divine Creator would say to you, "You do not look like Me any more. You have changed! You did not change evil to good. But you have changed. You look like images of things that are in the sky, birds. I see things that walk on the earth: beasts, insects, and

creeping things such as bears, lions, dogs, snakes, locust, scorpi-
ons. You look like images of things in the water, fish. You have
carved yourself into images that do not look like Me." Sin is deadly, so I see dead birds, dead four-footed animals (beasts), and dead
creeping things. You no longer act like me! You live like the animals, the birds, and the insects. You have no rules, no laws, no God
over you. You pay allegiance to no higher power than man.
Animals live by instinct and have no reasoning powers. You have
lost your ability to reason life out."

Sodom and Gomorrah, look back at God. When you look at
God, you need to understand He is not like you. You have changed
into things that are not like God. God does not think like you. And
He would not live as you do.

This commandment is the most powerfully worded and the
most graphic of all the commandments. Can you see the spiritual
condition of earth? It is now covered with these false images: dead,
stinking animals and birds, dead fish and creeping things? If God
were to look down from heaven today, He would not see the
human race He created. He would see an earth covered with these
animals, birds, fish, and creeping things. And throughout the
Bible, He often addresses the wicked as He sees them. The Bible is
God talking to us. He speaks to us from His viewpoint, from His
perception, in His language, as He sees it.

And so the Holy Book our Creator sent to earth is saturated
with references of birds, beasts, and creeping things. One example
calls man a swift dromedary. "'How canst thou say, I am not polluted, I have not gone after Baalim? See thy way in the valley,
know what thou hast done: thou art a swift dromedary traversing
her way" (Jer. 2:23). A swift dromedary is a camel, a beast. And the
cross-reference takes us back to Adam and Eve. "The woman thou
gavest to be with me, she gave me of the tree and I did eat" ('Gen.
3:12). God is asking this question to Adam and Eve, "How can you
say you are not a beast? a camel, a false image of God." How can

any man and wife who consent to commit original sin say they are not polluted. How can they say they have not become an image of a beast. Heterosexual marriage partners who consent to sin need to see their way, and understand what they have done. You both are false images, a false likeness of God. A false god. You are a beast. Neither of you thinks as God thinks.

God clothed Adam and Eve in skins before driving them from the Garden, which is saying God saw them as animals. "Unto Adam also and to his wife did the Lord God make coats of skins, and clothed them. So he drove out the man" (Gen. 3:21,24). God would never drive people. Spiritually speaking, God saw and He drove two animals out of the Garden. It is proper to lead people, and it is also proper to drive animals.

The countless biblical references to beasts, animals, birds, and creeping things are not all dealing with the sexually perverse, but a great number of them are. From Genesis to Revelation we read about beasts: dead beasts, burning beasts, stinking beasts. Seven verses from the end of the Holy Book we read in Revelations: "For without are dogs, and sorcerers, and whoremongers, and murderers, and idolater, and whosoever loveth and maketh a lie" (22:15). You will discover each word in this verse is a description of a sexually perverse individual, and a four-legged animal (a dog) is mentioned at the top of the list. God reveals to us much of His righteous anger directed at Sodom and Gomorrah in this commandment. You will not be allowed to enter the Promised Land of peace on earth in your present condition. In the beginning, you were removed from the Garden for this behavior, and at the end of time this abominable behavior must end before you will be allowed entrance into God's presence. Nowhere between Genesis and Revelation, the beginning and the end, does The Master of the universe change His mind.

In Psalms, the sinner is likened unto another animal. "Thus they changed their glory into the similitude of an ox that eateth grass" (106:20). Glory is goodness. When Moses asked God if he could see His glory, God answered him by saying, "I will make all my goodness pass before thee" (Exod. 33:19). To change glory is to change goodness. They exchanged goodness for evil. An ox is a beast of burden and eats grass when it is hungry. Man becomes a beast who carries a burden, the burden of sin, and eats sin when he is hungry. The carnal mind processes the sexual appetite in the same manner it processes the physical desire for food—when hungry, eat!—just like the animals.

"Thou makest darkness, and it is night: wherein all the beasts of the forest do creep forth" (Ps. 104:20). During the time of spiritual darkness, there are beasts everywhere. I have heard it said, "It is a jungle out there." Original sin makes the earth a jungle. "Its a dog-eat-dog world." Sin produces these conditions. When transgressors are removed from earth, these conditions will no longer exist.

"Ye serpents, ye generation of vipers, how can ye escape the damnation of hell?" (Matt. 23:33). Since I place the birth of Jesus at the end of time, Jesus will say to the religious leaders of today: You are serpents, creeping snakes who kill the righteous; vipers, venomous snakes who catch the innocent in your evil clutches and carry them to hell with you. You did not succeed in changing evil into good. "I'm okay, you're okay" is not truth. You are not the image of God, but instead false images of creeping things, snakes. You are just like the snake in the Garden, deceiving people with your lies, repeating Satan's same Garden of Eden lie, "Go ahead and sin." "Sin is not deadly." This whole generation is a generation of vipers, a generation of sexually perverse people passing this lie on from one generation to the next, even killing their young.

"And I will give peace in the land . . . and I will rid evil beasts out of the land" (Lev. 26:6). "Evil beasts" is always referring to the sexually perverse. When these beasts are gone, we will have peace in our land.

"For their vine is of the vine of Sodom, and of the fields of

Gomorrah: their grapes are grapes of gall, their clusters are bitter. Their wine is the poison of dragons, and the cruel venom of asps" (Deut. 32:32-33). "Their wine" is speaking of the wine of fornication, the sex of Sodom and Gomorrah. This thinking is poisonous and cruel, and as the poison of dragons and the venom of snakes, it is deadly; this is why the wicked are so often referred to as snakes, dragons, asps, cockatrices, adders, spiders, and vipers. God sees Sodom and Gomorrah as images of creeping things that have deadly bites that kill. They are a false image of God, creating a cruel, hurtful world. God is not like this.

"And makest men as the fishes of the sea, as the creeping things, that have no ruler over them" (Hab. 1:14) Peter fished for fishes. Fishes are wicked people. He filled the church with fishes. Jesus will tell Peter to go out into the deep, and then he will catch men. This old Christianity needs to get into the deeper matters of life, the law. When it does, the church will cleanse itself and then catch men (righteous men and women) instead of dead fishes. Dead fish make the church stink.

Think of yourself as an image, either a true likeness of God or a distorted likeness of God. Each one of us begin life as a true picture of our heavenly Father and do not become a false image unless original sin is committed. We begin life good, holy, and upright. We have been commanded by our Father to stay good, holy, and upright. Do not commit oral sex, for when you do, you change and no longer look like God. You do not live as God would live. You no longer think as the Creator thinks. You are no longer good, no longer holy, and you are no longer upright. You are no longer alive. God sees you as a dead animal: evil, profane, unclean, and fallen. All who follow you, are following a untrue likeness of God.

Grandma Moses once said: "Life is what you make it, always has been, always will be." God said that this way: "The kingdom of God is within you" (Luke 17:21). Mankind is capable of creating a scary, dark jungle where ravenous beasts devour and poisonous snakes strike and kill. We've proven that! But God tells us we are also capable of creating a lighted, peaceful, harmless world occupied by humans who live like and think like the Person who created them. We have the power within us to make the earth a Garden of Eden again. When mankind decides to make that choice, our home on earth will once again be a safe place, where no ravenous beasts or poisonous snakes roam. It is a choice! Everyone has this power within them, the power to choose good over evil.

If the false images think they have already made a bad choice and it is irreversible, they are wrong. Sometimes it's good to be wrong. The Bible repeats over and over again in various stories and in many illustrations how to come home to God. The story of the Prodigal Son is one. Phrases and words such as "the plan of salvation," "redemption," "deliverance from sin," "reconciliation," "being born again," "raised from the dead," "victory in Jesus," "repentance," and, of course, the new covenant promise that "God will write the law upon your heart." "If you stop rebelling, I will be your God and you will be My people." All promises to Sodom and Gomorrah from the God of goodness.

The argument mankind is having with the Creator over this issue will end when man agrees with God. You see, your heavenly Father is not going to change His mind. You are! You insult Him with this behavior. You also insult yourself, for you really are too intelligent to sin. When you insult your own intelligence, you are insulting the Godly part of you, your mind. Your mind and the mind of God should be alike. When they are not alike, you are not the image of God.

Do you see God? Do you see His basic character? Do you see His face? Can you see His mind? The Supreme Being is not going to change His mind about original sin. It is basic to His character. That's the way He is. It is called **goodness**!

It is called **holy**! God is good. God is holy. God considers His goodness and His holiness to be His glory. Goodness makes God holy, and goodness will make all who embraces it holy.

The false images need to correct their own minds so they will no longer be a false likeness, but will become a true likeness once again. This change will destroy the animals, snakes, and creeping things. The end of sin is an image correction. When this change has been made, God and man will be like-minded, meaning they will look alike and think alike once again. The animals, snakes, and creeping things will be gone, and God will once again recognize His children.

To change your image is to change your mind. "And have put on the new man, which is renewed in knowledge after the image [mind] of him that created him" (Col. 3:10). It is important to understand that to correct your image is to correct your mind. You need to think right. To be converted or to have the experience of conversion is to have a major change of mind, an about-face. To be renewed in knowledge means your mind is made new by new knowledge. This requires that you not only accept new information, but you must also be willing to reject the old familiar ways of thinking and living. This new information has the reasoning power to change the way you act. For when you adjust your behavior to correspond with the law, you change and achieve a new God-like image. Now you are a new person. Truth is once again in you.

Speaking of Jesus, "Who [Jesus] is the image of the invisible God, the firstborn of every creature" (Col. 1:15). Jesus is the image of God because He never committed original sin. He is the appearance of God because of the way He thinks and lives. When you see Jesus, He will not be sexually perverse. The Lamb of God will not believe in oral and anal sex. When you bring your mind into agreement with the mind of Christ, you become like Him. Christians are Christ-minded. Christ is God-minded.

Because the Scriptures have been misunderstood, we have not seen the mind of God the Father, so we will need to look at the mind of Jesus to see God. To see God's mind, we need to look at the doctrine of Jesus. What does Jesus believe? What does He think? How does He live? Jesus opens up (explained) the Scriptures, enabling man to see God.

Christ comes with a new doctrine, and that belief is the law of holiness. He believes in keeping the Garden Law, for it is the law of the new covenant. On this issue of original sin, He thinks and lives as God would live if God were human. Therefore, His image (mind) did not change. He did not argue with His Father. The mind of Christ and the mind of God are identical. God, Jesus, and true Christians think alike. They all agree together: oral sex is the original sin.

"And be not conformed to this world: but be ye transformed by the renewing of your mind, that ye may prove what is that good, and acceptable, and perfect, will of God" (Rom. 12:2). Do not yield yourself to Satan's world: Change your mind and think like Jesus. Satan began his "world" in the Garden of Eden, with oral sex being the doorway into that "world." When you end sin, you will be walking out of "the world." By putting new information in your mind and ending sin, you will be changed, reconciled to God, and disassociated from "the world" Satan invented. When Jesus states, "My kingdom is not of 'this world,' " He is saying that there is no sexual perverseness in the Kingdom of God.

Being conformed to the image of Jesus always involves a change of mind, new eyes that see differently. "And be renewed in the spirit of your mind" (Eph. 4:23). Believing in the same doctrine (law) as Jesus believes means you have God in you. "He that abideth in the doctrine [law] of Christ, he hath both the Father and the Son" (2 John 9). The law is truth, the truth of God. When this law is in your mind and lived out though your actions, you have both God and Jesus in you. You have truth in you.

Faith in Jesus is not blind faith, not a mindless faith, nor is it a faith without a solid belief foundation. To be anti-intellectual is not what Christianity is all about. Being a Christian embraces a great deal more than merely believing Jesus was a person, or making believe He comes into your heart. Christianity is believing in the teachings of Christ. It is a reasoning faith, designed to bring peace to earth.

Sit down and reason out your own salvation. "Come now, and let us reason together, saith the Lord: though your sins be as scarlet, they shall be as white as snow; though they be red like crimson, they shall be as wool" (Isa. 1:18). God is depending on the human race to reason our way out of this widespread confusion sin has created here in the wilderness, until we can once again live in peaceful harmony with God and with each other.

We are children of a reasoning God. Let us not be like the people in the days of Moses, who could not see the Promised Land as Moses did. For then the people chose to remain in sin, were comfortable hiding in the dark, and even said they wanted sin without restrictions, and God left them there. The Divine Creator even sent them quail (dead birds), all they wanted. To rebel was their choice. They spent a long time in the wilderness, just as we have.

This second commandment is demanding we do not change ourselves into a false, dead image of God. This can only mean that we are not false, dead images at birth. We think like God from birth, and from birth we have within us the common sense knowledge that oral sex is wrong; so the wrongdoer will hide, sneak, lie, and feel guilt and shame. Every person who has changed into an animal-like image, creeping thing, bird, or fish, needs to return to his original state of mind of thinking like God, having a holy sinless mind. Renewed!

ॐ

"Wherefore gird up the loins of your mind, be sober.
As obedient children, not fashioning yourselves
according to the former lusts in your ignorance."
1 Peter 1:13-14

CHAPTER THIRTEEN

Commandment 3

Thou shalt not take the name of the
Lord thy God in vain.
Exodus 20:7

The word God, by the nature of the word itself, underscores the reality that God is superior. He is above man. He is the Creator of the earth and of mankind, and this places God above and over the earth itself and everything on it, including mortals.

Vain means empty, or of no value: nothing, worthless, without force or effect, fruitless. To use the name of God as a swear word verbally reduces God to a nothing, a worthless person, and loudly announces an inappropriate placement of God, by exalting the user above God. Positioning oneself above God is backward, disrespectful, and the opposite of worship. This commandment demands verbal respect for our Creator.

However, this demand not only regulates how we should reverence the names of The Almighty in our speech, but it also requires of us a lifestyle that exalts God, for both our words and our lifestyle can demonstrate that we believe God to be of no value, a nothing, no one to be concerned with, offering worthless knowledge of no importance, and having no effect on us, thus elevating ourselves above God.

The lawbreakers, those who go whoring, announce a lifestyle that communicates their own superiority above God. One act of oral sex disregards God's basic law of good, and makes God a person of lesser wisdom than the lawbreaker.

Even if a person controls his or her speech and never uses the names of God in a disrespectful and vain way, a lifestyle of fornication exalts your own self above God, for it acts out your belief that what The Holy One states is of no importance to you. He is a nothing, a person of no significance, worthless, and no one to debate with, for you could actually tell God a few things. In your mind God is wrong on this issue of sin. He is wrong about how married people should relate sexually, for they are allowed oral sex. He is wrong about homosexuality, and bisexuality. He is wrong about human sexuality in general. You are right and God is wrong.

Many years ago, I said to myself, "I bet the sexually perverse will accuse Jesus Christ of being sexually perverse before they will admit they are wrong." I did not know how true that statement was until I discovered what a crown of thorns actually is.

This may be the best picture of reducing God to nothing that I am able to present to you. In Genesis we are told man comes from the dust of the earth. "And the Lord God formed man of the dust of the ground" (2:7). And again we are informed we come from dust: "For out of it [dust] wast thou taken: for dust thou art, and unto dust shalt thou return" (Gen. 3:19). Humans come from the ground. After Adam and Eve sinned, natural consequences occurred called curses. One such curse was that the earth will produce thorns and thistles. "Thorns also and thistles shall it bring forth to thee; and thou shalt eat the herb of the field" (Gen. 3:18). Once original sin was desired and acted out, the ground will now bring forth thorns and thistles, meaning mankind, not vegetation.

Those who overrule this first holy order are the thorns and thistles, and the Scriptures have much to say concerning thorns and
thistles, snares, brambles, tares, briers, prickles, and traps. All are
images of the many who offend as Adam and Eve did, and should
not be mistaken for or confused to mean literal vegetation.

Compare a literal thorn or thistle from a vegetable garden to
sinful mortals being thorns and thistles in the garden of life.

VEGETATION THORN	HUMAN THORNS
Hurtful	Hurtful
Nuisance	Nuisance
Bothersome	Bothersome
Creates work	Creates work
Fruitless	Fruitless
Unpleasant	Unpleasant

Now from the ground, where humans came from, will emerge
people who hurt people, bothersome people who disrupt the
peace, unpleasant individuals who do not have the fruit of the spirit of God (love, joy, peace, patience), persons who make necessary
all the work we do to try to eliminate the secondary problems of
our civilization.

Every area of our lives is affected by the thorns and the thistles,
resulting in personal mental torment, misunderstandings and dis-
trust in our daily relationships, considerable deceitfulness, all of
which are damaging and destructive to our marital relationships,
wounding to our children, and detrimental to our nation's well-
being. Thorns are the unjust, and they not only cause pain to the
just but also to each other. If humans were not thorns, life would
be much more pleasant, and peaceful; in fact, life would return to
being perfect.

Just as we prefer to have a vegetable or a flower garden without thorns and thistles, we should prefer to have an earth without

human thorns and thistles. Yet our earth is brimming with those who verbally, mentally, sexually, and physically injure people. The sexually perverse are the snares and the traps, the brambles and the prickles, the thorns and the thistles, and all who come in contact with them suffer.

Many of the thorns and thistles brought into existence the different church denominations which we call Christianity. Now, they openly promote original sin and then profess to be like Jesus and proudly proclaim Jesus is like them. This model of Jesus is a lie, projects a false image of God, and should not be believed by anyone. This incorrect likeness degrades and humiliates God. Holding Jesus up as a sexually perverse person makes God and Jesus vain, worthless, empty, and profitable for nothing, without having a worthwhile effect on our culture.

What you have actually done is make God into the image of sinful man (profane), and that is backward. Instead, you should have changed sinful man into the image of God, holy. It appears the sexually perverse have reversed almost everything.

A crown is placed on the head of a person as a sign of honor, to symbolize a person's high status and authority. The sexually perverse (the thorns and thistles) have "honored" Jesus by placing a crown of thorns on his head, making him their king. King of the thorns!

Mocking God? Yes! Before the sexually perverse will admit they are wrong, they will proclaim that Jesus is sexually perverse. This is contempt for God coupled with a stiff-necked, stubborn pride keeping them from admitting they are wrong, which forces them to carry this insult to such great magnitude. The scandalous reality I have experienced is, Christianity is a support group for the sexually perverse, and they exclude anyone who disagrees with them about this subject of oral sex. "But in vain they do worship me, teaching for doctrines the commandments of men" (Matt. 15:9). It is possible to worship God in vain: in a way that is worthless, meaningless, of no value, unprofitable, and destructive to the human race, having no lasting effect on our culture. Immoral church members, who commit original sin, declare they serve God, make up their own rules, and do as they please, are called hypocrites.

God is not going to change. He is the same yesterday, today, and forever. He is holy. He is not sexually perverse. You will need to change to be like God. When church-goers achieve this, when they are no longer fornicators, then they will experience having a healing effect on our culture.

In Hebrews, God reveals what will happen to the thorns, "But that which beareth thorns and briers is rejected, and is nigh unto cursing; whose end is to be burned" (Heb. 6:8). At the end of this age, you will be burned up by the law, brought to nothing. And in Isaiah: "And the light of Israel shall be for a fire, and his Holy One for a flame: and it shall burn and devour his thorns and his briers in one day" (Isa. 10:17). You are mistaken about Jesus. For Jesus is not the king of the thorns! He comes to kindle the fire that will remove you from the earth. He will not sneak you (just as you are) past God into heaven.

Blaspheming is another word that describes the breaking of the Garden commandment. To blaspheme is the act of cursing, slandering, or showing contempt or lack of reverence. To blaspheme God is to act out your own superiority over God, and that is done when you overrule God, disobey His law to be holy, and do as you please. This shows contempt for God.

"The foolish people have blasphemed thy name" (Ps. 74:18). The foolish are the sexually perverse. They blaspheme God by acting out cursing and show contempt for God.

"Speak unto the house of Israel, and say unto them, Thus saith the Lord God; Yet in this your fathers have 'blasphemed me, in that they have committed a trespass against me" (Eze. 20:27). The cross-reference explaining "to blaspheme" takes us to Romans where the sexually perverse are described: "And changed . . . God into an image . . . like corruptible man, and to birds, and four foot-ed beasts, and creeping things" ('Rom. 1:23). All who dwell in Sodom and Gomorrah are the ones who have blasphemed God. You have changed your image but think yourselves wise, smarter then God. Original sin insults God and you are blaspheming his name. Cursing God. Exalting yourself. Mocking God.

"But now ye also put off all these; anger, wrath, malice, blas-phemy, filthy communication our of your mouth. Lie not one to another, seeing that ye have put off the old man with his deeds" (Col. 3:8-9). When the commandment on the once missing stone tablet (the law) is observed, think of how it will change our cul-ture! No anger. No hatred. No swearing. No lying. No sexual per-verseness. No Blaspheming. Delightful! Yes!

CHAPTER FOURTEEN

Commandment 4

Remember the sabbath day, to keep it holy.
Exodus 20:8

Are we born holy or unholy? Knowing our spiritual condition at birth is essential. We need this vital information in order to know how to proceed in life. For if we are born holy, we need schooling on how to stay holy. If we are born unholy, we need instruction on how to become holy; for no man or woman will see God if they are not holy. "Follow peace with all men, and holiness, without which no man shall see the Lord" (Heb. 12:14).

What is holy? A definition of holy is key to the understanding of this commandment. Holiness is not just a New Testament term. Moses was instructed by God to show the people the difference between the holy and the profane. In that day they were also confused as to what the difference was.

Holy is not a state of being that can only be reached after the coming of Jesus. Holy, just, upright, righteous, God-fearing, and godly are all interchangeable words; and the Old Testament names many who fall into this category. A just person is holy. An upright person is holy. A righteous person is holy. A godly person is holy. In the Old Testament, Lot was just. Noah and Job were upright and godly men. David was upright and did not wickedly depart from God. Abraham, Isaac, and Jacob would fall into the category of holy men. Moses and Joshua were holy men. In the New Testament, John the Baptist, Jesus, and Mary the mother of Jesus were just and holy. What made these people holy? The absence of original sin made them holy. None of the above revolted against the law from Eden. And at the completion of this age when the remnant are separated from Sodom and Gomorrah, the remnant are holy and Sodom and Gomorrah are profane. When you see holy, you see God, for God is holy. When you see profane, you see Satan. This difference between God and Satan is original sin. The difference between holy and profane is original sin.

In the following Scriptures, God informs us we are holy before sin is committed: Born holy!

- "Thou wast perfect in thy ways from the day that thou was created, till iniquity was found in thee" (Eze. 28:15). Everyone is perfect until sin is committed. Perfect by God's standard.
- "Lo, this only have I found, that God hath made man upright; but they have sought out many inventions" (Ecc. 7:29). We are all made upright/holy. Not fallen. But inventions, sexual inventions, make a person fallen/profane. These inventions are man-made and come from the imagination. Fantasies.
- "Who leave the paths of uprightness, to walk in the ways of darkness" (Prov. 2:13). A person must abandon being upright in order to fall. You must forsake light (the law) to walk in darkness. You are holy and walking in light until you desert God by sinning. Then you are unholy, fallen, dead, in a grave, and in the dark.
- "Enter not into the path of the wicked, and go not in the way of evil men" (Prov. 4:14). God gave this wise advice to all. If we

do not go in the way of evil man, we will not be evil. That is clear and easily understood. If each person had followed this warning from God, the Messiah would not need to come to earth, for the people of earth would still be holy. Every individual who has sinned should stop blaming Adam and Eve. You need to take responsibility for your own actions. You have had the same choice as they had. You were born holy. You could have stayed holy. And you were commanded to do so.

God is holy! And we are born in the image of God. Therefore, we are born holy! Holiness at birth gives us the right to see God, making the right to see God our birthright. From the beginning of time, all people have needed schooling on how to remain holy. Since no instruction was given, the earth has become profane and dark.

As the result of misinformation or confusing information, many people have lost this prized possession called holiness which they had at birth. Many have unknowingly sold their birthright for the pleasures of sin. They have became unholy/profane. You could say they got burned. The misinformation that we are "born sinners" has been one of the most detrimental lies this old Christianity has told. You could call it verbal abuse against humanity, such a negative way to approach life. "We are unfit for God before we leave our cribs." "We need to be fixed." "We are born sinners." It is the opposite of the truth, and one of the most damning lies told to the human race. The plain truth is: We are born holy. And there is a sin that will make us unholy, and that sin is oral sex. When we are unholy we are unacceptable to God. We should not commit this one most despicable sin.

Both sides of an opposite need to be understood before either one can be. The opposite of holy is profane, and the opposite of profane is holy. Let us look at how a person loses his or her holiness and becomes profane. Everyone is either holy or profane.

"Lest there be any fornicator, or profane person, as Esau, who for one morsel of meat sold his birthright" (Heb. 12:16). Esau sold his right to see God for fornication. One act of original sin is all it takes to lose your holiness. This is an either/or situation: Either you have God and no fornication, or you have fornication and no God. And we know fornication is the sex of Sodom and Gomorrah. Esau was a fornicator, which made him unholy. He was like Sodom and Gomorrah. Jacob and Esau were brothers and represent the human family. And when our Heavenly Father states that He is the God of Jacob, He is also confirming that He is not the god of Esau, who made himself unholy.

If you have sold your birthright (your right at birth to see God) and are no longer holy, how do you get your holiness back again? You sanctify yourself. And this is how you do it:

"For this is the will of God, even your sanctification, that ye should abstain from fornication" (1 Thess. 4:3). It is God's will that all become holy. That means God wants you to become holy again. He wants you! You are His children, and He wants you to return to Him and to love only Him. You return by putting sin out of your life. Abstain from fornication. It took only one act of sin to become profane, and it will take the total removal of fornication to become holy again.

"But fornication, and all uncleanness, or covetousness, let it not be once named among you, as becometh saints" (Eph. 5:3). If you call yourself a saint, or a follower of Jesus, a child of God, or a Christian, then you should not commit fornication even once.

"For I am the Lord your God: ye shall therefore sanctify yourselves, and ye shall be holy; for I am holy: neither shall ye defile yourselves with any manner of creeping thing that creepeth upon the earth" (Lev. 11:44). Sanctify yourself. This is something no one else can do for you. It is a personal decision. Only you can remove yourself from "the world," and only you can abstain from committing sin. No one can do this for you. Either you will desire to please God or you will prefer to sin and please yourself. The Holy One tells you not to defile yourself with creeping things any longer.

Do not be a creeping thing, and do not serve those who are.

"For when ye were the servants of sin, ye were free from right-eousness. But now being made free from sin . . . ye have your fruit unto holiness, and the end everlasting life" (Rom. 6:20-22). You are either a servant of sin and have no righteousness, or you are right-eous and do not commit this offensive trespass. Freedom from original sin produces holiness, and your end will be everlasting life. You are now back to the same spiritual state-of-being you were when you were first born from your mother's womb—holy. Spiritually speaking, you can say, "I have been born again" because you are holy again, as you were when your mother birthed you. You have your birthright back, the right to see God, as you had when you were physically born. As you start over again, this time you know how to please your Heavenly Father.

"Whosoever is born of God doth not commit sin" (1 John 3:9). When you are born of God, "born again," you do not sin. You can be born again at any age, but regardless of your age, God consid-ers you a new babe. An infant with everything about life to learn over again. For a period of time you will be fed milk, but as you grow and mature in the things of God, you will need and desire the deeper truths of God. You will become wiser with age, and that is how it should be. Wisdom will help us solve the ills of this planet.

Jesus comes to sanctify the church. "Husbands, love your wives, even as Christ also loved the church. That he might sancti-fy and cleanse it with the washing of water by the word" (Eph. 5:25-26). At the close of this age, the church will need to be made holy: cleansed, washed with the word of God, made clean and sin-less. There will be fornication in God's house, making the church unholy, profane, and unclean. Prophet and priest and pastor will be profane/unholy. Yet this Scripture states that Jesus loves even this sinful church and will cleanse and sanctify it. When fornication is removed from God's house, The Almighty will stand with the church. This is an amazing message to such a sinful "house of

God." It is "good news," for this godless religion. The church will receive power at this time, and will truly have the ability to save the world. Power comes from the truth of the law. Remember, without the law there is not enough power to convert anyone.

Jesus comes to sanctify marriage. Husbands, love your wives as Christ loves the church. How will Christ love the church? He will sanctify it by removing fornication. Husbands need to do the same for marriage, sanctify your marriage. Remove fornication from your marriage. Make marriage clean, innocent, and holy. Wives were not given to you to debase, abuse, and use. As hatred should not be found in the house called The House of God, hatred should not be an ingredient of marriage either. Original sin is an act of hate.

God is holy. All people should desire to be holy. Holy is a way of life. However, there are two powers available for humans to serve: either God or the devil, and those who worship Satan are unholy/profane. Adam and Eve were the first devil worshipers. Unholy individuals commit fornication—the sex of Sodom and Gomorrah. Holy people do not commit such acts. When you see holy, you see God. And when you see profane, you see Satan.

Do you see holy?

Do you see a holy God?

Do you see a holy person?

Do you see a holy marriage?

Do you see a holy America?

Do you see a holy earth?

If you see a holy earth, then you see the Promised Land of peace on earth. You can also see how far we are from where we must go. To travel across this vast distance will require an organized forward movement out of sin. We will travel this distance by way of a mind change, powered by the Law from Eden. There is sufficient power in this statute to move us out of the wilderness into this new land. As I said in the beginning, "The problem is not where we are standing, it is how we are living."

Now that you understand holy, does this fourth commandment mean to be holy only on Sunday? Six days a week we need not be holy? No! There is a God-day and a man-day. God made man to scale. We are like Him in intelligence, but without a doubt with less intelligence. We are like Him in that we have a family, but obviously a smaller family than the family of God. Like Him in creativity, but evidence proves we have a lesser measure of creativity. We are like Him in that we are alive, and some of us live more then one hundred years. God lives forever. On a scale of a hundred to forever, I am not sure how long a God-day is. We know a man-day is twenty-four hours long. A God-day is much longer than a man-day. How much longer, I do not know.

God created the heavens and the earth in six God-day measurements. On the seventh day he rested. During this day of rest, God put man in charge of the earth. It is my belief God's Sabbath day is still ongoing. When he awakens he will not like what he sees. "As a dream when one awaketh; so, O Lord, when thou awakest, thou shalt despise their image" (Ps. 73:20). When the God-day Sabbath is coming to a close, our Father will hate what has happened to his children. He will hate seeing the images of animals, birds, and fishes. Where have all the children gone who should look like God their Father?

The parable of the vineyard in Mark 12:1-11 tells of the owner of a vineyard going away and leaving the vineyard in the hands of others, only to find upon his return they not only wanted the vineyard for themselves, but even had plans to kill the owner's son, who would inherit the vineyard, to accomplish this. The parable is depicting God as the owner of the earth. Thinking He left the earth in capable hands, He went away. But upon returning He found that those He left in charge were willing to kill the Son of God to possess God's earth.

I am not saying the Almighty has slept the day away. But as a general rule, He does not break His own commandment and work on His Sabbath Day unless He has an emergency. Jesus, while doing the work of His Father, will be questioned about working on the God-day Sabbath. He will answer man with a question about what would a man do if his ox fell in a ditch on man's twenty-four-hour Sabbath day. Of course, you would get the ox out of the ditch even if it meant working for a little while on your day of rest. God has a church in the ditch. It is an emergency. And He will work a little while on His Sabbath day to get His Church out of the ditch before everyone is deceived and the situation is hopeless. "They be blind leaders of the blind. And if the blind lead the blind, both shall fall into the ditch" (Matt. 15:14). Jesus is speaking to the leaders of organized Christianity and those who follow them. The church has fallen into a ditch. Let's get God's house out of the ditch!

We are almost at the conclusion of this one God-day, the seventh day, His Sabbath day. It was during this day of rest that the devil had free reign and was able to deceive almost everyone except a few, the remnant, who are not like Sodom and Gomorrah. God had to shorten this day or no flesh would be saved. Tomorrow is a new day, the Day of the Lord. Peter will deny Christ three times before the dawning of the next God-day. Then Peter will say, "Repent, for the kingdom of God is at hand." This new day is the day of salvation, and will bring deliverance from evil. The kingdom of God has no sin in it. If there were deliverance before the deliverer, there would be no need for the deliverer. The day before the day of salvation was a day of no salvation, or why have a day of salvation?

As I write this chapter, the Promise Keepers are planning their annual meeting. They are a group of men (men only), laymen and pastors from all denominations, who for a weekend in June fill the sports arenas in our major cities for the purpose of becoming more godly.

In 1997 at the Promise Keepers rally in Washington, DC, they sang about being holy, some laid on the ground face down, and asked to be holy. In songs, words, and actions you said this:

"Let this generation be the generation
to return to God and have peace."

There will be a generation (everyone an earth at a given point of time) who will see the Promised Land of peace on earth. Everyone will be persuaded to follow truth and will be brought into friendship with God and truth. Guys, do you truly want to be in that generation?

"We want America to be a holy nation.
Where the proud shall humble themselves."

Do you want America to be a holy nation? And now that you know what holy means, are you willing to be holy? Will the pride that keeps you from admitting you are a sinner be humbled so you can seek forgiveness from God and change your minds to agree with the mind of Christ? America will become holy, one person at a time. Only people make a nation holy or unholy. Animals, vegetable, and matter do not have the capability of being holy or unholy.

"With love we will speak the truth
to all the lost."

Would you be willing to speak the truth? Willing to speak the law given to Adam and Eve in the garden?

The wicked have had enough untruth; they have also had enough hate. They have already had enough hurt. The truth needs to be spoken in love to this lost generation. Everyone from the greatest to the least needs to hear the law delivered with love and mercy and forgiveness.

"Let us stand united
as we serve the Lord. "

Christianity needs to be united in truth. Truth should be the same for the Baptist as for the Roman Catholic, the same for the Mormon as for the Methodist, and so on. Individual church doctrine is man-made, for it came from the founder of your denomination. Every church needs to put aside its own doctrine and replace it with the doctrine of Jesus Christ: the law. The law is from God, and the law will unify the churches in truth. It is the only doctrine you need. Power to convert comes from this first commandment. Without this foundation you have not yet converted anyone, not even yourselves, but with this law you will be able to convert everyone.

True Christianity will also need a common language. Theologians have invented words that have divided the church on language alone. Harmonize your language as you replace your beliefs. When unified by the doctrine of Jesus, the law, truth, and language, the church will become believable and powerful. When explaining Scripture, remember who your audience is! Not everyone had the opportunity, the funds, or the ability to graduate from a four-year college and go on to graduate school. Do you want them to understand? Speak to the multitudes who did not, then everyone (those who do and those who do not have a degree) will understand what you are saying. Recently, I read a Protestant report using these words: hermeneutical, antinomian, commodification, exegetical, concomitant, eschatological, and clericalism. Honestly I had to look these words up in the dictionary before I could understand what this report was saying. I'm sure many others would have to also. When talking to the masses, use language they can all understand.

> "God let us be instruments
> for bringing peace to this generation."

Let us be the generation that returns to God. Yes! Let us be that generation! When I watched and listened to what you were saying, I wondered, if they understood "holy," would they be willing to be that generation? However, God will choose the generation to be holy, and let us hope it will be this one. If it is, then rise to the occasion.

God said he would put a quick end to iniquity, and your organization could play a major role in how quickly the church is sanctified. First, remove fornication from your own life. If you are married, sit down with your wife and discuss removing it from your marriage. Then eliminate it. Banish it from your family. Every child has the right to grow up without any sex until marriage, and then only righteous, holy, clean sex. It is their birthright. Remove fornication from the church. If your pastor is willing to climb out of the ditch, follow him. You followed him into the ditch, now follow him out. If he is not eager to climb out, follow someone who will lead you out of the ditch. If you are not willing to climb out of the pit, then leave the church. You do not belong in it.

The fourth commandment can be said this way: "While I have a day of rest, honor My Sabbath day and keep My earth holy." From the beginning until God returns at the end, we should have kept His earth holy. Most of you did not do this. Now all must keep this commandment and return to being holy. For peace on earth to become a reality, holiness must become a daily and permanent lifestyle of everyone on earth.

Sodom and Gomorrah, you need to be "born again." Then you will be holy again! It is your passport to heaven.

ॐ

May I add, understanding this commandment helps to explain how long the other six days of creation were. It is illogical to think God created the earth in six man-days. Why would God, who has the intelligence to make an earth, say, "Abracadabra, let it be?" God doesn't need magic. It seems to me He would want to see all the laws of nature He thought through and compiled relative to the creation of earth performed in the appropriate manner He planned. He did say, "Let it be." Let it be the way I plan it to be.

The Holy Book of Scripture God sent to earth. The book on how to make an earth He did not. God has left this marvel for man to wonder, discover, contemplate, meditate upon, theorize, and prove our own theories to be true or false. We call this learning, and learning is fun and exciting. With each new discovery about the laws that govern the earth and the universe, inventions have been born. Today, to name only a few, our refrigerator, automobile, radio, telephone, television, airplanes, computers, and space ships all come from understanding the laws of nature. These are relatively new inventions. There was a long time before the wheel was thought of. Conceivably there is no end to knowledge. We will continue to gain knowledge at a superior level, surpassing our present knowledge, during heaven on earth, and gaining even more wisdom in the next heaven. In eternity, with so much time to spend in learning, we may each someday have the knowledge to make an earth. Look at what God has made to understand the capabilities of what His children may someday accomplish.

CHAPTER FIFTEEN

Commandment 5

⅗

Honor thy father and thy mother:
that thy days may be long upon the land
which the Lord thy God giveth thee.
Exodus 20:12

The only possible way this commandment can be broken with one act of original sin would be if God were both our mother and our father. And yes, God is both mother and father, for if that were not true, this commandment would be eliminated from the one table of stone leaving only nine. This commandment has not been removed from the all-inclusiveness of how original sin breaks the law (all ten commandments at once). It is not logical to remove it from the others. "My son, hear the instruction of thy father, and forsake not the law of thy mother" (Prov. 1:8). Law is in the singular and is referring to the Garden Law, indicating it was given to us by both our God Father and our God Mother.

In Genesis when God created everything He spoke of himself in the singular until He created mankind:

Day 1: "And God said, Let there be light" (Gen. 1:3).

The sun.

Day 2: "And God said, Let there be a firmament in the midst
of the waters" (Gen. 1:6).
The earth in water.
Day 3: "And God said, Let the waters under the heaven be
gathered together unto one place, and let
the dry land appear" (Gen. 1:9).
The separation of water and land.
"Then He said, Let the earth bring forth grass,
herbs, trees, and seeds."
All vegetation.
Day 4: "And God said, Let there be lights in
the firmament of the heaven to divide the day from
the night" (Gen. 1:14).
The moon, the stars.
Day 5: "And God said, Let the waters bring forth
abundantly the moving creatures that hath life, and
fowls that may fly above in the open firmament of
heaven" (Gen. 1:20-21).
Fish and fowl.
Day 6: "And God said, Let the earth bring
forth living creatures . . . cattle, and creeping
things, and beasts of the earth" (Gen. 1:24).
Insects and all animals.

None of the vegetation or the animals are said to be created in
the image of God. Therefore, vegetation, animals, insects, birds,
fish and creeping things do not have the capability of being holy
like God, nor does The Creator expect holiness from them. It was
not until God made man, also on day six, does He refer to His own
image, and addresses Himself in the plural. "And God said, Let us
make man in our image, after our likeness: and let them have
dominion over all the fish of the sea, and over the fowl of the air,
and over the cattle, and over all the earth, and over every creeping

thing that creepeth upon the earth. So The Creator created man in
His own image in the image of God created He him; male and
female created He them" (Gen. 1:26-27). Once again our heavenly Father calls both male and female— him. Male and female are
created in God's image, making them the only life forms capable
of being holy. Godlike. Moral. Good. Truthful. Ethical. Moralistic.
Righteous. Upright. Just.

Man should not live like the animals, nor should we compare
ourselves to animals, for we are superior to the animals in both reason and morality. Animals are not made in the image of God.
Humans are. "What is man, that thou art mindful of him? For thou
hast made him a little lower than the angels, and hast crowned him
with glory and honour" (Ps. 8:4-5). Man was crowned with goodness and honor, and made a little lower than the angels: God—
angels—man. We are created at the bottom of the God chain, not
the top of the animal chain, and we should begin to identify with
our Heavenly Father and stop relating to the animals.

The spirit of God will never be placed in an animal, for an animal is not the image of a holy God. And all who believe in reincarnation should consider that fact.

Consider this: we are made as a scaled-down model of God.
Male and female become one when they marry, and birth children.
The father usually lays the law down. And when the children disobey their father, it is usually the mother who is the peacemaker,
reconciling the child back into an obedient relationship with their
father. In the spiritual realm of things, our parents are married and
are one. It is God the Father who laid the law down in the Garden
of Eden, and the children who broke it. It will be God the Mother
who will reconcile the children back to their Father, making the
New Jerusalem the Mother of us all.

On the human level, children should obey their parents.
However, this commandment does not promise us a long life if we
do this. We all know good children who obeyed their parents and

did not live a long life. Many children die young. This commandment is asserting a much greater meaning: the human race will live long if we obey the commandments of our heavenly Parents. The opposite of obeying and living long is to disobey and not live long. If the human race wants to avoid extinction, we will need to keep the commandments of our parents, God. If we continue in sin until no righteous person is left on earth at the end of time, this will kill Jesus, our deliverer, for our deliverer will be on earth at the end. With no deliverer, we will eventually self-destruct. The long-term results of serving Satan will play out in the annihilation of the human race. There are many ways this can happen: germ and biological warfare, disease, famine, depletion of our natural resources, pollution of our natural resources, war.

Once we have arrived at peace on earth and all earthly parents are holy, then when children obey their parents, righteousness will live on forever.

CHAPTER SIXTEEN

Commandment 6

⅗

Thou shalt not kill.
Exodus 20:12

Perhaps you feel we have already covered this commandment in
the beginning chapters, and we have. The fact we can fall is
proof we are born upright. The fact we can blaspheme the Holy
Spirit and become profane is proof we are born holy. The fact we
can depart from God and return unto Him is proof we begin with
God, for you cannot depart from or return to a place where you
have not been. And the fact we can spiritually die is proof we are
born spiritually alive. Yes, we are born holy, and we are born alive,
(spiritually alive), and we die a spiritual death when original sin is
committed.

Thou shalt not kill by using this weapon called "sin." This is an
order from God. As parents, we spend some time teaching our
children safety rules so they will not accidentally injure or kill
themselves. Don't play with fire. Don't cross the street without
looking both ways. Don't drink and drive. Don't stand on a rail-
road track when the train is coming. It is hoped we will spare them

physical pain and/or death. However, it is extremely important that every child be taught how not to die spiritually. Most have never been taught this most critical fact of life and happiness: how to avoid spiritual death and its rewards, pain and sorrow.

In this chapter, most of the emphasis will be placed on the death that occurs when the righteous die from original sin. Since this has been extensively covered in the first chapters, let us look at some other scriptures that add to our understanding of this subject.

In section one, we learned the unjust kill the just, the foolish kill the wise, and evil people kill good people. When you consider the fact the Bible is a story of good and evil, the living and the dead from beginning to end, you will find the living and the dead on every page. All the characters in the Word of God are either alive and good or dead and evil. The same is true for this present generation. Everyone on earth today is either alive or dead, and God is not the god of the dead, the sexually perverse.

The dead are sometimes called murderers. "Whosoever hateth his brother is a murderer: and ye know that no murderer hath eternal life abiding in him" (1 John 3:15). Original sin comes from Satan and is an act of hate. It kills, and when this act is carried out, the person requesting that an act of sin be performed is a murderer. You murder your fellow humans. They die from this act of sin.

"He [the wicked] sitteth in the lurking places of the villages: in the secret places doth he murder the innocent" (Ps. 10:8). Usually this kind of murder is done in secret. There are no witnesses. The wicked prey on the unsuspecting, and the innocent have been no match for these cruel and crafty evil ones. Their innocence and trustfulness have been used to the advantage of the murderer. Many die at the hands of their own relatives, many have been convinced to die by an evil spouse, and many are killed from those who call themselves friends and neighbors.

Those who kill are also called bloody men. David had much to say about bloody men, many times referred to as the men of Beliel.

He asked God to protect him from these men. In Psalms he asks God: "Deliver me from the workers of iniquity, and save me from bloody men. For, lo, they lie in wait for my soul" (Ps: 59:2-3). The wicked lie in wait for the souls of men. Sin is not a game, an activity one should make a sport of. Keeping score is fun and games, but it is not amusing, a thing to make wisecracks and jokes about. The sinner needs to see the seriousness of what is at stake, the souls of people. No one has the right to kill another man's soul.

David also asked God to slay these murderers, and this should be the prayer of all the remnant. The innocent few who survived the war between good and evil should pray for the end of immorality so the earth can return to righteousness. "Surely thou wilt slay the wicked, O God: depart from me therefore, ye bloody men" (Ps. 139:19).

Knowing the end of the wicked, David wanted nothing to do with their evil beliefs. And we all know, surely there will come a day when God will put an end to lawlessness, when He will end the bloodshed. The human race is doomed, and would perish in foolishness if it were not for the fact God will someday remove the wicked from among us. When asking for peace on earth, we are asking God to destroy the wicked. When we pray the Lord's Prayer, "Thy kingdom come," we are asking the Divine Creator to remove Sodom and Gomorrah from the earth, and we are requesting that Babylon fall and be no more. It is not wrong to ask for this.

One of the most blatant examples of this kind of blood-shed was played out in the well-publicized, televised Menendes trial. Eric and Lyle Menendes were on trial for physically killing their parents. Both brothers were born alive, holy, good, without sin, and had the one true God for their God, giving them both a birthright, the right to see God. But they had a wicked father. Mr. Menendez at some point in his life died when he first committed sin, for only the wicked molest their children. No one from the remnant would do this. He served Satan. Unable, unwilling, and blinded from this sin, too stubborn and with too much pride, he would not admit to his own wrongdoing and he molested, abused, and selfishly used his own sons. The first time his sons were forced to commit unnatural sex acts they died a spiritual death. They were murdered by their own father. This is a modern-day example of spiritual murder, and we should all ask God to end this. It is a cycle passed on from one generation to the next, but someday there will be a generation willing to break this cycle.

In Scripture the people who kill in this way are called bloody men, men of blood. "And shed innocent blood, even the blood of their sons and of their daughters, whom they sacrificed unto the idols of Canaan; and the land was polluted with blood" (Ps. 106:38). Of course this blood is not literal.

Years ago, when the Old Jerusalem, the Christianity of today, was begun, many who claimed to be converted would raise their hands during a service. Originally, the intent was to show that their hands were clean, to show they had washed the blood off their hands. But now we are aware that they did not wash but continued killing even in the house they built and called the house of God. The church has been deceived and sheds the blood of the innocent. "And shed not innocent blood in this place, neither walk after other gods to your hurt" (Jer. 7:6). Your hurt comes from following other gods. It is this bloody killing that causes all the damage, and is the root sin from which all social ills stem. If you sin, you suffer. Human sufferings increase in proportion to the increase of sin.

Biblical bloodshed is seldom literal. Blood is shed in the battles between good and evil. Can you imagine a war where only one side kills? In a literal war, such as World War II, physical killing is expected. What would have happened during World War II if only the Japanese had killed? If America had stood by without defending our men or our country, if we had killed no one, who would have won the war? The Japanese! If only one side kills, that side is certain to win the war. There is no contest. In the spiritual war between good and evil, however, that is precisely what happens. Evil people kill good people. The good shed blood when they die (spiritually speaking). Good people do not kill at all. It has been a mighty one-sided, destructive war. You can see how the earth can come down to the end of the age with most of the righteous murdered. The innocent, good, upright ones have been no match for the deceitful, clever, crafty, selfish, evil people. God said he had to shorten this period of merciless killings or no flesh would be spared, and it is why Jesus will work on the Sabbath day.

And so, as we near the outer border of the wilderness of sin, look back! It should not surprise you to see so many dead. At the end of this present age, almost everyone on earth is spiritually dead from the sin Adam and Eve introduced into our society. And the hurt is everywhere.

Spiritually speaking, where are the dead? In Babylon! "And in her [Babylon] was found the blood of prophets, and of saints, and of all that were slain upon the earth" (Rev. 18:24). All but a few have died in this city of fornication and abominations, this bloody city of spiritual drunkenness.

Satan has the power to birth the dead, and all the dead were birthed in Babylon. "And upon her forehead was a name written, MYSTERY, BABYLON THE GREAT, THE MOTHER OF HAR-LOTS AND ABOMINATIONS OF THE EARTH" (Rev. 17:5). Babylon is the mother of the dead. All of Satan's children are born in this city of abominations from the filthiness of fornication. Oral sex is the mark of the beast; it identifies the dead as belonging to Satan. All his dead children have this birthmark.

You have heard it said, "Vengeance belongs to God." It is time for God to take vengeance on Babylon. "Flee out of the midst of Babylon, and deliver every man his soul: be not cut off in her iniquity; for this is the time of the Lord's vengeance; he will render unto her a recompense" (Jer. 51:6). "And I heard another voice from heaven, saying, Come out of her, my people, that ye be not partakers of her sin, and that ye receive not of her plagues" (Rev. 18:4). "O thou that dwellest upon many waters, abundant in treasures, thine end is come" (Jer. 51:13).

All the spiritually dead have been slain in Babylon, this city of fornication. So it should not surprise us to learn that all of the dead shall die in Babylon. "As Babylon hath caused the slain of Israel to fall, so at Babylon shall fall the slain of all the earth" (Jer. 51:49). The dead will fall. The fall of Babylon is predicted both in Jeremiah and in the Book of Revelations. It is the fall of Satan's kingdom begun with Adam and Eve in the Garden of Eden. The Kingdom of God will overthrow this kingdom of the sexually perverse. These are opposing kingdoms, one is founded upon sin, and the other has no sin in it.

What will happen to the dead people in Babylon? How will God rid the earth of them? Jesus will judge them to be double dead wrong. This harsh and necessary judgment is for the purpose of seeing. The blind will see, and the killings will end. The dead will be raised from the dead. The foolish will be made wise, and the unjust will be justified, made just again. Jesus will begin a Christianity powerful enough to end sin by slaying the wicked with truth. The dead will also shed spiritual blood when they die.

"Neither yield ye your members as instruments of unrighteousness unto sin: but yield yourselves unto God, as those that are alive from the dead, and your members as instruments of righteousness unto God" (Rom. 6:13). In other words, your bodies should be instruments of righteousness so put an end to sin in your life, and you will be raised from the dead. You will be made alive again when you are baptized. Baptism will be correctly explained in Chapter Twenty-six.

CHAPTER SEVENTEEN

Commandment 7

⤳

Thou shalt not commit adultery.
Exodus 20:14

In Chapter Three, I listed several words the King James Bible uses to describe Sodom and Gomorrah. Many more have been added to that list as you have read on, and now we will add another. God sees you as adulterers.

God likens his relationship to us in different ways, and one is that of a an honest and faithful husband. "Turn, O backsliding children, saith the Lord; for I am married unto you" (Jer. 3:14). In marriage, there is a commitment to be faithful to each other. Both partners pledge themselves to each other in love and faithfulness. In this marriage union between man and God, God is faithful to man, and He never stops loving us. He does expect us to be faithful to Him. We should not love another god. Those of you who leave God (as Adam and Eve did) to serve Satan, are committing adultery against God.

"Surely as a wife treacherously departeth from her husband, so have ye dealt treacherously with me, O house of Israel, saith the

Lord" (Jer. 3:20). When original sin is committed, man is acting against God in the same manner as a wife when she departs from her husband. Departing from God is what the couple in the first paradise did. They loved God in Eden, but they loved the serpent when they left the Garden. All those who have been deceived by Satan have treacherously departed from the Holy One, and are adulterers. You have left the protection of God, to love a vain and empty god who will do you harm and cause you pain and doesn't know the meaning of the word faithful.

"I have seen also in the prophets of Jerusalem an horrible thing: they commit adultery, and walk in lies: they strengthen also the hands of evildoers, that none doth return from his wickedness: they are all of them unto me as Sodom, and the inhabitants thereof as Gomorrah" (Jer. 23:14). Once again this is speaking of the ministers and pastors in the Old Jerusalem, the Christianity of today. "Adultery," "lies," and "evil-doer" speak of the sins of Sodom and Gomorrah, and God sees the church today as Sodom and Gomorrah, sexually perverse. He sees this as a horrible thing. Organized religion is committing adultery against the God they verbally claim to love. "For from the prophets of Jerusalem is profaneness gone forth into all the land" (Jer. 23:15). Today, the church is promoting profaneness (unholy living), and all the land has been deceived. All the earth has been polluted.

"That they have committed adultery, and blood is in their hands, and with their idols have they committed adultery, and have also caused their sons, whom they bare unto me, to pass for them through the fire, to devour them" (Eze. 23:37). Blood is on their hands from this adultery which they commit with their idols, making this adultery the sex of idolatry, which is oral and anal sex. They kill children with fornication and burn them in the flames of the broken law.

"Ye adulterers and adulteresses, know ye not that the friendship of the world is enmity with God? whosoever therefore will be a

friend of the world is the enemy of God" (James 4:4). "The world"
at times is called Egypt, and at times Sodom and Gomorrah, and
at other times Babylon. "The world" is Satan's world of sexual perverseness originating in Eden. If you love "the world," you are the
enemy of God. "The world" is full of adulterers and adulteresses,
people who commit original sin and have left God to love the god
of "this world," Satan.

To grasp a better understanding of the difference between spiritual adultery against God and adultery against one's spouse, let us
look at two sinning biblical characters. One committed adultery
by vaginal intercourse, David. And one committed adultery by oral
sex (fornication) Esau. At the end of this age, when Jesus judges
the earth, both of these sins will be judged. "Marriage is hon-
ourable in all, and the bed undefiled: but whoremongers and adulterers God will judge" (Heb. 13:4). God will judge the Esaus and
the Davids.

David the adulterer. David broke one of the Ten Commandments
listed on the second table of stone, the one we are so familiar with.
It was a splinter-sized, gnat-sized sin—a wrinkle.

David is an Old Testament character who lived before Jesus
came to earth. God sent Nathan, a friend of David's, not Jesus, to
remind David of his evil. And David responded in this manner: "I
acknowledged my sin unto thee, and mine iniquity have I not hid.
I said, I will confess my transgressions unto the Lord: and thou for-
gavest the iniquity of my sin" (Ps. 32:5).

David was not too proud to admit he was wrong, or too weak
that he could not stop his disobedience. He did not hide his sin.
God listened to David's prayer and forgave him. David did not
need a Jesus or the new covenant. He prayed directly to God. His
prayer for forgiveness in Psalms went like this:

- "For I acknowledge my transgression: and my sin is ever before
  me" (51:3). He admitted his sin.

- "Against thee, thee only, have I sinned, and done this evil in thy sight" (51:4). He placed God above him; having authority over him.

- "Behold, I was shapen in iniquity; and in sin did my mother conceive me" (51:5). David is not excusing himself. He is not blaming God, saying You made me a sinner, God, what did You expect? However, "I was shapen in iniquity" *does not* mean his mother was a sinner because she had intercourse. It *does not* mean David was born a sinner, or that he had a sin nature when he was birthed. It does, however, mean that David was not born in the Garden of Eden when there was no sin. Nor was he born during the time of peace on earth where once again we will live without sin. It does mean he was born in sin, in the wilderness of sin, where little truth flourishes and sinning is the norm. Like David, we have all been born holy here in the wilderness of sin. David is stating that fact: "In sin did my mother conceive me." All of us can make that same announcement. Yet, it does not excuse us.

- "Purge me with hyssop, and I shall be clean: wash me, and I shall be whiter than snow" (51:7).

- "Create in me a clean heart, O God; and renew a right spirit within me" (51:10). When a person has a right spirit, a mind that thinks correctly, he or she will not commit adultery.

- "Cast me not away from thy presence; and take not thy Holy Spirit from me" (51:11). God did not cast David out of His presence as He did Adam and Eve, nor did He depart from him as He did Esau. David did not become profane, unholy. Vaginal adultery does not separate a person from God, nor does it make a person unholy. If he had committed fornication, he would have been profane/unholy, without God, and in need of a deliverer, just like all who commit original sin. And God would not have heard his prayer for forgiveness, just as He does not hear the prayer of any fornicator before the Savior. David did not need a Jesus to be the mediator between him and his heavenly Father. He prayed directly to his heavenly Father.

You could say that even in his sin, David acknowledged that God made male and female. He understood why. He did not think he was smarter than God and invent something new and different. He did not break the Garden Law. He did break one of the Ten Commandments, but this did not separate him so far from his Creator that God would not hear him asking for forgiveness. God heard David and forgave him, when he stopped sinning and asked to be forgiven. He was not a slave or a captive of adultery. He could free himself. It was not necessary to send a Jesus to David. He did not need the new covenant.

On Judgment Day, if David were there, he would not stand in Sodom and Gomorrah, for the sin of adultery does not place a person in Sodom and Gomorrah. He did not cross over the line into Satan's territory, nor did he receive the mark of the beast (oral sex) identifying him as one of Satan's followers. He did not sell his birthright, as Esau did. He did not become profane or unholy (unacceptable to God), as the fornicators do from the sin of fornication. Biblically, David is never associated with Sodom and Gomorrah, and he is called neither a whoremonger nor a fornicator in Scripture. He is never called an idolater, or identified as a follower of other gods.

The Holy Bible backs up the fact David never departed from God and God never departed from David, with these verses: "And yet thou [Jeroboam] hast not been as my servant David, who kept my commandments, and who followed me with all his heart, to do that only which was right in mine eyes. But [thou, Jeroboam] hast done evil above all that were before thee: for thou hast gone and made thee other gods, and molten images, to provoke me to anger, and hast cast me behind thy back" (1 Kings 14:8-9). When God states David kept the commandments, He is saying David never broke the Garden Law. Of course he broke a commandment, but not the law. He never served another god, or made himself into an image of an animal or creeping thing as Jeroboam did. "Blessed are the undefiled in the way, who walk in the law of the Lord" (Ps. 119:1). David walked in accordance with the Garden Law, and God would consider David to be undefiled. He would also call him a virgin, untouched by Satan.

If at the end of time you have sinned the sin of vaginal adultery but not the sin of fornication (oral sex), you will stand with the remnant who are not like Sodom and Gomorrah. You will stand with God for you are a virgin, one of the 144,000 virgins spoken of in Revelations. Does this surprise you? It surprised me. If you find yourself in this surprising situation, do what David did, repent and end your sin and prepare yourself to be in the first resurrection of the lambs.

Esau the fornicator. "Lest there be any fornicator, or profane person, as Esau, who for one morsel of meat sold his birthright" (Heb. 12:16). Esau and Jacob are brothers and represent the human race, male and female, as do the two sons in the story of the Prodigal Son. Jacob served God; Esau served Satan. Esau represents the fornicators, and as the verse states, he is profane, meaning unholy. God has left him. The Holy Spirit (truth) is gone. Esau gave up his birthright, the right to see God. And Jehovah announces: "Jacob have I loved, but Esau have I hated" (Rom. 9:13). Esau broke the Garden Law, and cursed are the defiled who break the law of God.

All those like Esau will need a Jesus. You would not listen to a friend, nor would you listen to the prophets God sent to you. In fact, you have killed all the prophets God sent to you, not physically, but spiritually by sin. For Esau vowed to kill all his brothers. "Then will I slay my brother Jacob" (Gen. 27:41). The fornicators have been killing their brothers since we left the Garden of Eden. This is not brotherly love!

In Scripture it is said that the wicked are slaves to sin. You are in bondage and imprisoned by sin. You have been captured by the enemy who has placed you in darkness and holds you captive by chains, and you are unable to loose yourself or to see your evil ways to find your own way out. Many of you still hide, as Adam and Eve did. You do not admit you have sinned, nor do you repent and stop sinning as David did. You do not believe oral sex is an insult to God, therefore you do not end it. As long as you sin, wipe your mouth, and say you have not sinned, you will remain in error. "Such is the way of an adulterous women; she eateth, and wipeth her mouth, and saith, I have done no wickedness" (Prov. 30:20). An adulterous women is any male or female who commits original sin, and all of you are in need of a Jesus.

This bondage to original evil will continue until the end of time, for God will conclude the world in unbelief. As I stated before, if there was deliverance before the deliverer, then there would be no need for a deliverer. You need a Jesus and the new covenant. Jesus will come to open your eyes, to set the captive free, to judge you for the purpose of seeing, to give you life, to heal the broken-hearted, and to bring you back to God.

Christ comes specifically to judge the fornicators. "And saviors shall come up on mount Zion to judge the mount of Esau; and the kingdom shall be the Lords" (Obad. 21). Christ comes to earth to judge and overthrow this adulterous kingdom of Esau. When these two opposing kingdoms meet, the Kingdom of God will overthrow the kingdom of Esau, for the victory belongs to Jesus. "And the seventh angel sounded; and there were great voices in heaven, saying, the kingdoms of this world are become the kingdoms of our Lord, and of his Christ; and he shall reign for ever and ever" (Rev. 11:15). Jesus will conquer Sodom and Gomorrah and possess everything they have built. Fornication will end, making all people holy, and it is holiness that will bring us into the land of peace on earth.

David committed vaginal adultery with a man's wife. Esau committed oral sex—adultery with another god. On Judgment Day, when the remnant are separated from Sodom and Gomorrah, those of you who have committed adultery, like David, will stand with the remnant. Those of you who have committed adultery by fornication, like Esau, will stand with Sodom and Gomorrah/Babylon/"the world"/the mount or kingdom of Esau, also called Edom. This dividing of humanity at the end is also called separating the wheat from the tares, and the dividing of the lambs from the goats.

THE REMNANT	SODOM AND GOMORRAH
Lambs	Goats
Wheat	Tares
David	Esau
Adultery	Fornication

You will discover that the remnant will not be perfect. They will also fall short of what God commands of His children. "For all have sinned, and come short of the glory [goodness] of God" (Rom. 3:23). I do not know why this was necessary, but by the time we reach the end of the wilderness, with moral corruption everywhere, no one will stand perfect. All humans will fall short of how good God expected us to be.

Some years ago, I took a community college class on human anatomy. While examining the "stinky monkey" from the refrigerator, our instructor pointed out a small, insignificant part of the monkey in a rather trivial manner. It was never mentioned again, nor was it in our textbook. Yet she put it on the final exam. Everyone missed that question, and when we asked why she put it on the test, she said, "I didn't want anyone to get one hundred percent on my test." Although God has been honest and aboveboard with us, for some reason He is not going to let anyone achieve one

hundred percent on the test He gives us on how responsibly we
live out our human sexuality. Maybe, so no one can "lord it over"
on another? Maybe, because of the length of time we have spent
here in the wilderness it could be no other way, a natural law of
evil? Maybe, He waited for a generation who did not make their
own choices, like the Menendez brothers?

Everyone has either violated one or more of the laws from the
commandments we are so familiar with, or they have transgressed
the standard given in the Garden. Breaking one of the Ten
Commandments is a splinter-sized sin; biblically it is also called a
wrinkle. Committing original sin is a beam-sized sin; biblically it is
also called a spot. When both of these sexual sins are removed
from the church, we will have a church without spot or wrinkle.

When adultery by fornication ceases, the environment that
causes adultery by vaginal intercourse will end. Fornication came
before adultery and is the root problem behind even adultery.
When the law is kept, there is no need for ten more commandments. Eventually the human race will return to having one commandment, as it was in the Eden. Perfection will return. Life will
be as God planned it to be, as He describes it in Genesis. Good!

Many times I have heard the self-righteous, professing-to-be-
Christians say, "You can't get to heaven on your morality." Blind
ignorance! That statement always disturbs me, and I feel anger
inside every time I hear it. I announce to you that you will not
enter the Promised Land unless you are moral. The human race
will never arrive on this most desired shore living in immorality.
We all need to take full responsibility for how we live out our
human sexuality, with the good of everyone in mind. When we
master this area of our lives, we will be spiritually mature, perfect.

Moses repeatedly reminded the people that to enter the
Promised Land both sets of commandments must be kept. These
moral principles are an expression of the moral character of God;
therefore, for us to be the image of God, we must be moral.

On one table of stone this commandment can be stated: you shall not commit adultery by fornication, oral sex. On the other table of stone it can be stated: you shall not commit adultery by vaginal intercourse. Moses placed both tables in the ark and put the ark in the temple. We must do the same. Both set of commandments belong in the House of God.

CHAPTER EIGHTEEN

Human Sexuality

⅗

Human sexuality is and always has been a subject of controversy. Someday, when wisdom rather then foolishness is the
norm, that will not be the case. When the just are considered to be
normal, proper, and holy, this will end much of the controversy.
One thing I have noticed about children is that they like to be
treated fairly and equally. And when oral sex is sin for everyone,
husbands and wives, the bisexual, and the homosexual, this is fair
and equal for all of God's children and should end all argument.
However, other uncertainties in the area of human sexuality exist,
which we will view from a biblical perspective.

But first, let's emphasize one more time the Good Book's
proof of original sin. "Wives, submit yourselves unto your own
husbands, ¹as it is fit in the Lord" (Col. 3:18). Wives, you must
ask yourselves this question: "What could I do with my husband
that the Lord would consider to be unfit?" The answer is given to
you in the cross-reference. "But fornication, and all uncleanness,
or covetousness, let it not be once named among you, as
becometh saints" (¹Eph. 5:3). Again, this leaves no room for
doubt. A man and his wife are not exempt from being classified
as sinners if they commit fornication. To be a saint, this activity

must not be part of a person's life even once, even if married.

For Eve there were two other immediate curses besides spiritual death and expulsion from the paradise.

The first was the loss of control over conception. "Unto the woman he said, I will greatly multiply thy sorrow and thy conception; in sorrow thou shalt bring forth children" (Gen. 3:16). To greatly multiply is to greatly increase conception. God had created a perfect union between a man and his wife. There was no difference in desire, no difference in participation, no difference in pleasure, and no difference in satisfaction. Add to this control of conception.

In the Garden of Eden, Adam and Eve had control of everything and all things were perfect, so it is not unreasonable to believe they had control of conception. However, this would require a perfect love for each another. Sin is an act of hate, and all the perfection God planned was disturbed and thrown out of kilter when an act of hate entered their love relationship.

Before sin, they could have intercourse with control of conception, indicating to me that intercourse was designed primarily for pleasure and secondly for procreation. One of the major concerns facing the future of civilization is overpopulation. Can you see how original sin is the rudimentary source of this predicament?

The second curse for women: "And thy desire shall be to thy husband, and he shall rule over you" (Gen. 3:16). Women lost their equality. Now men would rule over women. In a wicked society, this curse is an advantage to women who are righteous and married to a righteous husband, as they have the protection of a righteous mate. But wicked men have abused this power to an unbelievable degree.

As long as we live in the wilderness of sin, these curses will exist. The women's liberation groups trying to remove these curses with an equality agenda, and the rights of abortion permitting women to have control of their own bodies, will never achieve a desirable solution. Only when sin is removed from earth will these two curses be removed naturally and correctly.

To live without these two curses is a legitimate desire for females. Of course, both of them have been unpleasant and troublesome. But it would be more logical for us to replace the women's movement with a forward movement out of sin. When this is accomplished, and we have reached the Promised Land, these two curses will end.

Let me add, if you are a young girl or a women who never committed original sin, but you did have an abortion, consider this: When the remnant is separated from Sodom and Gomorrah, abortion alone does not place you in either of those cities. You will stand with the remnant, standing with God. The remnant will not be perfect, but they will not be sexually perverse. God has not departed from you because you have had an abortion.

All of you who have committed original sin should also consider this: God did depart from you! The worst sinner is once again judging a lesser sinner. Oh! How you do judge! Yet you want no one to judge you. How convenient!

To Adam, God said, "In the sweat of thy face shalt thou eat bread, till thou return unto the ground; for out of it wast thou taken: for dust thou art, and unto dust shalt thou return" (Gen. 3:19). Working for a living is a curse. But like Eve's curse, which dealt with a change in body function during intercourse, I believe this curse also pertains to Adam's love life. Intercourse became work.

I asked my family physician if he had any ideas how Eve could have had control of conception and how intercourse would not be work for Adam. He gave a quick answer, "Woman have a muscle they use to deliver babies." When you consider the location of this muscle, and the fact labor and climax both involve involuntary contractions, there could be a connection. The fact this muscle delivers a six- to ten-pound infant through a very small canal, with no help whatsoever from the infant, makes this a very powerful muscle. If used during intercourse, it would hug the penis and it could play a role in the control of conception and also in eliminating most, if not all, of the work, not to mention increasing pleasure. Presently, many women never use this muscle during intercourse. Some may use it occasionally and some more often than others. But in this present moral muck, I doubt if anyone experiences anything remotely close to the perfection of sexual intercourse God designed for a man and his wife, two bodies working together in unison as one. God did design it; therefore, it was perfect.

Men, the desire to have effortless climax, and to have the penis tightly hugged are two legitimate desires. But, the inventions you have come up with, oral and anal sex, will never satisfy nor will they come close to the perfection of God's way. They do provoke God's wrath, and it is not wise to provoke God to anger.

Satan gives you climax without work, sex without pregnancy, and sex for pleasure only. Anal sex gives you more hugging. Adam and Eve had all of this in God's perfect intercourse. Satan always imitates God in his own perverse way. But Satan's way is called sin. A more intelligent course of action would be to move out of sin and back to God.

Intercourse before marriage. Women have often complained about the double standard men set up for themselves. Men took advantage of their position over women when they set up the double standard; men need experience before marriage, but women should be virgins when they marry. In the 1960s women decided there should be no double standard, and they embraced the same standards as the men. I saw this as backward thinking! This only made life more difficult. Love and trust were never easy, and love and trust have become more difficult since the sixties. Divorce has increased. Relationships suffer now even more than they did in the past under the old double standard. That is not saying the old was right, but for women to follow the standards of men only lowered those of women, making an overall lower standard of morality for all.

The ideal solution to this moral chaos is for men and women both to be virgins when they marry. Men have made selfish rules, being extremely lenient on themselves while demanding a higher moral standard for the women they marry. Forward movement would have taken place if men had adopted the same morality they set for women. Then all would have reached a higher standard of morality.

This double standard will end in the Promised Land. The days of the "good-ole-boys' society" will end. Both men and women will believe in being virgins until they marry. Being male will not be an excuse for being immoral.

Admit what original sin is. Know that those who commit it are the wicked. Remove original sin from the life of everyone and put into place one sexual standard of purity for both male and female. Then you will be able to understand what the Bible is saying about human sexuality.

God sets the standards this way: "But if any man think that he behaveth himself uncomely toward his virgin, if she pass the flower of her age, and need so require, let them do what he will, he sinneth not: let them marry" (1 Cor. 7:36). The next verse, verse 37, states: "Nevertheless he that standeth steadfast in his heart, having no necessity, but hath power over his own will, and hath so decreed in his heart that he will keep his virgin, doest well." And the conclusion comes in the next verse, verse 38: "So then he that giveth her in marriage doth well; but he that giveth her not in marriage doeth better." God does not consider the couple who have intercourse before marriage to be sinners, if they then marry. One has done well; the other has done better. It is better to wait until the marriage vows are taken before having intercourse, but if a couple loses control and they lose their virginity before the vows are taken, they have not sinned. Let them marry. This indicates to me that both men and women should marry the first person with whom they have intercourse if this intimacy should happen before marriage.

Growing up in the fifties, I often wondered why such a fuss was made over a couple who needed to marry because the girl was pregnant. Isn't marriage what they should do? While at college, one of the basketball stars returned after the summer break married to his sweetheart, whom he had met the year before. Their child was born in just seven months rather than the customary nine. He was made a public example and removed from the team, even though neither had done wrong in the eyes of God. They did well. They could have done better, but they did well. Well enough for God. Why isn't that well enough for us? They were not sinners in the eyes of God.

This happened before I knew people committed whoring, oral sex. It now seems to me that those who commit this most horrendous sin of whoring and consider it unthinkable that someone would judge them have no reservations when it comes to judging someone else. Those who commit original sin have made themselves judge and jury, while at the same time they ward off any judgment against themselves by saying, "Who do you think you are, that you can judge me?" "It is a sin to judge." "Who died and made you God?" They need to be challenged on this. Jesus Christ himself will judge all those who have broken the first set of laws given in the Garden, and when He judges them, they will know they have been judged.

When the righteous marry the righteous. "And unto the married I command, yet not I, but the Lord, Let not the wife depart from her husband" (1 Cor. 7:10). No divorce should happen between two righteous, married people. However, if a separation should happen: "But and if she depart, let her remain unmarried, or be reconciled to her husband; and let not the husband put away his wife." If they were to divorce, they would both need to remain unmarried or they would be committing adultery should they marry someone else. They can also be reconciled back to each other.

When the righteous marry the wicked. Here in the wilderness of sin there are those who commit the sin Adam and Eve introduced and those who do not. This is a collision of two different and intensely opposite worlds. Those who believe in oral sex should not marry those who do not. When the righteous marry the wicked they are unequally yoked together. "I wrote unto you in an epistle ¹not to company with fornicators" (1 Cor. 5:9). The cross-reference teaches a clearer understanding of what it means "not to company with fornicators." "Be ye not unequally yoked together with unbelievers: for what fellowship hath righteousness with unrighteousness? and what communion hath light with darkness?" (¹2 Cor. 6:14). Do not keep company with fornicators. If you are not a fornicator, do not marry a fornicator. If you do, you will have little companionship or mutual sharing with each other. There will be no deep communion or understanding between you, no genuine closeness, no friendly association, or same mind-set. Fornicators will not be faithful. They are not honest. Trust is impossible. They will crave and commit original sin outside of their marriage. What communion does light have with darkness? None! As you leave the altar, one will walk toward God, the other will walk away from God, going in the opposite direction. The longer you are married, the farther apart you will become.

Communion or conversation is also speaking of the act of oneness a married couple experience during intercourse. This area of your marriage will also be noncommunicative. No real closeness, as God planned. No oneness.

You will experience a pull from the fornicator to be like him or her, a nagging, an underlying sense of disapproval. And no matter how hard you try you will always fall short of being what your partner wants unless you please by committing the act or oral sex.

Righteous Job had a fornicator for a wife, and she said the same thing to Job that Eve said to Adam. "Then said 'his wife unto him, Dost thou still retain thine integrity? curse God and die" (Job 2:9). The cross-reference tells us what Job's wife said to him. "And when the woman saw that the tree was good for food, and that it was pleasant to the eyes, and a tree to be desired to make one wise, she took of the fruit" ('Gen. 3:6). Job's wife said exactly what Eve said to Adam. "Why don't you blaspheme God (commit fornication), lose your holiness, and die? Die a spiritual death and be profane like me." Many wicked spouses have said the same to their partner. Job didn't react the way Adam did. Job said, "You talk like a foolish woman." He knew the difference between wisdom and foolishness, and he did not join his wife in her foolishness. Job was unequally yoked together with a non-believer.

Jesus will change the grounds for divorce from adultery to fornication. Moses said adultery was grounds for divorce, but that is in the Old Testament and Jesus added, adultery was only grounds for divorce because of the hardness of your hearts. You were hardhearted. The whoring partner gives him or herself permission to have sex outside of marriage, but if their normal spouse has a normal sexual encounter outside of the marriage that is grounds for divorce. How hardhearted! Selfish!

New Testament grounds for divorce is fornication, sexual perverseness. However, divorce is not your only option. God gives you three alternatives. All three fall short of giving the righteous mate an ideal solution to their situation.

1) You may divorce and marry again. But you must marry a righteous person. What point would there be in marrying another fornicator? If you do end your marriage and then marry a righteous person, you will not be committing adultery. "But I say unto you, That whosoever shall put away his wife, saving for the cause of fornication, causeth her to commit adultery: and whosoever shall

marry her that is divorced committeth adultery" (Matt. 5:32). If the divorce is for any other reason than fornication, both the divorced and those who marry the divorced will be committing adultery.

2) You may stay married to the wicked person. But do not participate in the foolishness. The daughters of Lot were unequally yoked together with men of Sodom and Gomorrah. Yet, they were delivered from these wicked cities, but their husbands were not rescued. That is because Lot's daughters did not participate in the sex their husbands believed in. They did not win over their husbands, but you may win over your spouse by your righteousness. "And the woman which hath an husband that believeth not, and if he be pleased to dwell with her, let her not leave him. For the unbelieving husband is sanctified by the wife, and the unbelieving wife is sanctified by the husband. But if the unbelieving depart, let him depart" (1 Cor. 7:13-15). The righteous spouse may stay in the marriage, but do not argue if the unbelieving spouse wants to leave the union. He or she will be looking for a like partner to commit sin with. If the evil spouse leaves, the righteous one may marry again. The reason for the divorce would be fornication, giving the righteous mate biblical grounds for dissolving the marriage and the right to remarry.

3) You may divorce and remain unmarried. I cannot find a verse that actually states this. But it is a logical conclusion to what we have already read. And certainly, there would be nothing wrong with this decision.

When the wicked marry the wicked. Under this cover of darkness now blanketing our home-place, the fools are marrying the foolish. There aren't many good people left from whom to choose a life-mate. Marriage is suffering more now than ever before. When the wicked marry the wicked, God gives you no advice. Why should He? You do not listen to Him. You think you are wiser than God. Your god is Satan, so ask the devil for advice or help in your times of trouble. I find little advice given to the wicked from God except to return unto God. "I will hide mine eyes from you: yea, when ye make many prayers, I will not hear: your hands are full of blood. Wash you, make you clean; put away the evil of our doing from before mine eyes; cease to do evil" (Isa. 1:15-16). First return to God by ending your rebellious behavior, then He will hear you. Come out of "the world." This is the fundamental spiritual principle God gives to all the wicked. First, acknowledge who I am, make Me your God, come home! Then I will listen to you, and I will help you. I will heal. But returning to God must come first. "But seek ye first the kingdom of God, and his righteousness; and all these things shall be added unto you" (Matt. 6:33). The deepest, most wholesome desires of all humans will be met by God when we seek His kingdom on earth and His righteousness. We should pray: God, please bring Your kingdom to earth, and establish Your thoughts and Your character in the minds of all who inhabit our planet. This will end fornication. The kingdom of God will bring heaven to earth; and the righteous will reign.

Take one wife. Underlying all this information about marriage is a truth mankind has paid little attention to.

The last verse in the Old Testament book of Ezra adds another phrase to the list that identifies the sexually perverse. Strange wives. "All these had taken strange wives: and some of them had wives by whom they had children" (Ezra 10:44). If strange wives could not have children, they would be same-sex wives. A male can be a strange wife; a female can be a strange wife: same-sex partner. An entire land of people had taken strange wives (same-sex partner in marriage), and when they understood God disapproved of this lifestyle, they put them away and ended this idolatrous practice. Then they took only one mate, one by whom they had children, an opposite sex partner. No same-sex, strange wife was taken again. And then this land of heterosexual couples should not commit original sin, as Adam and Eve did.

In the days of Noah, they were marrying and giving in marriage. In those wicked days before the flood, men also took two
wives right up to the time the rain came. And we are told this is
the way it will once again be at the end of the age. Only a few, a
remnant, are not guilty of this today.

ॐ

For clarity concerning God's use of the words "men" and
"women," "sons" and "daughters," let me add that God often calls
all His children sons. And He will at times, not all the time but at
times, call those who serve Satan women. This is expressed in
Genesis, "That the sons of God saw the daughters of men that they
were fair; and they took them wives of all they chose. And the
Lord said, My spirit shall not always strive with man" (Gen. 6:2-3).
When those who serve God (the sons of God) marry those who
serve Satan (the daughters of man) and learn the ways of Satan
(sin), God states His spirit will leave. Those persons will no longer
have God.

Satan began sin with a male and a female, but it wasn't long
before wickedness increased to include bisexuality and homosexuality. Many times the Bible will refer to Satan's followers (male and
female) as women, whorish women, strange women, strange wives.

At other times God will call all those who serve Him (male and
female) sons. This may sound negative toward women, but when
you stop to think, it is equal. Both men and women are the sons of
God, when they serve God. Both men and women are called
women when they serve Satan. God does not discriminate against
one sex or the other.

The followers of Satan will once again be called sons when
they return to God. "Behold, what manner of love the Father
hath bestowed upon us, that we should be called the sons of
God" (1 John 3:1). This is a promise to all who have sinned,
females as well as males.

CHAPTER NINETEEN

Happiness

The answer to the question "Where does happiness come from?" should be answered in this section. God began the human race with a man and his wife. There was happiness in this relationship. I think it is safe to say that most of us greatly desire the happiness that comes with a lifetime of love and companionship, as designed by God. When love and marriage fail to fulfill our desires, we experience some of our greatest emotional pain. Although original sin brings about the most severe and long-lasting damage, betrayal and deception in marriage brings to us some of our deepest hurts, and both leave us scarred and emotionally affected in any future relationships for the rest of our lives.

The happiness in the Garden of Eden and in the Promised Land has one common denominator—no original sin. This means there is no hate in those two lands. Between these two lands of no sin is a land of sorrow, pain, tears, anguish, and fears caused by this first transgression. Love and marriage have had great difficulty here in the wilderness. Hate is an enemy to all relationships, especially the marriage relationship. Unhappiness, even that of a damaged or broken marriage, ultimately comes from this continuation of base living. Removing sin from all relationships, including marriage, will play a major role in restoring happiness. In this approaching land of peace, a holy man will again take one holy wife and marriage will be perfect. This union will be lasting and both partners will be faithful. Sin and hate will be absent. Love will be true. Trust will return.

The Bible gives us definitions, many of them different from the ones I sometimes hear conveyed to us from behind the pulpit. One example is the fear of the Lord. By using the one standard drawn between good and evil in the Garden we can understand what the fear of God means. "The fear of the Lord is to hate evil" (Prov. 8:13). Since we know what evil is, this can be stated: A God-fearing person hates original sin. If you believe the God who said sexual perverseness is deadly, then you believe in God. If you obey God, and abstain from disobedience, you are showing that you have a healthy fear of God. He has authority over you. If you defy God and disregard this first law, you demonstrate that you do not have the fear of God. You ignore God. You act out, "Who is this God who can tell me what to do? I will do as I please." This is not a healthy, respectful reverence of God. Disobedience is the opposite of worship.

So when the Scriptures speak of God-fearing men and women it is speaking of those who do no evil by rejecting the sin of Adam and Eve. Whenever you see the words "fear of God," they can be changed to hating evil, for that is what the fear of the Lord is—to hate evil.

Here are a few examples:

- "Blessed is the man that feareth the Lord, and delighteth greatly in his commandments" (Ps. 112:1) can be changed to "blessed is the man who hates evil and loves his commandments." And of course, cursed are those who do evil.
- "The fear of the Lord is the beginning of wisdom" (Ps. 111:10). This can be changed to "hating evil is the beginning of wisdom." As long as you see sin as a wise thing to do, you have not reached the place at where wisdom begins. You are foolish.

- "Let us cleanse ourselves from all filthiness of the flesh and spirit, perfecting holiness in the fear of God" (2 Cor. 7:1). Holiness is perfected by hating evil. When evil is removed from a person's life, he or she is clean, and this cleanness makes a person holy. God is holy. We should also be holy; we should live without doing evil.

- "The secret of the Lord is with them that fear him; and he will show them his covenant" (Ps. 25:14). The secret of the Lord is with those who hate evil. The law is with the people who hate evil, for they keep the Garden Law. God will show secrets to those who do not commit original sin.

- "Let us hear the conclusion of the whole matter: Fear God, and keep his commandments: for this is the whole duty of man" (Ecc. 12:13). The final truth about this whole matter of life is to hate evil, for only then do we keep the first commandment. Keep the Garden Law and then keep the Ten Commandments we have been taught. This is man's whole duty. Think about that! If all did this, life on earth would be perfect, and we would not need a "do-gooder." It is more important to be good than it is to do good.

Another example is the word "understanding." Behold, the fear of the Lord, that is wisdom; and to depart from evil is understanding" (Job 28:28). Hating evil is wisdom. Understanding is departing from evil. "Happy is the man who gets understanding" does not mean that a man is happy when those who know him understand he needs to be evil. Biblical understanding is just the opposite. It is departing from evil.

And those who live by the commandments have good understanding. "A good understanding have all they that do his commandments" (Ps. 111:10).

I have said all that to give you God's formula for happiness. I sat in a class once and listened to a group define happiness. No one used a scriptural reference. Everyone had an opinion, but everyone spoke from their own viewpoint, not even giving a Webster definition. Each was trying to sound more wise then the other, even though they were all blind and foolish.

We have always had an answer to this question in our reach. God's formula for "happiness" is stated this way: "Happy is the man that findeth wisdom, and the man that getteth understanding" (Prov. 3:13). Happiness comes when a person finds wisdom (hates evil) and gets understanding (departs from evil). Why are there so many people who pay no attention to the answers from God?

Wisdom begins with the fear of the Lord (hating evil). Understanding is departing from evil. When a person recognizes evil and departs from it, common sense is beginning to surface. God accepts you back, and this sure knowledge of knowing you are pleasing to God is basic to your mental well-being. We are made to love God. Until we do, we will not be content. We are made to love and to be kind to each other, and until we do, we will not be happy. The greatest commandment is to love God and to love our brothers as ourselves. Translated that means: Do not commit this first sin the serpent introduced and do not ask anyone else to perform original sin. Obeying this commandment is for our own happiness.

The personal relationship between a man or a woman and God must be restored before any other relationship can be restored. Each one of us needs to live according to what God requires. We must put an end to evil. This requirement needs to be met before we can be happy or have a loving and meaningful relationship with another human being. Sin is not loving or meaningful. We are responsible for removing it from our behavior.

"The fear of the Lord is clean" (Ps. 19:9). Hating evil and departing from it will make a person clean. You will have been washed with the Word of God in clean water when you stop sinning. Clean is the opposite of filthy.

When people know they are clean, holy, accepted, and pleasing to God, this brings an inner peace and true happiness. This knowledge is unmistakable and based on facts, truth. You can be sure you are a child of God. Of course the facts come from God, making a belief in God a prerequisite for believing the facts. First believe in God. Then believe the truth of God. Accept His truth, adjust your life to it, be obedient to the truth in your actions, then you can know beyond a doubt that you are holy and acceptable to the God who created you. You will know that you please and love your heavenly Father, and that He is no longer angry at you for rebelling against Him in sin. There is great peace of mind in knowing this.

In the days of Moses, Pharaoh (the government) stood in the way of the people leaving sin. I do not know if that would happen today. But if our government were to do the same, the Declaration of Independence and the Bill of Rights both give protection to the people along with the right and the privilege to abolish such an administration. The Declaration of Independence declares "that all men are created equal, that they are endowed by their Creator with certain unalienable Rights, that among these are *Life, Liberty,* and the *pursuit of Happiness.*" We are promised the right to life and liberty. And we are promised the right to pursue happiness. This is a promise to the American people that our government will not stand in the way of anyone who desires to pursue happiness by leaving sin and coming out of "the world."

The Declaration of Independence goes on to say, "to secure these rights, Governments are instituted among men deriving their just powers from the consent of the governed. That whenever any Form of Government becomes destructive of these ends, it is the Right of the People to alter or to abolish it, and to institute new Government, having its foundation on such principles and organizing its powers in such form, as to them shall seem most likely to effect their Safety and Happiness." The common folks have the right and obligation to alter or abolish any government that stands in the way of our pursuit of happiness, and then we are given the right to create a new government which will secure and protect the safety and happiness of the people. Remember the passage, "When the wicked rule the people mourn, and when the righteous rule there will be rejoicing (happiness)." Honestly, I prefer rejoicing to mourning. We have an obligation to abolish a wicked government.

Protection also comes from the Constitution of the United States where all citizens are promised certain rights. The first amendment of the ten amendments to the Constitution, The Bill of Rights, gives every citizen freedom of speech, the right to voice their opinion in the marketplace of free ideas. This amendment also promises that our government will not interfere with religion or of the assembling of ourselves together.

A minute segment of our society identifies itself as a member of the Freemen, Vipers, and Militia movements. I see them on the front page and in the editorial section of my newspaper more often then one would think. I would suggest to them, if you were to follow a peaceful, forward movement out of sin, you would achieve what you desire much sooner.

I find nothing wrong with longing for rulers who do not over-tax us and then waste and/or spend our tax dollars for the politicians' gain and for special interest groups. We are not wrong when we yearn for a government that does not over-control the people it governs, or when we desire to have honest, moral people in high positions of leadership. And there is nothing wrong with craving a government that will take the good of all those they rule over into account. Many of us have become nauseated when viewing "politics as usual."

However, there is something amiss when you believe military might will remove this type of governing. In foreign countries governments have been replaced in this manner, but without any guarantee the new regime will be any different from the one just removed. It will be the wisdom of the believers in holiness that will remove corrupt governments. Wisdom is better than weapons of war. And I will predict that when we have new Christianity, biblically described as the New Jerusalem, there will be no separation of church and state. At that time the church will be in control of church and state. The church will not be corrupt; therefore, the government will not be corrupt. The church will be just; therefore, the government will be just. When the just rule, the people will rejoice.

May I just add: We do not want the Moral Majority to run our nation, for they come from the Old Jerusalem. They would not provide for us a "just" governing body.

A simple movement out of sin in the pursuit of happiness will abolish any corrupt leadership if the movement is large enough to be the majority. Either the church will become the governing body or all people will vote only for a just or a justified person, ones who have come out of sin and make up the body of Christ, the church. Either way, this will obliterate any government that would practice and defend sin. This can happen, and it will happen without weapons of war. The battle between good and evil is a battle of two mind-sets, the just and the unjust. The final battle will be fought with words. In the end, the just will win the war. Then they will govern. Mourning will end.

CHAPTER TWENTY

Commandment 8

Thou shalt not steal.
Exodus 20:15

This seems like a simple commandment. Do not take what does not belong to you. Most of us see this as: do not take things, money, reputation, spouses, or possessions that belong to someone else. That explanation is correct when viewing the commandments we are so familiar with.

But in this book we are examining the set of ten commandments written on the other table of stone. This set goes deeper into the matter, commanding us not to steal what belongs to God.

When reviewing the eighth commandment from the Garden, Adam and Eve were in charge of everything. In this story they were alone. There was no property to steal, no money, or spouse of another person, or possessions. So, how did they break this commandment and steal from God? and what did they steal?

The Creator gives us a list of his possessions: "The earth is the Lord's, and the fullness thereof; the world, and they that dwell therein" (Ps. 24:1). Here the earth and "the world" are two separate entities, and this verse leaves no room for doubt, for God clearly identifies His property. The earth itself belongs to God. This includes every thing and very person. "The world" and those who dwell there belong to God. Even those who live in Satan's world of fornication belong to the Creator.

All humans belong to the One who created them, God their Father. His children can be stolen from Him. Adam stole Eve, and Eve stole Adam. Neither committed sin alone. It takes two. If Eve was deceived and committed sin first, then Adam was a willing partner and is responsible for Eve's death and submission to Satan. He stole her from God. Adam committed sin next. Eve had to be a willing partner and is responsible for the death of Adam. She stole Adam from God and turned him over to Satan. When they left the Garden, they no longer belonged to God, but were the property of the serpent. They had been deceived, captured, and stolen and had become part of "the world," the devil's world of fornication.

Yet, Almighty God tells us those who dwell in "the world" still belong to God. Do you know you do not belong to Satan? He is not your creator. The devil fathered no one. He is in possession of stolen property, and has a plan to steal all of God's children.

The prince of darkness cannot create! He cannot design and bring into existence an earth. He cannot form a people, not even one person. The only way Lucifer can have children, a home, or be a king ruling the earth is to steal it all from God. He gives birth to his children by this method: "The field is the world; the good seed are the children of the kingdom; but the tares are 'the children of the wicked one. The enemy that sowed them is the devil; the harvest is the end of the world" (Matt. 13:38-39). The cross-reference, telling us who the "children of the wicked one" are, takes us to Eden to explain how the devil has children. "And the Lord God said unto the women [Eve], What is this that thou has done? And the woman said, The serpent beguiled me, and I did eat" ('Gen.

3:13). The devil captures all of his children in this same manner by which he deceived both Adam and Eve, by original sin. Oral sex does birth children: the wicked children of Satan. Yet, before sin you belong to God, and after you have been deceived, you are still God's children, but you have been stolen.

This commandment is dictating that no man steal God's children from Him, and is proof we begin our existence with The Creator being our God and our Father. If we are not deceived, we never leave God, and God never leaves us. But those of you who learned fornication were stolen from God; if you taught, forced, deceived, enticed, or convinced another person to commit fornication, you too, are guilty of stealing one of God's holy children. You do Satan's work.

Those of us who have children consider them our most treasured possessions. If a thief were to steal from us, we would prefer he stole our money, car, television, camera, silver, or jewelry. We would not want our children stolen. God feels the same way. The stealing of God's children is a greater sin than the stealing of someone's possessions.

Jehovah God addresses this kind of stealing, and states that the law is written for the following people: "For whoremongers, for them that defile themselves with mankind, for mensteaters, for liars, for perjured person, and if there be any other thing that is contrary to sound doctrine" (1 Tim. 1:10). All the above words describe the sexually perverse. The law is written for you menstealers. You steal men and women from God. However, stolen property still belongs to the person it was stolen from. "Yea, they sacrificed their sons and their daughters unto devils" (Ps. 106:37). Your sons and daughters belonged to God before you stole them and gave them to Satan. It is good news that God still considers all those stolen from Him to be His children and has a plan to redeem them. A plan to get them back.

Even the remnant is robbed by Satan's people. David, who

would stand with the remnant if alive at the end of time, said, "The bands of the wicked have robbed me: but I have not forgotten thy law" (Ps. 119:61). David did not break the Garden Law, yet he is robbed of a safe, peaceful, sinless place to live. Robbed of a society where truth is the norm. Robbed of living without being wounded.

And when the wicked marry the righteous, you rob that person of a righteous spouse. If you convince the holy spouse to commit original sin, you steal that person from their Creator. You steal their birthright (the right to see God) from them. If you have children, you deprive them of a righteous mother or father. You deny our youth respectable role models. You rob our civilization of morality.

God is the Creator. Satan is the destroyer. If the earth and the human race were completely taken over by Lucifer, the earth and its people would someday self-destruct. That would be its end. Satan has a plan to capture all of God's children and rule the earth. However, The Supreme Being has a plan to return all His children and the earth to Himself. For before God made the earth, and before He made the human race, He put a plan in place that if the stealing of His children should occur, He would have a plan of redemption: a way, a process, a method, a course of action to bring His children back to the safety of their own Father. It is the plan of salvation, deliverance from sin, and will be offered from the New Jerusalem. Sometimes it is referred to as the plan of redemption.

Redemption: Webster's definition states: "To buy back, to get back, to recover by paying a fee, to make worthwhile, to justify." Here Webster agrees with the Holy Bible in definition. God sent Jesus to buy back the stolen, to make the unjust just again, and to return them to God. The price He paid, to reach mankind with the light (law), was coming to earth and dying on a cross made of sin. The truth was made flesh. He brought truth to a people in darkness.

"He [God] sent redemption to his people" (Ps. 111:9). His

"people" means everyone. God sent the truth in Jesus for the purpose of getting you back. The truth will make you whole and will
bring you back to your Father. God will send it in His own time.

"For with the Lord there is mercy, and with him is plenteous
redemption" (Ps. 130:7).

"And when these things begin to come to pass, then look up,
and lift up your heads; for your redemption draweth nigh" (Luke
21:28). What we are to look for in knowing our redemption is near
are the signs the age is drawing to an end. Here are some of those
signs: the church will be full of wickedness; nations will be in dis-
tress; many false Christs will have come; the sea and the waves will
roar. The sea and the waves are Sodom and Gomorrah, and they
are presently raging, making a great amount of noise. They are the
ones exhibiting so much anger and havoc. We are seeing these
signs today, indicating that redemption is near.

"And he saved them from the hand of him that hated them, and
redeemed them from the hand of the enemy" (Ps. 106:10). The
enemy is Satan. The devil does not love you. God will recover you
from the god who hates you. You will understand this better when
you see peace on earth and compare it with what the serpent has
offered you in sin.

ॐ

To clarify "waves," and "roaring sea" let us look at the book of
Jude one more time. Describing Sodom and Gomorrah, "These are
spots . . . clouds they are without water, carried about of winds . . .
twice dead. Raging wave of the sea, foaming out their own shame
. . . wandering stars" (Jude 12-13). When speaking of the storms of
life, Sodom and Gomorrah create a storm with clouds, a wind of
doctrine that forms raging waves on the sea of life. Many times
when we think the Scriptures are speaking of the weather, the
truth is they are describing Sodom and Gomorrah. If you expect a
Jesus who can control the weather, you will be disappointed.

Instead, He will calm the raging sea: Sodom and Gomorrah. Their wind (doctrine) will cease, the sea of life will no longer rage, and these clouds (people) will once again have water, holiness.

It is said Jesus will come in the clouds, but not in the clouds without water. He will come with the clouds (people) that do have water—the holy remnant. Don't look for Jesus in the clouds in the sky.

CHAPTER TWENTY-ONE

Commandment 9

࿓

Thou shalt not bear false witness
against thy neighbour.
Exodus 20:16

Just as we are all an image, either the true image of God or a false image of our heavenly Father, the same is true about being a witness. Everyone is a witness, either a true one or a false one to all those around about us—our neighbors. We are children of God; therefore, to be a witness of truth, we must first believe the truth and then live it out. To be a witness for God is to live by the law.

When the lie Satan told in the Garden is believed and original sin committed, your life and your words, opposing truth, will make you a false witness. Do not, through lifestyle or words, tell your neighbors lies about God. This court order from the Highest almost needs no further explanation, but let us look at a few verses supporting this commandment.

"Thou shalt not raise a false report: put not thine hand with the wicked to be an unrighteous witness. Thou shalt not follow a multitude to do evil; neither shalt thou speak in a cause to decline after many to wrest judgment" (Exod. 23:1-2). The wicked are unrighteous witnesses. Do not join them, for those who do evil clash with common sense and wisdom by their life and in their speech.

"A faithful witness will not lie: but a false witness will utter lies" (Prov. 14:5). He who serves God does not live a lie, while a person who serves Lucifer not only lives the lie but is usually a master of the art of lying and deceit. People like this, I have heard, teach themselves to lie in ways that do not seem to be lying. For example, if they put two negatives in a sentence, that means "yes" to them, but not to those who think it means "no." One of the laws governing electricity is two negatives make a positive. To many, "No, I did not" is a yes. They can pass a lie-detector test this way, or tell a jury "no" when the truth is "yes." "Did you see anything unusual?" "No, I did not" can mean, "Yes, I did."

Another way to be deceitful is when every tiny detail must be correct or they will claim the entire statement is false. "Be more specific" can mean: "I'm looking for a way out." "Did you have a twelve-year affair?" "No." The slight difference in time permits the person to say "no" to the entire question, for it was only an eleven-year affair.

"A man that beareth false witness against his neighbour 'is a maul, and a sword, and a sharp arrow" (Prov. 25:18). A "maul" is explained in the cross-reference: "They have sharpened their tongues like a serpent; adders' poison is under their lips" ('Psalms 140:3). The lies people tell concerning original sin are like poison. They are sharp as a sword aimed at the innocent like an arrow, and kill quickly like the sting of a deadly serpent's bite.

In Revelations, we are told no liar will enter the New Jerusalem: "And there shall in no wise enter into it anything that defileth, neither whatsoever worketh abomination, or maketh a lie" (21:27). Lies have to be made for there were none in the beginning. Truth must be altered to manufacture a falsehood. No one who has changed truth or made null and void the Garden Law will enter into the New Jerusalem.

We know that Jesus will come as a judge. Judges listen to witnesses. Scripture tells us He will not judge after the hearing of His ears. In other words, you will not be judged on what you say. The hypocrites verbally claim they believe in Jesus. Words! But they will not be judged on their claimed status, rather on how they lived out their lives. They will be judged on the law they broke.

In Jeremiah, God declares: "Behold, I am against them that prophesy false dreams . . . and do tell them, and cause my people to err by their lies . . . therefore they shall not profit this people at all" (23:32). Ministers who tell us lies will not profit our land. In America, I believe we are beginning to see this come true. The United States leads the industrialized world in the majority of all crime. Yes, we are richer than most countries, but what have we sold for money: our sons and daughters, our morals, our goodness? Our nation is presently reaping what we have sown. Immorality. Drugs. Crime. Gangs. Children who kill. Divorce. Ever-mounting taxes. Government corruption. Widespread disillusionment. Over the long haul, vain living is unprofitable, for a person or a nation. Ministers who do not tell us the truth, do us no lasting good.

The Jesus at the end of this age will be a true witness for God. He will not only live by the law, but His truth will bring to light the true facts about God. "Behold, I have given him for a witness to the people" (Isa. 55:4). And in Matthew, "And this gospel of the kingdom shall be preached to all the world for a witness unto all nations; and then shall the end come" (24:14). When the doctrine of Jesus is preached, the root of all confusion made known, and original sin is recognized and shown to all peoples, then we can see God, and we can expect the end of "the world."

ॐ

The terms of this commandment order us to be witnesses of the one true God of the Garden Law, with our lives and our words.

If, in a court of law, you were required to testify for your god by your actions alone, would your testimony prove your allegiance to God or to Satan?

CHAPTER TWENTY-TWO

Commandment 10

ॐ

Thou shalt not covet thy neighbour's house,
thou shalt not covet thy neighbour's wife, nor
his manservant, nor his maidservant,
nor his ox, nor his ass,
nor any thing that is thy neighbour's.
Exodus 20:17

To covet: to have an intense desire to possess something or someone, to want it ardently, to long for it. We have already been ordered to refrain from taking what does not belong to us, not to steal. This last command addresses only the desire to possess what is not ours.

This final command states it is a sin to desire to sin, to long to commit fornication, or to ardently want to bow to Adam's first sin. Some may think this is impossible, but if it were not possible, then it would not be required of us. What God demands, He supplies.

In our culture, many have been misled to believe that it is all right to entertain the desire to be homosexual, as long as the craving is not acted upon. That is a lie! This commandment states it is sin to even have the desire. God is speaking to more than the homosexual; He is speaking to everyone, and affirms the fact it is a sin for anyone to desire or to have a longing to commit original sin. All people belong to God, and it is sin to wish or want them to leave Jehovah to serve you, for when they serve you, you have stolen them. You should have no desire to steal God's children from Him.

Cancer and AIDs are modern-day diseases no one craves to have. Leprosy is a dreaded physical disease no one wants. However, in Scripture, leprosy is not a physical disease, but a spiritual one. "The garment also that the plague of leprosy is in, whether it be a woolen garment or a linen garment" (Lev. 13:47). The word "garment" is better explained by the cross-reference and takes us to the Book of Romans where the sexually perverse are described beginning with verse 21 through 31. The cross-reference includes all eleven verses. I will list a portion of these passages: "God also gave them up to uncleanness through the lusts of their own hearts, to dishonor their own bodies [garments] between themselves" (1:24). "God gave them up unto vile affections: for even their women did change the natural use into that which is against nature. And likewise also the men, leaving the natural use of the women, burned in their lust one toward another; men with men working that which is unseemly" (1:26-27).

Garments are our bodies and sexual perverseness is the plague of leprosy. The day will come when the desire to have the spiritual plague of leprosy will be as unattractive as having a dreaded physical disease. There is only one known cure for spiritual leprosy and that is a strong dose of unaltered truth. You should have such a intense disgust for sin that it would be unthinkable, repulsive, abominable, shameful, and as undesirable and as unwanted as the physical diseases of cancer, leprosy, or AIDS.

With new eyes you will see sexual perverseness as a spiritually deadly plague spreading throughout our land, and it will lose its seductiveness. Your vision is still impaired as long as the yearning to sin is there, for you do not have the mind of God yet. God would not desire to disobey this first law of life and wisdom. You need a deeper comprehension of the devastating, destructive repercussions original sin has on our culture and our future. You need to see as God sees.

Others Scriptures tell us more about covetousness: "For the love of money is the root of all evil: which while some covet after, they have erred from the faith, and pierced themselves through with many sorrows" (1 Tim. 6:10). Money is not evil: but to love it so much you will leave God and bow to Satan to get it is. The above verse warns of much suffering, misery, and woes as a result of loving money this much. Has America loved money this excessively?

And again in that controversial portion of Scripture about the sexually perverse, we learn that they covet.

"Being filled with all unrighteousness, fornication, wickedness, covetousness, maliciousness; full of envy, murder, debate, deceit, malignity; whisperers" (Rom. 1:29).

Although some believe these verses in Romans are the only ones that speak of the sexually perverse, these same expressions are used throughout the Word of God and are found in 1 Corinthians 6:9-10. Here is a long list of the people who will not inherit the Kingdom of God: fornicators, idolaters, adulterers, effeminates, abusers of themselves with mankind, thieves, covetous, drunkards, revilers, and extortioners. All these words describe those who live in the two dark cities of Sodom and Gomorrah. Those who desire to sin (the covetous) are on the list. But deliverance is possible for in the very next verse we read: "And such were some of you: but ye are washed, but ye are sanctified, but ye are justified in the name of the Lord Jesus, and by the Spirit of our God" (1 Cor. 6:11). When deliverance is offered to mankind many who desire to be evil and those who act out sexual perverseness will be cleansed

by the washing of the word, sanctified and made holy, and justified by returning to the ways of the just.

The same list is also found in Ephesians: "For this ye know, that
no whoremonger, nor unclean person, nor covetous man, who is
an idolater, hath any inheritance in the kingdom of Christ and of
God" (5:5).

As long as you believe these lies: Adam and Eve ate an apple,
original sin is human nature, the sexually perverse are born that
way (sexual orientation), boys will be boys, sin is normal adoles-
cent behavior, fathers are wise to pass this evil on to their sons, oral
sex is a wifely duty, and Satan's sex is impossible to overcome, we
are all doomed to remain here in the wilderness of sin.

None of the above is true, for when you remove sin from your
life, you become holy, just, and clean. Then you become a true
Christian, fit for the Kingdom of God.

To understand the mind of God better, look at one more explanation of His plan to remove this first offense from the earth. The
words "elements" and "rudiments" are interchangeable in Scripture.
Webster's dictionary defines "rudiments" as: the fundamentals of a
subject learned. In the Bible, the words, "elements" and "rudiments"
both mean "the fundamentals of a subject learned." When you
learn the fundamentals of "the world," you learn original sin. Satan
founded his world on this first wrongdoing, and it has been
learned by many.

"Even so we, when we were children, we were in bondage
under the elements of the world" (Gal. 4:3). God considers those
who live in "the world" children in bondage. Held captive by the
lies you believe, and by what you had to learn to enter "the world,"
oral sex. When you come out of the world you will begin to grow
up. Spiritually speaking, you will be a mature Christian when you
learn how to live out your human sexuality in a way that will bring
harm to no one. You become sexually accountable. Only selfish
people request sin, for they are considering no one but themselves.

"Beware lest any man spoil you through philosophy and vain deceit, after the tradition of men, after the rudiments [elements] of the world, and not after Christ" (Col. 2:8).

Men made sin a tradition, passing worthless knowledge from one generation to the next. They spoil their youth and teach them the fundamental sin Satan built his world on. If you have learned the sin of "the world," you do not belong to God.

"Wherefore if ye be dead with Christ from the rudiments of the world" (Col. 2:20). When you are dead with Christ, you have died to all wrongdoing. You have rejected the foundation of sin you had to learn to enter Satan's world. Now you are released from bondage and from the devil, and you have returned to God.

"But the day of the Lord will come . . . and the elements shall melt with fervent heat, the earth also and the works that are therein shall be burned up" (2 Peter 3:10). The "elements will melt" is not the earth literally burning up. It is not a nuclear meltdown. It is Satan's kingdom burning up from this first law of fire. The fire will begin at the foundation of the world, the subject learned— oral sex. The day of the Lord is planned for the sole purpose of ending Lucifer's world. To fight fire with fire is to fight the breaking of the Garden Law by conforming to this first most important set of commandments. Surrendering your will in submission to the law will destroy Satan's world from its foundation upward.

Seeing that "the world" will be dissolved, melted down to nothing by the fiery law from the Garden, you should abandon your desire to be partakers in what God is so absolutely against and has plans to destroy so utterly. You should see as God sees, think as God thinks. A desire to participate in what God totally opposes is illogical.

ॐ

To sum up this first table of stone, the first Ten Commandments given to Adam and Eve, then to Moses, and lastly to Jesus in one verse, "For all the law is fulfilled in one word, even in this; Thou shalt love thy neighbour as thy self" (Gal) 5:14). All ten command-ments state: love one another! Do not commit hate/original sin. Love God, love yourself, and love your neighbors. This is the great-est commandment. Disobeying this greatest commandment give us a greatest sin.

"Then the eyes of
the blind shall be opened,
and the ears of the deaf
shall be unstopped."

Isaiah 35:5

Spiritual Eyesight

Beginning again is as simple
as getting rid of the old
and starting over.

Truth   Truth   Truth
The trinity

God is the author of truth
Jesus brought God's truth to earth
The Holy Spirit is the truth within you.
When spoken,
The Holy Spirit will go everywhere.

CHAPTER TWENTY-THREE

The New Jerusalem

৶৵

A merica is a nation of people who practice evil, and we have certainly been traveling in the wrong direction if we want out of our many troubles. "Ah sinful nation, a people laden with iniquity, a seed of evil doers, children that are corrupters: they have forsaken the Lord, they have provoked the Holy One of Israel unto anger, they are gone away backward" (Isa. 1:4). God made some serious demands of his children, but we as a people have ignored those requirements and have forsaken The Holy One to do evil. Sin always brings suffering to all those who break the Garden Law as well as those who do not. Everyone suffers from sin, and is lost because of it. Sin is where the lost wander aimlessly, in shame and confusion. "They shall be ashamed, and also confounded, all of them: they shall go to confusion together that are makers of idols" (Isa. 45:16). Bewildered, baffled, puzzled, confused best describes our culture today. So many views come at us from all directions, invented by the makers of idols who stand perplexed together. What are we to believe?

Jesus comes to seek and to save those who are lost in idolatry, sin, and confusion. "For the Son of man is come to seek and to save that which was lost" (Luke 19:10).

What does it mean to be spiritually "lost"? I tried to understand how a person literally becomes "lost," and in my mind's eye I drove to the mountains in northwest Washington state, to the breathtaking North Cascade mountain range where the tall evergreen trees grow and thick underbrush covers the mountainside. I parked my car and took a walk in the woods. As long as I could see my car, I was not lost. I could easily return to it. Once my car was out of sight, if I had remembered the path I had taken, then I could simply walk the same course back to my car, and I was not lost. I was only lost when (1) I could not see my car, and (2) I did not know the path I had taken to arrive at where I stood. Both conditions needed to be a reality before I became lost.

Biblically speaking, I believe human beings became spiritually lost in the wilderness of sin because the same two conditions were present in their relationship to God. First, in the darkness man lost sight of God and could not see what God was like or where He stood on serious issues. Second he did not know the path he had walked that took him so far away from God and into this present murkiness. Mankind is now hopelessly doomed here in evil, wandering in the darkness, tormented by guilt and shame from the sin that took him here. He is presently lost and confused. Blind and in the dark. Confounded. Without being rescued or without a deliverer to show the doorway back to God, man will remain here in waywardness. For he is lost.

When I hear people ask, "What's gone wrong in America?" "Why is there so much hurt and unhappiness?" and "Why is there suffering?" they really do not know the answers. They do not know how they arrived here, why they remain, or what the root source is behind all the heartaches. Without help, these questions will continue on forever.

That is why I have taken us back to the beginning so you may see God. God is good. God is love. God is HOLY, HOLY, HOLY. He is not evil, He would not commit an act of hate (fornication),

which would make Him profane (unholy). Now you see the goodness of a holy God. When you are good, you are holy. And when
you are holy, you are good. This now-visible holy God is the one
true God.

And, because the first definitive line drawn between good and
evil, distinguishing God from Satan, has also been made known,
you can see the course of evil the human race has traveled and continues to travel to this very day. It is the path of immorality, the
practice of original sin.

The road taken, this path of evil, original sin, has led to pain,
suffering, and the confusion experienced since we left the Garden.
Remember it. Recognize the danger points and the pitfalls, and
don't take it again. Turning truth around, thinking sin is wise, is
going in a backward direction away from Holy. It is moving us farther from peace and rendering us helpless and lost without the
ability to see God or your way back home.

But now, because you know the first definitive line drawn
between good and evil, distinguishing God from Satan, you can
recognize the God of truth.

And you also see the passageway that took you so far away
from your heavenly Father and into the most shameful, hurtful
areas of life and into the darkest part of this snake-infested jungle.
It was the path of evil, original sin. So, with God in sight and the
path you walked clearly laid out before you, returning to God and
moving forward into the Promised Land where once again there
will be no sin should be reasonably easy.

Do you understand you are no longer lost? For you see God
and the path home. You are at a point where you must make a decision to remain in evil or walk out of the wilderness. In the days of
Moses, the people chose to remain in sin. They felt comfortable
there in familiar territory. Some expressed the fear that they would
be deprived; for in sin, they could eat their fill. You are free to
make the same choice, to remain evil, or you can walk the path

home. To find your way back home and dwell with your Father will require a belief in truth.

By now you either believe or you have rejected what you have read. You have already seen many new truths, and those who believe will find this section full of new ways of looking at some old familiar texts. Understanding Scripture correctly is having spiritual eyesight. We will examine some of the fables we have heard repeated again and again until we believed them to be truth without questioning what we were told. Because the law was left out of the church, none of the Scriptures could be understood correctly, so fables became the principal foundation upon which the Old Jerusalem was built.

The Old Jerusalem. "They build up Zion with blood, and Jerusalem with iniquity. Therefore, shall Zion for your sake be plowed as a field, and Jerusalem shall become heaps" (Micah 3:10,12). Bloody men built a bloody city. People who believed in a lifestyle of iniquity built a church that commits iniquity. For your own sake plow it all under and begin again from the foundation up. The leaders of the Old Jerusalem should lead the people and begin the plowing, replanting, and rebuilding.

In 1995, the Evangelical Lutheran Church of America finished a seven-year study titled "The Church and Human Sexuality: A Lutheran Perspective." This study ended with members of the church arguing over what constitutes sexual morality, especially in the area of homosexuality. The Lutheran denomination, the first Protestant movement, is more than five hundred years old and is just now sitting down and trying to decide what morality its members should live by. This is backward! Morality should have been the foundation of the church. Think how many immoral persons may have joined the church during this period, when no basic moral code of conduct was required for membership.

The New Jerusalem. Morality will be the foundation of this powerful, genuine, authentic Christianity, biblically called the

New Jerusalem. "Awake, awake; put on thy strength, O Zion; put on thy beautiful garments, O Jerusalem, the holy city: for henceforth there shall no more come into thee the uncircumcised and the unclean" (Isa. 52:1) First, Jerusalem will be holy, meaning no fornicators will be allowed there. No one like Adam, Eve, Cain or Esau, who commit oral or anal sex, will be permitted to enter. This new Christianity will be clean and holy. Notice the city is also called Zion. In other passages it is called the City of God, the Mountain of the Lord's House, and the Kingdom of God.

Remember the law all the people wanted removed from their hearing? The Garden Law. It is this order from Eden that will be the foundation of the New Jerusalem: "Jesus saith unto them, did you never read in the scriptures, The stone which the builders rejected, the same is become the head of the corner: this is the Lord's doing, and it is marvelous in our eyes" (Matt. 21:42). The law given in Eden, the one written in stone, the one the church ignored and rejected, the law Jesus brings to us in the new covenant will be the cornerstone of the New Jerusalem. A cornerstone is a stone placed at the corner where two walls meet, joining the building together. It helps to align the building and tie it all together. "In whom all the building fitly framed together groweth unto an holy temple in the Lord" (Eph. 2:21). All denominations will be fitly joined into one true holy church by this cornerstone of truth. With this mandate in place, all those who enter will find it provides a moral foundation for them. Those guilty of breaking this law will not be accepted until they wash themselves clean. A "master's degree" in morality will be required of everyone in this new Christianity. Here the human race will learn sexual responsibility and become holy.

Moses brought two tables of stone down from the mountain. Both of these tables of stone will be in the New Jerusalem, the Garden Law being the first and most important of the two.

Before planting a new crop, farmers plow the residue of the old crop under. In newly plowed, broken, and prepared soil, new seed is planted. This needs to be done with the Old Jerusalem, then plant with new seed—new truth. Break up the stubborn, stiff-necked, hardness of your hearts and prepare your minds for new truth. I think it will surprise you how fast the new seeds will grow.

"I am returned unto Zion, and will dwell in the midst of Jerusalem: and Jerusalem shall be called a city of truth" (Zech. 8:3). All truth will come from this new and holy city, and the arguing over what is truth will end. There will be no more divisions in Christianity. All nations will flow to this city of truth, meaning all nations will believe the same truth and all other religions will cease to be. In the days of Moses, everyone ate the same spiritual food and drank the same spiritual water, meaning everyone had the same truth. So shall it be at the end of this age.

"But ¹Jerusalem which is above is free, which is the mother of us all" (Gal. 4:26). The cross-reference for the word "Jerusalem" tells us more about that city. "And it shall come to pass in the last days, that the mountain of the Lord's house shall be established in the top of the mountains, and shall be exalted above the hills; and all nations shall flow unto it" (¹Isa. 2:2). Mothers give birth. In the last days in this New Jerusalem (the house that God builds) all people from every walk of life will be "born again." The church will be our mother, giving spiritual life to everyone. Earthly mothers have a loving, tender, and compassionate touch which draws from a love deep within the heart. This is affectionately expressed when their own wounded, hurt children are in need of comfort. From Jerusalem comes the perfect love of our heavenly Mother, who will comfort and cuddle her children held captive for so long in sin. This love will heal the wounds, take away the pain, and turn tears into laughter as it brings mankind back to a righteous, holy, and obedient relationship with their heavenly Father.

In everyday life, mothers are often the ones who bridge the gap between wayward children and their fathers. They are the peacemakers. The New Jerusalem will be the mother who bridges the gap between God and His children.

The wilderness of sin has been emotionally painful for everyone, and for many physically painful. The Book of Isaiah informs us that Jerusalem will be as a mother's love. "As one whom his mother comforteth, so will I comfort you; and ye shall be comforted in Jerusalem" (66:13). God will be a mother to us, and her love will be comforting: soothing, warm, and welcomed. It is a promise that will happen in the last days, and the promise is for everyone. Truth will begin with one person, believed by one nation, and from one nation spread to all the earth. God does not have favorites. He has a plan that begins small and grows to include everyone, for God is the God of all the earth.

Some of the promises associated with the New Jerusalem are:

- "I set my king [Jesus] upon my holy hill, of Zion" (Ps. 2:6). There is no Jesus on earth until this new and holy Jerusalem.

- "Come ye, and let us go up to the mountain of the Lord, to the house of the God of Jacob; and he will teach us of his ways, and we will walk in his paths: for out of Zion will go forth the law, and the word of the Lord from Jerusalem" (Isa. 2:3). From Jerusalem we will learn the ways of the God of Jacob. And from this mountain of the Lord the law will go out to all people and will be commonly accepted.

- "And I John saw the holy city, new Jerusalem, coming down from God out of heaven. Behold, the tabernacle of God is with men, and he will dwell with them, and they shall be his people, and God himself shall be with them, and be their God" (Rev. 21:2-3). The holy Jerusalem will come down to earth and God will walk with mankind, as he did in Eden, and we will be the people of God.

- And "Upon mount Zion shall be deliverance, and there shall be holiness; and the house of Jacob shall possess their [Esau's] possession" (Obad. 17). No deliverance is offered to the fornicator until the New Jerusalem. It is here in the city of Jerusalem that God overthrows those who are wicked.

- "But ye are come unto mount Sion, and unto the city of the living God, the heavenly Jerusalem. And to Jesus the mediator of the new covenant" (Heb. 13:22,24). It is here from the heavenly Jerusalem that the new covenant will be offered. Jesus will come with the law God gave to Adam and Eve and write it in your hearts, just as the new covenant promises. A mediator settles an argument between two parties, and Jesus will end the dispute between God and his children. Deliverance and reconciliation will come, for the law converts. All this and much more is promised from this new Christianity. I do not see how anyone can honestly believe this happened two thousand years ago.

    The twenty-first chapter of Revelations describes the New Jerusalem, and in the first verse it states: "There was no more sea." The word "sea" is better explained by saying there will be no more wickedness. "But the wicked are like the troubled sea, when it cannot rest, whose waters cast up mire and dirt" (Isa. 57:20). Many times in the Bible, "sea" refers to the wicked. Here we are told once again that God plans to put an end to this sea of wickedness. Sodom and Gomorrah, Babylon, "the world" that the prince of darkness began in the Garden will end and be removed from the earth. When that happens, joy will return to our planet, for it is Sodom and Gomorrah that create all the filthiness and cause all the hurt. They produce the anger, fear, confusion, shame, and torment. They could someday bring about our ruin, but God will not allow that to happen, for He will stop them. Jesus will calm the sea.

- "And God shall wipe away all tears from their eyes; and there shall be no more death, neither sorrow, nor crying, neither shall there be any more pain: for the former things are passed away. Behold I make all things new" (Rev. 21:4-5). The New

Jerusalem is new Christianity, new beliefs, and new "truth" meaning the old will no longer remain.

Satan's followers gave us a worthless counterfeit when they organized today's Christianity, the Old Jerusalem. Jesus will give us the genuine. He will begin a new Christianity built by God, the New Jerusalem. The Jerusalem we find on the map of the world in the nation of Israel is not the Jerusalem of the Scriptures, nor are the Israelites the Jews who literally crucified Jesus. Since Jesus did not come to earth two thousand years ago, there has been no literal crucifixion.

God's promise to Abraham. From this new Christianity, God will be fulfilling the promise He made to Abraham, Isaac, and Jacob. "And thy seed shall be as the dust of the earth, and thou shalt spread abroad to the west, and to the east, and to the north, and to the south: and in thee and in thy seed shall all the families of the earth be blessed" (Gen. 28:14). From this New Jerusalem all people will believe in the God of Abraham, Isaac, and Jacob, and all the families of the earth will be blessed.

"Know ye therefore that they which are of faith, the same are the children of Abraham" (Gal. 3:7). When the law breakers return to God by faith in Jesus, they become as the children of Abraham, thus fulfilling the promise that from the seed of Abraham shall all the nations be blessed. Everyone will someday serve the God of Abraham for his God is the God of Creation. The one true God.

I believe I have shown you many new things. And in the following chapters I will show you new ways of looking at the very foundation this present Christianity was built on. The old groundwork will need to be re-examined and then plowed under and replaced with a truthful, spiritual understanding of truth, creating a New Jerusalem.

When this has been accomplished, The Holy One will rejoice and approve of this new clean and holy Church. "And I will rejoice in Jerusalem, and joy in my people: and the voice of weeping shall be no more heard in her, nor the voice of crying" (Isa. 65:19). The New Jerusalem will bring joy not only to God, but also to all people. When the church is clean and holy, everyone will profit. Christianity will be everything the Scriptures have said it would be. And it will accomplish what has been expected of it. The end of sin. Peace on earth.

ॐ

All nations will come to believe the truth published from the City of Truth creating one religion on earth.

CHAPTER TWENTY-FOUR

No Wooden Cross

ॐ

The law is light. When the law is missing from a person's knowledge, that individual is blind to spiritual matters. Then the Scriptures are seen through blind eyes and are storied to us incorrectly. When we know the law, we have new eyes. We see new things. "Open thou mine eyes, that I may behold wondrous thing out of thy law" (Ps. 119:18).

We have already examined some of the messages told by the spiritually blind, and learned how a personal comprehension of the law enables us to see them differently. For example:

Blind eyes: Being drunk with wine only happens when we drink too much of the wine man makes from grapes.

New eyes: Spiritual drunkenness occurs from being drunk with the wine of fornication, whoring, which is sexual perverseness.

Blind eyes: Being sober is when we do not drink the wine man makes from grapes.

New eyes: Spiritual soberness is when we do not drink the wine of fornication. Moral soberness is required for leaders of the church, and for all who proclaim to be Christians.

Blind eyes: Literal fire will burn up the wicked and the earth.

New eyes: Biblical fire is not real fire. The law is a fire that will burn up the wicked. Neither the wicked nor the earth itself will burn in the flames of a literal inferno.

Blind eyes: Moses physically killed an Egyptian.

New eyes: Moses killed a wicked Egyptian with the truth. All the rest of the wicked Egyptians said, "Who do you think you are, Moses? Do you think you can kill all of us?" Moses left. He spent some time with God when he saw the enormous task ahead of him.

Blind eyes: The battles in the Bible are literal battles, fought with literal swords.

New eyes: The battles in Scripture are spiritual battles between good and evil, and they are fought with swords, which are the words of God and the words of false gods. Truth is a sword. "And he hath made my mouth like a sharp sword" (Isa. 49:2). Lies are also called swords. You can kill with a philosophy, a belief, a lifestyle of sin, a wind of doctrine if it is a false doctrine.

Blind eyes: Animal, birds, and creeping things are literally animals, birds, and creeping things. Locusts are locusts.

New eyes: Animals, birds, and creeping things are people who live in Sodom and Gomorrah, and have changed themselves into images that are not like God. Locusts are creeping things, people from Sodom and Gomorrah, and they covered the earth in the days of Moses.

Blind eyes: David literally killed a lion, a bear, and a giant with stones.

New eyes: David killed false images of God, first a lion, and then a bear with the law written in stone. Then he killed a military giant with the same commandment. No physical death occurred.

Blind eyes: Mary was a virgin, a person who had never had sexual intercourse.

New eyes: Mary was a virgin, a person who never committed an act of original sin. She was untouched by Satan.

Spiritual eyesight is absolutely the most necessary ingredient needed in understanding the Word of God, and it comes from accepting the Garden Law as truth. With the law in place as the foundation of the New Jerusalem, many passages will be explained differently from what you are accustomed to hearing. All people will be confronted with new ideas and will be challenged to change their minds about many old, familiar, heavily fortified traditional beliefs.

One of those familiar beliefs common to all denominations and central to, or you might say the groundwork of, the old Christianity is the physical death of Jesus on a literal cross made of real wood. New eyes will see that: crosses are not made of literal wood, the death of Jesus is not a physical death, he did not come out of an actual grave. This may sound unbelievable at first. But you will plow the wooden cross under, along with many other church doctrines, when your spiritual eyesight is restored.

To explain this, I need to start back at the beginning, looking at Moses as the example Jesus will model. Moses judged the people. "Moses sat to judge the people." He states, "I do make them know the statutes of God, and his laws" (Exod. 18:13,16). The purpose of judging the people by explaining the two tables of stone was to show the people the ways of God so they could exit the wilderness and enter the Promised Land. Jesus will come to earth with this same purpose in mind: to judge all the earth and show the people the law and the laws of God so they can leave sin and have heaven on earth. We learned that God left this final day of judgment in the hands of Jesus. "For he cometh to judge the earth: he shall judge the world with righteousness, and the people with his truth" (Ps. 96:13). His truth is not the truth He will find on earth at His coming, and that is why all things become new. Some will say, "What is this strange doctrine—this new truth?"

Yes, Jesus will judge the entire earth, all living people, with His truth. Not with what man believes to be truth, but with Jesus' truth, which is the truth from God. He will not judge the physically dead from the graveyards, for the earth is inhabited by those who are physically alive. He will judge all who are physically alive, but spiritually dead from sin.

However, before judgment can take place on earth it is appointed unto man once to die and then to be judged. "And as it is appointed unto men once to die, but after this the judgment" (Heb. 9:27). All humankind will die a spiritual death before this day of judgment. We will all die from original sin or from one of the sins listed on the other set of commandments. Since Jesus, Himself, will come to earth as a human, grow, learn, live, and be tempted in like manner as every other mortal before this day of judgment, He must also die. Judgment (wisdom, discernment) will come after all have died, requiring Jesus to die and then judge Himself when He judges all people.

When Jesus left heaven and agreed to come to earth and live as a mortal being, for the purpose of redeeming all mankind, and to ensure the continuation of the human race, He knew He was going to die a spiritual death. This does not mean that He committed the sin Adam and Eve committed, for indeed He was without sin, without original sin. But it does say He broke one of the Ten Commandments.

Jesus disagrees with those of you who call Him good. For He states that He is not good. And the Bible backs Him. I confirm this reality with the following three examples:

1) **Spots and wrinkles.** "As Christ also loved the church, and gave himself for it. That he might sanctify and cleanse it with the washing of water by the word. That he might present it to himself a glorious church, not having spot, or wrinkle, or any such thing;

but that it should be holy and without blemish" (Eph. 5:25-27). Jesus comes to wash the church. The church is unclean. The Savior will accomplish this by washing the Old Jerusalem. When it has been made holy by the removal of fornication and made perfect by the removal of all other lesser sins, it will be without spot or wrinkle. To understand Jesus' desire to have a church without spot or wrinkle we need to know what is a spot and what is a wrinkle.

Every word in scripture has a definition, and "spot" is no exception. We need a clear definition of the word spot and in Deuteronomy, we are told, "They have corrupted themselves, their spot is not the spot of his children, they are a perverse and crooked generation" (32:5). We presently live in a deceitful and perverse generation, and those who are crooked and perverse have corrupted themselves. This immorality caused them to have spots. Their spots come from original sin, and the marks are proof that the crooked and the disobedient are not the children of God. Moses called these spots leprosy—spiritual leprosy. Both Noah and Moses lived in a crooked and perverse generation as does Jesus.

And in Job we learn, "If iniquity be in thine hand, put it far away, and let not wickedness dwell in thy tabernacles. For then shalt thou lift up thy face without spot; yea, thou shalt be steadfast, and shalt not fear (11:14-15.) Those who commit iniquity, the sin of Adam and Eve, and have leprosy can be without spots if they end their sinfulness. Put it away, put it far away from your mind and your life, and the spots will be gone. You will also be steadfast, unmovable, and no one can deceive you again. Webster defines "steadfast:" "fixed, settled, not changing, established." You will be established and settled in the truth of God, and the fear of rejection from God is gone when you remove evil from your life.

"Woe unto them! For they have gone in the way of Cain. . . . These are spots in your feasts of charity, when they feast with you, feeding themselves without fear" (Jude 11-12). Those who follow Cain are spots, and we know Cain is like Sodom and Gomorrah, sexually perverse. Here the sexually perverse are said to be spots, not to have them, but to be them. The book of Jude is exclusively speaking of Sodom and Gomorrah, and verse 23 requires us to do this for those who live there: "And others save with fear, pulling them out of the fire; hating even the garment spotted by the flesh." Their garments are their bodies, and the lust of the flesh has caused them to have spots in their flesh—not literally, but spiritually. They have leprosy. Even so, they are family and we must rescue them. We are all children of the same God.

In the days of Moses, these marks in the flesh were called the spots of leprosy. Moses called leprosy a deadly plague spreading throughout the people. It was and still is a deadly spiritual plague, and unlike a physical plague, such as the bubonic plague that killed many of those it touched in the Middle Ages, the plague of spiritual leprosy kills all who embrace it. Moses cleansed the lepers. Jesus will cleanse the lepers.

Now that we have a definition for the word "spot," we can partially understand what Jesus requires of us for entrance into this New Jerusalem, when He states He wants a church without spot. We can sense the tender, warm affection being expressed in the Song of Solomon when it speaks of the church's loveliness this way: "Thou art all fair, my love; there is no spot in thee" (4:7). God will love a spotless church. It is another way of saying the New Jerusalem will be a holy city, without the perverseness of fornication.

We do know this: Jesus offered himself to God without spot. "How much more shall the blood of Christ, who through the eternal Spirit offered himself without spot to God, purge your conscience from dead works to serve God?" (Heb. 9:14). This is not the first time we have seen proof that Jesus is not part of Sodom and Gomorrah, and why He makes known to us, "My kingdom is not of 'this world.' " When you enter the kingdom of God, the New Jerusalem, you will not find sexual perverseness in it. And if this were the only requirement for admission, Jesus would be qualified to enter. But He could only claim to be without spot. He could not with honesty declare to be without spot and wrinkle. So before He could enter Jerusalem, meet the high standard of morality both God and Jesus desire and demand in the New Jerusalem, and not pollute this new church, He would need to wash Himself of a wrinkle. That is why He will be baptized in the Jordan River.

Yes, I am saying Jesus was not perfect. He was without original sin. But He did have a wrinkle. He broke one or more of the Ten Commandments written on the second table of stone, a splinter, gnat, wrinkle sized sin, but not a beam, camel, spot-size sin. We can violate the Garden Law, the greatest affront to God. And we can disobey one of the Ten Commandments, written on the other table and this is a lesser offense. Jesus offered himself to God as a person who never broke the Garden Law. He was without spot. But, He did have a wrinkle, which means He did break one of the Ten Commandments we are so familiar with.

2) Jesus Himself declared He is not good. "Why callest thou me good? there is none good but one, that is, God: but if thou wilt enter into life, keep the commandments" (Matt. 19:17). God in heaven is the only good person. This holy God will conclude the world in unbelief, and then have mercy on everyone. Jesus tells us that only God is good. He, Jesus, is not as good as God. Then He adds that if you want life and not death, you must keep the com-mandments—both sets of them. And, Jesus implores of us, "Be ye therefore perfect, even as your Father which is in heaven is perfect" (Matt. 5:48). We must be as perfect as God in heaven, therefore we must be more perfect than Jesus. That sounds like a mighty tall order, and impossible for a human to attain. Yet it is exactly what we must achieve in order to enter the New Jerusalem. And it is reachable, or it would not be asked of us. Jesus learned obedience, and all of us will willingly submit to the demands of God and return to right living. We will conform because we want to obey, because it is the most reasonable course of action to take. You will

220 OF EDEN A LAW FROM EDEN

exit the world when you comprehend the happiness and uprightness it will bring to the human race. We will obey the law and the
ten commandments when we understand obedience brings heaven
to earth and will replace the present hell on earth. "Though he were
a Son, yet learned he obedience by the things which he suffered"
(Heb. 5:8). Jesus also learned submission. He understood that it is
only through obedience to all the laws of God that we become as
perfect as God our Father.

   3) Jesus confessed His sins. In your mind's eye take this verse
and put on a two-act play, then sit down and watch it. Speaking of
Jesus "Who needed not daily, as those high priests, to offer up sacrifices, first for his own sins, and then for the people's: for this he
did once, when he offered up himself" (Heb. 7:27). Act one: The
priests walk across the stage and offer sacrifices for their own sins,
and then for the sins of the people. The priests do this every day,
over and over again, day after day. End of act one. Act two: Jesus
walks across the stage and offers a sacrifice for His own sins and
then for the sins of the people. He does this once. End of Act two.
End of play. Jesus offers a sacrifice for His own sins and for the sins
of the people.

   Before Judgment Day, all have sinned. And when we sinned we
died. We died on a cross. Crosses are made out of sin or sins, not
wood. Therefore, since all have sinned, everyone has a cross. Jesus
will pick up His cross first, and then He will ask everyone to pick up
their crosses and follow him. "Whosoever will come after me, let
him deny himself, and take up his cross, and follow me" (Mark 8:34).

   Each one of us has a cross, the burden of a sin we died from.
No one can go back and change the past or undo what has been
done. That simple fact nails each person to his cross just as Jesus is
nailed to His cross. He cannot get off of His cross. And when He
judges you, Jesus nails you to yours, and you cannot get off of
yours either. Every individual has a cross, a sin, to reveal. And
when we strayed we died and shed spiritual blood.

"And whosoever does not bear his cross, and come after me, cannot be my disciple" (Luke 14:27). If you believe Jesus carried a literal wooden cross to His physical death and that you must follow, then why isn't your cross made out of wood?

Let us for a moment make all crosses out of literal wood. Make the death on the cross physical. If everyone were to follow Jesus and become a Christian in this manner, this form of Christianity would end sin, for it would abolish the human race. I do not believe this to be an intelligent process by which to end sin. Just as it is not reasonable to remove sin by ending childbirth, it is not rational to eliminate transgressions by physically killing off the human race. Yes, sin could be ended in this manner, but who would be left to enjoy peace on earth? This reasoning is illogical. Are you sure you want crosses to be made of literal wood? or the death on the cross to be a physical death? Because you will pick up your cross and follow Jesus to His death and resurrection.

Then let us make all crosses, yours and mine and the cross of Jesus, out of original sin or sins. And let us make the death on the cross a spiritual death and not a physical one. Jesus died a spiritual death when He broke one of the Ten Commandments and fell short of being as perfect or as good as God. When we say we are bought with a price, we are. Jesus paid a high price to save mankind. He left a perfect heaven and came to an imperfect earth at the darkest, most sinful hour in time, when mankind was in the depth of sin. He lived with the wicked and died from a sin He committed before it was time to judge the inhabitants of earth, for all will die (including Jesus) before the day of judgment.

On Judgment Day, all will be dead, for it is appointed unto man once to die before the judgment. In the first two chapters, we looked at the remnant and Sodom and Gomorrah as we examined the division of mankind in the end times. Jesus will stand with the remnant at the close of this age. The remnant will be dead from sins, wrinkles (not from sin, spots), and Jesus will be the first to be raised from the dead. This will happen at His baptism, for when He is baptized, He will confess his wrinkle. Or you could say He will bear His cross (reveal His sin). Then the rest of the remnant will be baptized and raised from the dead. You will also reveal your sin when you bear your cross.

I don't believe I have yet met anyone from the remnant, maybe one. I would like to. "The remnant of Israel [the earth] shall not do iniquity, nor speak lies; neither shall a deceitful tongue be found in their mouth: for they shall feed and lie down, and none shall make them afraid" (Zeph. 3:13). I would like to meet the people who do no wickedness, speak no lies, and are not deceitful. How refreshing. They are the ones who did not commit original sin, and only a few are left. Hello out there. I would like to meet you.

After the remnant is raised from the dead, Sodom and Gomorrah will be raised likewise. You will also bear your cross (confess your sin). The only logical way to remove original sin from our planet, as I see it, is to first identify it. Know what sin is. Understand what Adam and Eve did. Deal with this great affront to God and self the way the Scriptures tell us to. Face it. End the denial. Stop allowing pride to keep you from admitting you have done wrong. If you have committed this greatest of all trespasses, admit it by confessing it, one to another. When sin is done in secret and the guilty remain silent, the plague quietly spreads throughout the land. Overcome and conquer sin until it is no longer a part of your life. Keep the law and the commandments. By doing this we have the right to say we are now as perfect as our Father in heaven is perfect. Then the earth will be inhabited by righteous people; hell on earth will cease to be, and will be replaced with heaven on earth. The human race will live on in peace and happiness.

ॐ

"For this saith the Lord that created the heavens; God himself that formed the earth and made it; he hath established it . . . he formed it to be inhabited: I am the Lord; and there is none else" (Isa. 45:18). God created the earth for one purpose: to be inhabited by the humans into whom He breathed life. I do not believe He needed us. He did not need someone to communicate with. Neither was He lonely. I believe he wanted to share. He possessed all truth and knowledge, a reasoning mind, creativity, never-ending space, and limitless time, and out of the generous goodness of His heart, He shared all that with us. He gave us life, love, and His creativity. He shared His possessions, His mind, reasoning power, and space. Think of what we would have missed if He had not created us. He asked only to be respected as the Creator. We prove our belief in our Creator by submission to a few basic laws of life He gave to us for our own well-being and happiness. He does deserve our obedience and is counting on our godlike ability to reason well enough to come to that conclusion. God is holy and He made us to be holy. When we are holy, we are acknowledging by our lifestyle that we believe our Creator to be a holy God.

CHAPTER TWENTY-FIVE

The Virgin Birth

᠙

"For it is written, I will destroy the wisdom of the wise, and will bring to nothing the understanding of the prudent" (1 Cor. 1:19). God will destroy the wisdom of all those who think they are wise, of all who believed the same lie as Eve believed: sin will make one wise. He will bring to nothing their understanding of truth. In their blindness they learn how to be cautious and manage their wickedness carefully with their own self-interest at heart. They trust in their lies, and then digest the word of God incorrectly and give us fiction. But God will remove from earth the "wisdom" they have supplied us.

Not only will the legend of a literal wooden cross be destroyed, but the traditional story of the virgin birth, given to us from the "wisdom" of the foolish, will also be replaced. We will see that Jesus, the person, was born the same as you or I. He had a human mother and a human father. He was man in every sense of the word. If this were not true, then how could He be a true representative of mankind? Couldn't we all have lived a better life if our biological father was God? if we were half human and half God?

God informed us that He will raise up one person and that person will be like everyone else—human. Moses said, that Jesus will be like himself (like Moses). "A prophet shall the Lord your God raise up unto you of your brethren, like unto me; him shall ye hear in all things whatsoever he shall say unto you" (Acts 3:22). If Jesus is like His brothers (all of mankind), then how can He be half God and half mortal? Aren't all His brothers mortals? If He is like Moses, then He is all human, for Moses was human only.

Again, the prophetic Scripture describing Jesus states: "God will raise up unto thee a Prophet from the midst of thee, of thy brethren, like unto me; unto him ye shall hearken" (Deut. 18:15). "Of thy brethren" can only mean another human being, an ordinary individual like any other person, conceived and birthed the way every person is physically conceived and delivered. This is why Jesus is called a "kinsman" redeemer. He is one of your kin.

Then what is the account of a female virgin conceiving a son from God—a God-man? There is a spiritual explanation to even this story of conception. The meanings of three words need to be understood:

1) **Virgin.** I believe we have already been introduced to a new definition of the word "virgin." The individuals who stand with the remnant are all virgins. They are untouched by Satan, meaning they were not deceived as Adam and Eve were deceived. Those of us who have never engaged in an act of original sin are biblically called virgins. At the end there will only be a few of us left.

2) **Bethlehem.** Most biblical words have a meaning of their own. Names of people have intentional meanings. The name Moses means "drawn out." Names of towns and places also have biblical definitions. Bethlehem means "the house of bread." And bread means "the word of God." Bethlehem is the word of God, truth, the Scriptures. Jesus was birthed in Bethlehem. Meaning that he was birth from the word of God, and He will feed the people pure truth. Jesus said, "I am the living bread" (John 6:51). He is a living person who knows truth.

3) **Conception.** Conception can be the power of conceiving mentally: thought, philosophy, a reasoned doctrine, a critical study, and logic. Conception is the beginning of a process, a formulation of ideas, and can also be an original idea, design, or plan. Jesus through reason and logic in the study of truth (the word of God) conceived the plan of salvation and deliverance. You would call this study of the word intercessory prayer, a deep communion with God.

Combine these three spiritual definitions of the words virgin, Bethleham, and conception and you can see a human, (Mary, the mother of Jesus), who is a virgin, and who through an in-depth study of truth conceived a plan to deliver mankind from sin. This is a mental process, not a physical one. God is close to Mary, gently, patiently encouraging, with persistent urging until through the study of the word of God truth is found. This person then becomes a Jesus, the Messiah, which means the anointed one, and the Deliverer as Moses and Jesus are both called.

Yes, the entire foundation on which our present Christianity is based will vanish, and a new foundation will be laid. "All things will become new," making it necessary for the new Christian to become as a child who has everything to learn over again.

This brings me to an explanation of why I have used the King James study Bible throughout this book. According to *Publisher's Weekly*, some 450 English translations, paraphrases, or rewordings of all or part of the Old and New Testaments have been published. The first attack upon the King James Bible was in 1952, only a few short years ago, when the Revised Standard Version was published. Think of how quickly we have become accustomed to rephrasing the Word of God to fit our own ideas of truth. When you consider the fact that God will conclude the world in unbelief and spiritual blindness, who had the eyesight to make so many changes in the Word of God? Only a virgin would have the qualifications—vision and the love of truth. Many who translated the Scriptures have changed or adjusted the truth to their own understanding. If I had in my possession a Bible that had had the word "fornication" removed from its pages or one that made all sin equal, the next time I had an occasion to build a bonfire I would use it for dry paper under the kindling.

Place Jesus at the end. If the King James Bible was tampered with until essential truth critical to the birth of a Jesus was distorted, a Jesus could not be born, because truth would have been lost. Changing truth to this magnitude does occur when all sin is made equal, and the words fornication and whoring are meddled with and redefined.

Have these many translations given us a better understanding of truth? It doesn't appear to me they have. America is more wicked now than in the fifties. We lead the world in the major crimes. We have the highest divorce rate of any nation. America is a nation where children are murdering each other. Violent crime has increased dramatically since the sixties.

These translations have, however, destroyed the common language whereby all devout Bible students can communicate with each other. A common language is important. And if the Bible is without error, then why change it in so many ways? Are these paraphrased editions why so many people no longer believe the Bible is without error? I think so.

In a duel between two persons, a common instrument is selected; it may be a knife, a gun, or a sword. In a duel between two mindsets, a common tool must also be chosen. If any of you want to challenge my interpretation of Scripture use the King James Bible. When the darkness passes over, and light returns to the earth, and you can see, then you may want to make the King James Bible more readable, or we may not.

In the New Jerusalem the practice of eating a small piece of unleavened bread and drinking red wine or a red juice to represent wine needs to end. Jesus is truth, bread. His doctrine is new wine. When you have communion in the New Jerusalem, you will share bread and wine—truth and the doctrine of Jesus. This truth needs to be digested and then lived out, and shared with those who have not heard.

Your ritual of pretending to eat someone's body and drink someone's blood is barbaric. It is a self-indulgent show, a pretense designed as a public display, feeding only one's self-righteousness.

Does this practice of communion, which is also called the Eucharist by many, do the wicked any good? No! But sharing truth, and fellowship, by exchanging godly ideas and the doctrine of Jesus, will bring goodness and holiness to earth. Communing the truth will eventually bring us peace.

Share! If you are a member of a church, ask your pastor to read this book. If you are a pastor, ask your congregation to read it and send a copy to you superiors. Then sit down and reason together.

The Almighty has promised a quick end to iniquity (sin), and every one of you can play a part in how quickly this truth goes out. Tell your family, friends, and even your enemies about this book.

CHAPTER TWENTY-SIX

Baptism

The Lutheran Church recently completed a study of human sexuality, and in the year 2000 the United Methodist Church began to examine their stand on baptism. It is an encouraging sign that churches are beginning to question their beliefs.

In the past, they believed they had all the right answers. Now they are not so sure! They are looking, inquiring, and preparing themselves to examine new truth. This is forward movement, for a willingness to investigate and explore new ideas is a humbling change of attitude suggesting that a change of mind is possible.

Logic should tell us the church needs a definition for sin before making such an effort to eliminate it. Morality and baptism need to be understood before building the house of God. And holiness needs to be comprehended. Unless the meaning of these four essentials is mastered, church members do not know if they are sinners, or if they are moral, or if they have been baptized in the proper manner. They do not know if they are holy. All of these qualities are basic to the character of Christianity. Real Christians are sinless, moral, baptized, holy people. Because a correct answer to these questions: what is sin? what is morality? what is baptism? what is holy? was missing, the Old Jerusalem never had sufficient wisdom to move anyone out of sin, to reconcile us back to God, and to bring us to the peacefulness of the land God has promised us, peace on earth.

The Christians of today invented their own righteousness based on their own perception of truth. "But we are all as an unclean thing, all our righteousness are as filthy rags" (Isa. 64:6). The mortal body is a garment for the spirit, and body and mind should be clean. The mind gives a person much torment when the body is dressed in filthiness. A make believe self-righteousness will give a person false hope, false peace, and a false since of security as it dresses you in filthiness.

In the New Jerusalem where all things become new, an understanding of how everyone will become sinless, moral, and holy through baptism will be clear, thus giving birth to sinless, moral, baptized, holy, genuine, clean Christians. Genuine righteousness.

"He that believeth and is baptized shall be saved; but he that believeth not shall be damned" (Mark 16:16). Here are the two essential requirements to become a Christian—believe in Jesus and be baptized. It is that simple.

1) **A belief in Jesus.** This means you must believe He has been sent from God. If you do not believe this, why do anything He asks you to do? Why be baptized? Why build a church with the cornerstone He provides? Why believe what He says? Why believe His definition of original sin? You must believe "His truth" is truth or why follow Him? His strange doctrine sounds foreign because it is so different from the "truth" that has come from the darkness while hiding in sin, which was not truth at all.

A belief in Jesus is more than a verbal statement. Simply declaring, "I believe in Jesus," or asking "Come into my heart, Lord Jesus," means nothing, for that is make-believe. Faith in Jesus is more than believing He is a person, and He existed. It is a belief in His doctrine, the Law, and a belief that His truth is the truth sent to us from God. Believing He was sent from God is primary. God is truth and Jesus is the truth made flesh, and you must have no doubt that what He says is truth.

2) **Then, you need to be baptized.** First believe truth, then be baptized. After trusting in the truth of Jesus Christ, baptism is the second necessary component of salvation. You are not saved from sin or raised from the dead without it.

Baptism: what is it? The original meaning of the word "baptism" is to be cleansed from breaking all the laws written in the Old Testament, those we broke while living under the old covenant. "And now why tarriest thou? arise, and be baptized, and wash away thy sins, calling on the name of the Lord" (Acts 22:16). Baptism will wash your sins away. They must be removed from your life. And when Jesus washes the church, it will be washed by the word of God. "Christ also loved the church . . . That he might sanctify and cleanse it with the washing of water by the word" (Eph. 5:25-26). The word of God is at times called the bread and water of life, and Jesus comes to earth to speak God's word. His words are the water that washes and sanctifies and purges until the sinner, the church, and the earth are clean and just again. This is achieved with the baptism of repentance as Paul states. "Then said Paul, John verily baptized with the baptism of repentance" (Acts 19:4). You are baptized when you repent. Baptism is repenting of your sins. Repenting is confessing your rebellious behavior with your mouth, and then putting an end to disobeying the laws of God. When you have done this, then you can say you have been baptized.

Jesus was baptized. "Jesus came from Nazareth of Galilee, and was baptized of John in the Jordan" (Mark 1:9). This is when Jesus repents of His wrinkle. He confesses His own sin, and He dies, is buried, and then raised from the dead at His baptism. "Therefore we are buried with him by baptism unto death: that like as Christ was raised up from the dead by the glory of the Father, even so we also should walk in newness of life" (Rom. 6:4). Your own baptism will be likened to that of Jesus. You, the sinner, will die and be buried at your baptism. Then a new creature will be raised (resurrected) from the tomb and walk in newness of life. You, the person, will not die a physical death, but the sinner has died. The baptized person is a new creature. He has been washed clean, is now sinless, made alive, made holy. He has repented, confessed and forsaken his sins, and has been restored to the true holy image of God. Backward thinking "sin is wisdom" ends here. Forward movement begins.

Who needs to be baptized? Everyone! We learned that God will conclude the world in unbelief, and that all have sinned and come short of the glory (goodness) of God. And it is appointed unto man once to die, and then the judgment comes. Everyone is spiritually dead and must be baptized. No one is excluded, not even the last Jesus who is the true Christ, who will judge Himself.

A righteous human dies a spiritual death when he or she sins. Then these spiritually dead wicked people die when they are baptized. The sinner dies, not the person. The transgressor will volunteer to die at his own baptism. The evil person dies and sheds spiritual blood and is buried in a grave, not literally. He is then raised from the death-of-sin to new life and is alive again, raised from the dead, to enjoy being a justified (just) child of God. This is the only resurrection of the dead I can find in the Scriptures. The church must plow under the falsehood about coming out of a literal grave after physical death. You storied to us a fable, a tale.

When Jesus builds the New Jerusalem He will require that everyone be baptized. From this city whose builder and maker is God, spiritual life will return to the earth, rewarding us with heaven on earth. Baptism is a spot remover. It will remove the spots and also the wrinkles.

"For he that is dead is freed from sin" (Rom. 6:7). Baptism kills the sinner. Having died to sin, you are no longer in bondage to Satan. You are set free.

Please note: there is no literal bloodshed in either the death of the righteous or the death of the sinner. Most of the bloodshed in Scripture is spiritual bloodshed. Plow under the story about Jesus shedding visible literal red blood, on a wooden cross, and then coming alive out of a tomb prepared for the physically dead.

As we approach an end of all things as we know them, all have fallen dead. Again, to re-emphasize the fact that all are dead and to explain a new point more easily, I take you back to the division of mankind at the end of this age. There are only two groups and both are dead. The remnant have wrinkles, and Sodom and Gomorrah have spots.

THE REMNANT	SODOM AND GOMORRAH
Just	Unjust
Adulterers	Fornicators
Sheep	Goats
Wheat	Tares
Wrinkles	Spots
Once dead	Twice dead
Holy	Profane

Resurrection means a rebirth, awakening, renewal, and revival. There will be a resurrection of the just and the unjust and that is everyone who is physically alive on earth at the close of this age. And all of us will be dead in trespasses and sins. But there is hope. "And have hope toward God . . . that there shall be a resurrection of the dead, both of the just and the unjust" (Acts 24:15). Both the just (the remnant) and the unjust (Sodom and Gomorrah) will be raised from the dead.

Baptism will be an awakening of mankind, a rebirth, a revival. Yes! This is the only resurrection of the dead I can find in the scriptures. Put Jesus at the end—at the close of this age. He will show us the way out of sin. He will also stand with the remnant (the just). He will confess a wrinkle and be raised from the dead at His own baptism.

Humans have traveled a long way in the bondage of sin, held prisoners by their own lies and backward thinking. As promised, in our sightseeing adventure of the mind we have reached the far edge of the wilderness. We stand on the banks of the Jordan River which separates two lands, the Wilderness of Sin and the Promised Land of peace. The only logical move is to cross the river. The generation willing to bathe in the Jordan will enter into the Promised Land as the people did in the days of Joshua.

The Jordan is not a literal river, but the spiritual river of life. It is here in the Jordan where everyone will be baptized. Sin ends here.

In the story of Joshua, God gave Joshua an orderly, workable plan, and the same plan will work for us today. Joshua was commissioned by God to lead the people to the Promised Land. "Moses my servant is dead; now therefore arise, go over this Jordan, thou, and all this people, unto the land which I do give to them, even to the children of Israel" (Josh. 1:2). Joshua, the high priest, led the way; the priests followed; then all the people followed the priests until all had crossed to the other side. "And all the Israelites passed over on dry ground, until all the people were passed clean over Jordan" (Josh. 3:17). On one side of the river they were not clean, and on the other side they were clean, for the Jordan River is where they all "came clean." They repented of their sins. "And were baptized of him [John the Baptist] in Jordan, confessing their sins" (Matt. 3:6). Baptism is when you confess your sins in the Jordan River.

Who will be baptized first? Jesus, the high priest, will be first, and then the priests, meaning all of our religious leaders. The priests, pastors, ministers, rabbis (the clergy) will pass over Jordan before the people. They will confess their sins before the people. "Before" has two meanings: first, and in front of. The clergy will be "first." They will confess their sins before the people confess theirs.

And before: meaning out loud in front of or in the hearing of the people. "And Joshua spake unto the priests, saying, Take up the ark of the covenant, and pass over before the people. And they took up the ark of the covenant, and went before the people" (Josh. 3:6). The religious leaders will at this time have the ark of the covenant containing two tables of stone (the law and the Ten Commandments), manna (spiritual food from God), and Aaron's rod of correction. This complete information will give the religious leaders of our day the power to correct and bring our nation back to God. God equipped the priests with the correct wisdom and then granted them the privilege of leading the people out of the wilderness.

Then the people will follow the priests until all have been baptized (raised from the dead) and life will begin to return to the earth like springtime after winter, until all have crossed the Jordan and the fullness of summer renews the earth with righteousness. An awakening. A revival. A rebirth. A chance to begin again.

We are closer to arriving in the Promised Land than ever before, and if we want to gain entrance, we must be baptized in the Jordan and pass over to the other side where we will all be clean/holy. No one can escape this crossing. Everyone will face, confront, confess, and overcome their spots and wrinkles. Each one of us must wade in and let the cleansing waters of the word of God cover us in baptism. The wicked die here in the Jordan. If baptism (repentance of sin) does not remove all misbehavior from your life, then you have not been baptized. Nor are you a Christian. Fornication (sexual perverseness) and adultery end here. All disobedience to all God's commands must be overcome or you have not been raised from the dead, for if you continue to violate the laws of God, you are still dead in your sins.

Common sense tells us that before we can enter the Promised Land where once again we live in obedience to God's laws, it is essential we put an end to the original act of defiance that took us from the Garden of Eden and put us in the wilderness of sin in the first place. The end of original sin (oral sex) will be the end of the wilderness. The human race will once again live in agreement (covenant) with God.

Jesus will be baptized in the Jordan, just as everyone will be. "And it came to pass . . . Jesus came from Nazareth of Galilee, and was baptized of John in the Jordan" (Mark 1:9). Here He confesses His wrinkle for that is what a person does at their baptism, they confess (tell, admit, own up, acknowledge) their sins. Jesus, who stands with the remnant, repents of breaking one of the Ten Commandments and is buried and raised from the dead. At this time He will begin to count His spiritual age, for it is at His baptism that God the Father will say, "This day have I begotten thee." "And lo a voice from heaven, saying, This is my beloved Son, in whom I am well pleased" (Matt. 3:17). Jesus will not begin His public ministry until after His baptism, when He confesses His own disobedience.

It would be unthinkable for Jesus to ask anyone to follow Him without knowing His past and His sin. So many times we have put our trust in a person only to find out later about hidden evils in his life, at which time we lose faith and trust in that person and choose not to follow.

As sheep follow the shepherd, the clergy will follow Jesus and the people will follow the clergy. The doctrine of Jesus will unify Christianity, making it a powerful force to be reckoned with. The human race has followed sin to its ultimate. When the tide turns, and a west wind blows (an opposite doctrine), righteousness will become the way of life, for all will follow righteousness to its fullness.

As today's Christianity begins to question itself and acknowledges it has failed to save "the world," church leaders must grasp the truth that morality through baptism is the key to saving the world. Your present-day baptism is not the real thing. Do not bring your baptismal bowls or tubs of water into the New

Jerusalem. Stop submerging your members in the local river or lake, or sprinkling them with tap water. Baptism, as I have just explained, will be a workable, constructive, active, forward movement out of sin. For it is the formula for the saving of mankind. For peace on earth.

Jesus will accomplish his mission to eliminate all sin through baptism. But pastors, may I suggest before you begin baptizing yourself or your congregation you ask all those who attend your church to first read this book and then sit down and reason together. Talk it over first.

〄

Remember!

As you talk it over, remember the purpose of Jesus. "He that committeth sin is of the devil; for this purpose the Son of God was manifested, that he might destroy the works of the devil" (1 John 3:8). Sin is once again in the singular, meaning the original transgression in the Garden of Eden. It is only logical for Jesus to begin putting an end to sin at the same point where Satan began it—with a man and his wife. Jesus comes to earth to destroy what Satan began with Adam and Eve. He will not fail to put an end to this first act of defiance that has become a way for almost everyone. Ending this original violation will ultimately end all disobedience.

Remember! Christ comes to sanctify the church. The church is wicked, unholy, filthy, and needs to be cleansed. "That he might sanctify and cleanse it [the church] with the washing of water by the word" (Eph. 5:26).

Remember! In the beginning those in hell (Sodom and Gomorrah) will give you some trouble. Expect it, but don't let them discourage you. Biblical wind is a wind of doctrine, a belief. Sodom and Gomorrah are said to be an east wind. God is a wind from the west. These two beliefs oppose each another. And this is why God states, "I will remove your sins as far as the east is from the west." The inhabitants of Sodom and Gomorrah will have a change of mind from one extreme to another.

CHAPTER TWENTY-SEVEN

My Baptism

§

In view of what I have learned about being baptized, repenting of one's sins, I believe I was raised from the dead (baptized) in 1969. Awakened. Re-birthed. Renewed. For it was at that time I repented of the sin I committed, and have been free from sins ever since. In 2001, I will be thirty-two years old, spiritually speaking, from the year of my baptism. I will be sixty-four years old from the year of my physical birth.

I lived the first thirty years of my life not seeing or knowing Sodom and Gomorrah existed. I was a member of a local church, sang in the choir, worked in the nursery, and taught Vacation Bible School, but I never felt part of the church. I was always not quite "in." I was always treated as though everyone felt I needed what they had and didn't have it. My mother- and father-in-law were both ministers and expressed their disapproval and disappointment in the wife their son chose. I wasn't godly enough! I just didn't quite make the grade. Sometimes I put on slacks and not dresses, sometimes I wore makeup, and sometimes I didn't agree with them. I played bridge. Obviously I was not godly. But at the time I was not aware of the difference between the just and the unjust or the remnant and Sodom and Gomorrah. And I had no knowledge of what original sin was, and so I thought I was the one off base, in need of repair. I was told and I believed that all people are born with a sinful nature bent toward sin and all have sinned. This made me a sinner in need of salvation.

At this time in my life, I believed the fundamental beliefs this Old Jerusalem was built on: Jesus died on a wooden cross, His death was physical, and He came out of a literal tomb at His resurrection. I believed in the resurrection of the dead from the literal graveyards and that everyone who has died since the beginning of time will at the resurrection of the physically dead come out of their earthen grave sites and go to heaven or hell for all of eternity. I believed in a heaven or hell after my own physical death.

I was told we can sin a sin that will separate us from God forever by blaspheming the Holy Spirit. My pastors would often repeat we can blaspheme the Holy Spirit by refusing His call to repent so many times that He stops calling us. I believed I had done that, and I had gone so far away from God that He did not speak to me. No question about it, I would surely spend eternity in hell. I was resigned to that certainty; yet, I decided to live the best I could and be as good as I could be, and I remained in the church.

While remaining in the church, my husband and I had several good friends, couples whom we invited over for Sunday dinners. We celebrated our birthdays and anniversaries together and enjoyed picnics and socializing. The husband of one of these couples began to call on the phone for rather innocent reasons during the day while my husband was at work. From time to time he would stop by during the day time to borrow or return what we had lent him, and on occasion he would stop just to chat, or call on the telephone. I mentioned the frequency of these calls and visits to my husband with the concern this friend might have other motives in mind, and my husband saw no reason to worry.

This turned out not to be the case, however; on one of these visits, a friendly rape occurred. A friendly rape is not usually violent, just forcibly persistent, no matter how many times the other person says "No." And most men are physically stronger than women. Because he was a good-natured, likable person and a close friend for more than five years, I did not resist to the point of causing him bodily harm. He suggested an ongoing affair.

Although I did not mention the rape at that time, I did discuss with my husband the desire his best friend was suggesting. My spouse said, "Why not? Go ahead." And he promised he would not divorce me because of it. Once, in the past, my mate had suggested the four of us exchange partners, but I had said, "No!" I thought he was joking. To this day, I believe we did exchange partners, although my husband still insists that was not the case.

Now I was faced with a decision. Do I willingly commit adultery or not? The next time he drove into the driveway, I could bolt the front door and make my "no" final. It was at this point that I learned a person must give him or herself permission to sin. The decision to sin is deliberate and personal. If I agreed to commit adultery, I had to change my "no" to a "yes," and that would be a deliberate, conscious decision. It was my choice, not my friend's, nor my husband's. I was well aware of the commandment not to commit adultery, and I take full responsibility for my actions. However, I based my reasoning on the belief that since I was beyond hope and would spend eternity in hell, no matter what I did, what difference would it make? Hell is hell if you go there for one sin, twenty-one sins, or one hundred and twenty-one sins. Add to that a promise of no divorce, and not having to lie, be secretive, or worry about being found out. Why not?

There was an element in this equation I had not factored in. Guilt. I had never experienced guilt before, and did not realize the degree of guilt and torment I would feel. I did not like guilt. For even though I had permission from my husband, I knew neither God nor the other wife gave theirs, and I was always aware of that fact. Shame, guilt, and torment always exist when any command-ment is broken. From time to time, I would ask my husband to say something to his friend, but he would only tell me, "You got your-self into it, you can get yourself out of it."

About three years into this affair, my husband had a business trip to San Francisco, and I went along. It was there, in San Francisco, that I met business associates and others who spoke about life in a world that was strange to me. I sat in a nightclub filled with what appeared to be men and women, but in reality were only men, some dressed as women. Whorehouses were men-tioned. One gentlemen spoke about how open San Francisco was compared to New York. "Easier to find what you want in San Francisco. Here it is all out in the open."

Someone asked my husband if he had been to a certain night-club on this trip. I remembered the name, looked it up in the yel-low pages, got the address, and said I wanted to go there. At this club, women danced nude and waited tables topless. This was a surprise to me, since my husband had become angry with me once because I had said, "Darn it," which to him was just as bad as swearing. He once refused to join me on a Sunday family picnic because it was a sin to have a picnic on a Sunday. He never played cards or pool because both were also evil and he always claimed to be innocent of this kind of nightclub activity. Someone men-tioned lesbianism (these were college graduates, and I was not) a new word to me. I ignored the conversation, not wanting to show my ignorance.

I became angry, threw a little fit—excuse me, I threw a big fit. I didn't even know I could throw such a big fit. When we got home the fit went on, and my husband, who refused to bring his pastor-father into the discussion, said we should talk to our local minister. He was new, a stranger, since our minister of eleven years had just left. But it was this stranger who explained to me what two men do together, and he said all men do it. I didn't believe him then, but have come to realize he was close to telling me the truth.

Certainly, I am not the only one who has had a shock like this. But for a while, about two years, I wished the earth were flat so I could walk to the edge and step off. If space travel had been perfected, I would have taken my two children to another planet. I felt, and I will put it exactly like I believed then: "This is just too dumb of a place for me to live." I wanted off this earth. I thought of suicide, but would not leave two children without a mother. I would not kill myself and my children, killing was not in me. About that time, I read of a young mother who dropped two small children off a bridge to their death, and I felt I knew exactly what she must have thought. She was making sure her children would reach heaven. My children would have no chance of reaching heaven in this appalling dreadfully disgusting environment. I believed they would be better off dead, not only so they could go to heaven, but also so they would never be sexually perverse.

I divorced my husband, but we remarried in three months. In retrospect, I feel that if there is no physical abuse, remain married as the scriptures say, but let the fornicator leave if he or she wants to. And divorce would not accomplish what I wanted—to protect my children from a wicked father. For he had the means and the legal right to see his children and to take them to see his parents. I could not protect them. When I look at the divorce rate and see the mixed families, I do not believe that is the best thing to do. I settled down to the fact I could not leave this planet, but determined in my heart to stay away from the foolishness.

For me, I began to believe in God. Not the god of today's Christianity, not the god of the sexually perverse, but the God who created the universe. I decided to put my trust in Him. And even though I could not understand what was going on, I would believe that the God who made all things still knows what He is doing. So I'd wait. Watch. Listen. Ask questions. I would find my own answers. And I would leave a church where all men are immoral.

From then on, I decided to take control of my own life, do my own thinking, and not listen to anyone, especially not anyone from the church. The next time I sat in the pew and looked the minister behind the pulpit, I thought, if he believed all men commit oral sex, he must be including himself in that picture. It was at this time I took my membership out of the church, and have never joined one since. I have never registered to vote since then, for I will not vote for the sexually perverse to govern the country I live in.

I said to my partner in adultery, "I'm not half that bad." But I still ended the affair. I locked the front door, stood in plain view, and just said "No." Deciding not to break a commandment is also a premeditated and personal decision. A choice. No one made that decision but me. However, it was many years later before I realized David, the adulterer, would stand with the remnant and not with Adam and Eve, Cain, and Esau in Sodom and Gomorrah, and David wasn't half as bad as those in Sodom and Gomorrah. He was wrinkled but not spotted. I didn't comprehend at the time who the twice dead were. It took me a long time before I thought I had the right to say anything.

It has been thirty-two years since I saw Sodom and Gomorrah. And like King David, I can honestly say that I enjoyed the years I lived blind better then the years since I can see. For the past thirty years I have been exploring the wilderness. It has been a long and sometimes painful journey, but I do believe, with all my heart, it is within the reach of a sanctified church to conquer the wilderness of sin. Priests, when you cross the Jordan (and you must), you will not sit down and declare, "We have arrived," but you will go forth and conquer the land for God. In your blindness, if your motives and desires to recover those who are lost have been honest, God is going to give you the desires of your heart.

From then until the present, I have made a decision not to break the law or any one of the Ten Commandments. I was sorry enough for my sin that I ended it. I crossed the Jordan thirty-two years ago, but today I cross the river again in full view of everyone. When you cross the Jordan, you will not do so in private, nor will you confess your sins under your breath. No one will: "Confess your sins one to another," cannot be done alone or in silence.

CHAPTER TWENTY-EIGHT

Leaving the Wilderness Behind

🙣

S atan has had his day! Now God is going to have His day! The day of the Lord is the day of salvation, when all the earth returns to God. As it so often does, the Bible will speak of the same subject in several different stories and with many different word usages. This is also true of the day of salvation. For example, when you study the Battle of Armageddon, Judgment Day, the fall of Babylon, the end of "the world," crossing the Jordan, peace on earth, the Promised Land, the day of vengeance, the day of the Lord's wrath, and the Kingdom of God, they are all referring to when sin ends and a new day dawns or a new age begins.

Nowhere in the Bible is this day referred to as Doomsday in the sense we have been taught—terrifying, sure destruction of humans. It is the end of wickedness, and the removal of the wicked. When they are judged on Judgment Day, they will tremble as they see the darkness they brought to earth and their great rebellion against God.

In both the Old and the New Testaments the prophets scold the wicked and advise them to return to God. "Therefore also now, saith the Lord, turn ye even to me with all your heart, and with fasting, and with weeping, and with mourning. . . . And turn unto the Lord your God: for he is gracious and merciful, slow to anger, and of great kindness" (Joel 2:12-13). And in the New Testament it is said this way: "He that overcometh shall inherit all things; and I will be his God, and he shall be my son" (Rev. 21:7). Overcoming evil is the key issue of salvation. You cannot return to God without removing all sin from your life.

All the above may be thought of as belonging to a single event at the end of time, when we leave the wilderness of sin. We will have a new age. A holy age. The dawn of a new day.

Literally, in one of our man days, we say it is the darkest before the dawn. Spiritually speaking, it is darkest before the dawn of the next age. Near total darkness will cover the earth before the day of salvation, as it was in the days of Noah. Almost everyone will be wicked. The first light to shine in this all-encompassing darkness of wrongdoing will be the truth Jesus brings, and is why He will be called the bright and morning star. His truth is the first light that shines in the night, signifying the dawn of a pure, sinless age.

God will correct His children. Judgment is for the purpose of correction. If He did not correct us, He would not be treating us as though we were His children. God's judgment and correction are proof that we are his children and He loves us. "As many as I love, I rebuke and chasten: be zealous therefore, and repent" (Rev. 3:19). To rebuke is to scold in a sharp way or to reprimand for the purpose of repentance. "For whom the Lord loveth he chasteneth, and scourgeth every son whom he receiveth. If ye endure chastening, God dealeth with you as with sons" (Heb. 12:6-7).

Those of us from the remnant, as well as those of you from Sodom and Gomorrah, this correction comes from a God who loves His children. All His children. This is not a promise to males only. Many times God will call all males and females His sons. I am not sure why. God will teach right living to His children. "Come, ye children, hearken unto me: I will teach you the fear of the Lord"

(Ps. 34:11). "I will teach you the fear of the Lord" means: I will teach you to hate evil.

"Behold, the day of the Lord cometh . . . to lay the land desolate: and he shall destroy the sinners therefore out of it" (Isa. 13:9). Baptism will achieve the removal of the sinners from our land. God's only plan to destroy the sinner is through baptism. This is good news! The day of the Lord is good news, and when it begins to happen, we should be glad and rejoice in it.

As we are being baptized in the Jordan, repenting of our sins, there is an abundance of advice given to us from the Word of God. We should look at it carefully, for by now we know God gives us good advice.

When the transgressor responds to God's call to be baptized (to repent) it is important to remember confession is not enough. "He that covereth his sins shall not prosper: but whoso confesseth and forsaketh them shall have mercy" (Prov. 28:13). Sin must be uncovered. Stop hiding. Come out into the open. Only those who confess and forsake will have mercy from God. Confess your sins, one to another, and forsake them. While proceeding to do this, we should remember, first, to be kind one to another. "And be ye kind one to another, tenderhearted, forgiving one another, even as God for Christ's sake hath forgiven you" (Eph. 4:32). If God forgives you, you must forgive others, even the ones who may have mistreated you by sexual abuse. We must realize that all fornicators have been under the influence of Satan and are prisoners of sin, slaves bound in chains, unable to recover from the control of evil, captured by lies, and with no deliverance offered until now. Now it is time to return to God, and in so doing be kind, compassionate, and tenderhearted toward each other. Forgive each other. You will be forgiven in the same manner in which you forgive others. "For if ye forgive men their trespasses, your heavenly Father will also forgive you" (Matt. 6:14). Your own forgiveness from God depends upon whether you forgive others.

I listened to a young minister who had been removed from his church because he admitted he had sexually abused two young female members. They were in the process of suing him for the harm he had done them. During the course of the conversation, the minister explained how he, when a youngster, had been molested by an older neighbor boy, and also by an uncle. He could have sued the uncle and the neighbor for the damage they had done to him. It is possible the uncle and the neighbor boy could sue someone who had abused them. When confession of sin begins, and many of these kinds of sins will be revealed, suing is not forgiving. No one should sue anyone. God is telling us to be kind to each other and forgive each other.

A movie for television aired some years ago with the purpose of encouraging children who lived in a sexually abusive home to tell someone. In the movie, when they did tell, the abusive father was removed from the family and put in prison. The children were placed in foster care, and the mother, who had never worked outside the home, could not pay the bills. If I were an abused child watching the movie, I would not have told anyone, for that is not what a child wants. They want the abuse to end, naturally, but not at the expense of seeing the family destroyed. When these types of sin are confessed and the abuse ends, the family should not be destroyed, the father should not be placed in prison, and the children should not leave the home. When sin is ended, none of the above needs to happen. The family members need to forgive and the abuse should never happen again. If Christianity cannot end this sin, then let us forget about peace on earth, for God cannot accomplish it, and the earth will never be a safe place. But God can accomplish it. The child molester can be restored to a perfect relationship with God and society. The reason society has not been able to rehabilitate the sex offender is because the offender has not been instructed to remove original sin from his or her life. Original sin is the source of all our social ills, even child molesting.

Moses put cities of refuge on both sides of the Jordan river, safe places to confess transgressions. Some sins would result in prison sentences for the confessors, if they were known. But when a person becomes a Christian and all sin is ended, there is no need to place anyone in prison. In fact, when those in prison can prove that original sin has ended, that homosexual activity is no longer a part of prison life, and that they can be kind to each other and live in peace, it will be safe to open the iron gates and let the prisoners out. They will no longer be a threat to society. They will have learned love and will have put an end to hate.

Good advice is also given in Luke. "Be ye therefore merciful, as your Father also is merciful. Judge not, and ye shall not be judged: condemn not, and ye shall not be condemned: forgive, and ye shall be forgiven" (6:36-37). It is time to stop judging. Stop condemning. Forgive and be forgiven. Have mercy on one another. Remember the definition of mercy? Pity. Refrain from harming or punishing. No punishment. Kindness in excess of what is deserved. Compassion. God will give mercy to the sinner and the sinner will give mercy to his brother.

More good advice is given to us about how we should think. Control your thoughts, for it was your vain imagination that took you so far into sin. Today they are called fantasies. Members of our society have been acting out all their evil sexual fantasies, and have been encouraged to explore and experiment in this area. This should end. "Finally, brethren, whatsoever things are true, whatsoever things are honest, whatsoever things are just, whatsoever things are pure, whatsoever things are lovely, whatsoever things are of good report; if there be any virtue, and if there be any praise, think on these things" (Phil. 4:8). When I was a teenager, my pastor said that this way: "Be careful what you think about. What you think about today you will be doing tomorrow. So if you find yourself thinking about something you know you should not be doing, stop thinking about it." I consider this to be the best advice I was ever given. Because I have come to learn that a person's thought-life plays a significant role in how he or she lives out their life. Over the years, I have always remembered this advice. From a young age, I have censored what I read, what I will look at, and what I am willing to listen to.

During the time immediately after my return from San Francisco, I was eating lunch with a friend when I said to her, "I have never even thought of oral sex." I felt a wave flow from the base of my neck upward, and a memory surfaced. I had thought of oral sex, probably three or four times, at the age of twelve, thirteen, or fourteen. I can't remember exactly when. And I also remembered what I did about it. The words of my pastor, who said be careful what you think about, came to mind. I also remembered the Bible verse that told me to resist the devil and he will flee from me. And in the unsophisticated manner of a young child I said, "Get away from me, Satan, and leave me alone." Then I determined in my mind never to think of oral sex again. I knew it was wrong without having to be told by anyone. I never thought of it again, and had forgotten I had thought of it at all, until that moment I sat at lunch many years later.

I believe we are born knowing original sin is wrong without having to be told. We are born with the knowledge in us. And sometimes we call this common knowledge plain old horse sense. That is why it causes so much guilt and torment. Being mentally equipped with this knowledge means we are born good and holy. No one becomes unholy until they commit original sin. Only after transgressing the law is a person profane. This profaneness produces a moral sickness, and when an entire civilization believes in being profane, moral sickness permeates our culture.

Another way to look at this is: We are born with the basic truth of what is good and what is evil already in us. As long as this basic truth remains in us, we have God in us. When we commit oral sex, truth leaves us, for we have believed a lie. God is truth, so God is gone. With God gone, holiness is gone. When this lie from Eden is believed, Satan is present.

The generation willing to respond to a call to be baptized, to return to the truth, and to be holy again is given many promises from our heavenly Father. Life, love, purity, holiness, and peace on earth have been mentioned, but it is not possible to list then all. The baptized are also called overcomers, for they are people who have overcome original sin. God's promises to the overcomer are many. Here are but a few:

Victory over the mark of the beast. "And I saw as it were a sea of glass mingled with fire: and them that had gotten the victory over the beast, and over his image, and over his mark, and over the number of his name, stand on the sea of glass, having the harps of God" (Rev. 15:2). It is possible to have victory over the one sin that identifies Satan's people, oral sex, and it is a requirement for entrance into God's presence. The overcomer has victory over original sin, over the mark of the beast.

A promise of a white robe, and your name written in the Book of Life. This is not a literal robe, but the white robe of righteousness, symbolizing purity and cleanliness. Saints are dressed in white linen robes. This garment will replace the filthy rags you wore while living in sin. It will remove the spots of leprosy. And your name will be written in the Lamb's book of life. "He that overcometh, the same shall be clothed in white raiment; and I will not blot out his name out of the book of life" (Rev. 3:5).

God promises to forgive and forget. "For I will be merciful to their unrighteousness, and their sins and their iniquities will I remember no more" (Heb. 8:12). Forgiveness without punishment. I believe this is called a pardon. Your heavenly Father will forget the wicked part of your past.

Eat of the tree of life. "To him that overcometh will I give to eat of the tree of life" (Rev. 2:7).

Eat hidden manna (truth). "To him that overcometh will I give to eat of the hidden manna" (Rev. 2:17).

To be with Jesus and God: "To him that overcometh will I grant to sit with me in my throne, even as I also overcome, and am set down with my Father in his throne" (Rev. 3:21).

Power over nations. "And he that overcometh . . . I will give power over the nations" (Rev. 2:26).

God will be your father, and you will be His son. "He that overcometh shall inherit all things; and I will be his God, and he shall be my son" (Rev. 21:7).

God will answer our prayers. "The Lord is far from the wicked: but he heareth the prayers of the righteous" (Pro. 15:29). God will hear when we pray to Him. When you have overcome sin and have returned to being just, upright, alive, and holy, then pray to God. He will hear you. And when you pray the Lord's Prayer, this is what you are praying for:

The Lord's Prayer
Matthew 6:9-13

**Our Father which art in heaven,
Hallowed be thy name.**

Pray to your Father, saying, HOLY, HOLY, HOLY. You are a Holy Father. Holy is Your name. We acknowledge and now recognize Your holiness, God, and we bow to You, our Holy Creator. (Hallowed means holy.)

Thy kingdom come.

Please bring Your holy kingdom to earth. Jesus tells us, "My kingdom is not of 'this world' and we now understand what that means. We know Your kingdom, God, has no fornication in it, and we pray for a earth with no sexual perverseness in it. Yes, we earnestly pray: Thy kingdom come!

Thy will be done

Let Your will, oh Holy God, be done on earth. Let all of mankind bow to Your holiness and keep Your commandments. It is Your will that no one perishes, and it is also our prayer that no one will perish.

in earth, as it is in heaven.

Let all the earth do Your will just as it is done in heaven, for it is then the earth will be holy and like heaven. Heaven on earth. We are ready for a new heaven and a new earth for we see our foolishness.

Give us this day our daily ¹bread.

The cross-reference that defines bread is speaking of spiritual truth as the following verse shows. "Remove far from me vanity and lies: give me neither poverty nor riches; feed me with food convenient for me" (¹Prov. 30:8). Give us food for the mind. Give us truth, not lies. We do not want to be fed falsehoods any longer. We are a nation of people who have put our trust in how well we can lie. Deceit is everywhere. We pledge to end our belief in lies. Give us bread from heaven, the word of God, manna, for this is now what we want. As the day of the Lord dawns, we will unstop our ears; we can see, we can hear, and we will listen.

And forgive us our debts,

Oh, Holy Father, forgive all of us, for all have broken one

. or more of the Ten Commandments, and forgive all who have committed original sin. We understand all offenses must be forsaken before Your forgiveness will come to us, and we comprehend the promise that when sin is forsaken, You are faithful and will forgive us just as You have promised. You will pardon us. No punishment.

as we forgive our debtors.

We promise to forgive all those who forsake sin just as You have forgiven us. We will follow Your example of forgiveness. We will pardon others, also.

And lead us not into temptation,

Lead us out of the wilderness. There will be a time when temptation is not a part of everyday life, as it is here in the wilderness.

but deliver us from evil:

Deliver us from all evil. Give us the power to be over-comers. Give us victory in Jesus. Deliver us from original sin which is the root of all wrongdoing. Lead us out of the wilderness where sin is everywhere to where it is no more. We understand it is within our power to control our minds and forsake evil habits.

For thine is the kingdom,

For Your kingdom is the only kingdom we want on earth. It is the only honest and good kingdom accompanied by kindness and integrity. We know Your kingdom will bring peace and happiness to earth and end all misery. We do not see the kingdom of Satan, "the world," as being the kingdom we want any longer. There is only one good God. There is only one true God and we acknowledge You to be that God. Have mercy on us. Forgive us. Show kindness toward us. Be our God, and bring Your kingdom to earth.

and the power,

There is a negative destructive power of evil which comes from sin, and a positive profitable power of good which comes from You, God. It is your positive power of good which we desire. Your kingdom has all power and might and You deserve to rule the earth. Good is more powerful than evil, and we know You can overpower evil. You are the all-powerful God, and deserve our honor and praise which we prove only by our obedience to Your laws.

and thy glory, for ever."

God's glory is His goodness. Your kingdom is full of goodness. Let Your kingdom of goodness reign on earth, and give goodness to all Your children forever and ever more. Let goodness be our standard always. End evil.

Amen.

Truly. We are serious, eager. We understand what we are asking, and after considerable deliberation and careful examination of Your truth, we will adjust our lives to meet Your requirements for being a holy people. We will forsake all sin, for we strongly desire Your kingdom to replace the kingdom of Satan's world on earth.

Let it be so!

CHAPTER TWENTY-NINE

Physical Death

I have directly or indirectly answered all the questions I asked in the preface, except one, and that is, "What happens when we die a physical death?"

The falsehood we have listened to so many times about how we will come out of the grave someday is just that, a fable. The primary reason for the spread of this misconception comes from having no knowledge of original sin. Without this wisdom man depended on the Ten Commandments to explain sin. Then, because Scripture tells us Jesus was without sin, He could not have died from a sin. This left no other explanation for His death but to explain it in a literal way, resulting in a belief that Jesus' death was physical. The next logical conclusion could only be He came back to life after physical death, resurrected from the dead.

This myth will continue as long as original sin remains a mystery. But when the mystery is solved and the weightier matters of the Garden Law go out, it will open up our understanding, and offer new insight revealing another plausible explanation to the death and resurrection of Jesus. Then this old tale will lose its credibility.

With an answer given to what is original sin comes an understanding of beams and splinters, camels and gnats, and spots and wrinkles. From this additional information will emerge a spiritual explanation of how Jesus was raised from the dead. Yes, Jesus could be without spot (original sin) and still have a wrinkle. Therefore, He could die a spiritual death on the cross from a wrinkle and come out of the grave at His baptism, raised from the dead.

"And you hath he quickened [made alive], who were dead in trespasses and sins" (Eph. 2:1). Those who are dead from spots (Sodom and Gomorrah, the unjust) and those who are dead from wrinkles (the remnant, the just) are made alive again when sins end. You have been raised from the dead. I have found no proof we will be raised from the dead twice, once at our baptism and again after physical death.

So what happens when we die physically? I began my thinking on this topic back in the sixties when I acted out this play in my mind. Three infants were born on the same day just prior to the day of salvation. One died having lived three hours, the second died a sinner at the age of twenty-five in an accident, and the third, who also committed original sin, lived to be ninety years of age. He lived to see Jesus come to earth and bring salvation. He repented and was delivered from sin, became an overcomer, and then realized all the promises given to the overcomers.

Our present-day Christianity would tell us the infant (with special provisions made by God) would go to heaven. The one who died wicked would go to hell, and the oldest one who lived to see Jesus would go to heaven. If this were true, we should all be so lucky and die an infant so we will be sure to go to heaven. The twenty-five year old could surely stand up and scream and holler that he was treated unfairly. For if he had died an infant, he could spend forever in heaven, and if he could have lived as long as the other, he could have repented and gone to heaven. He had no control over his birth or death, but had he been able to choose he most certainly would not have chosen to die a sinner.

This analogy is not fair to any of us. Is it fair for a person to live on earth three hours and go to heaven for eternity having never experienced one temptation, while others spend years on earth and are exposed to a variety of temptations and evils? No! Is it fair to be born into a wicked society and die before salvation is offered, while others live longer or are born at a later time when God moves to save mankind? No! Obviously this is not fair, nor is it a correct way to look at life and death.

Consider this: Between the Garden of Eden and peace on earth lies the wilderness of sin. Therefore, all the people who have died since Adam and Eve have died in the wilderness of sin. They have died under the old covenant before they were offered deliverance from evil. Some died holy; some died profane. They died before Jesus brought deliverance. Will all those who died profane miss heaven? No!

As we approach the end of this wilderness, darkness covers the earth as it did in the days of Noah, and almost everyone on the planet is a transgressor. This is a big earth. When you stop to think of the number of people who die each day, the number is large, and the majority of them are dying sinners. Does this mean all today's dying sinners will miss heaven? No! Will they go to the eternal hell we have been conditioned to believe in by today's Christianity? No! Will all the infants who have died spend all eternity in heaven having never been tempted? No.

If this last animal-look-alike, grossly carnal, brazenly defiant, proud, and blind generation is the chosen generation to see the light and move out of the wilderness and experience an end to sin on earth, is that fair to all who have died before this generation? No! Wouldn't it be wonderful if all our relatives were alive to experience the light, forgiveness, deliverance, and a full pardon from God, for certainly most of them were no worse than most of us. Is it fair for only one generation to have such favor with God? No!

A better understanding of what happens when we die would

provide answers to what is fair for everyone. The following passage offers us valuable insight. "Then shall the dust return to the earth as it was: and the spirit shall return unto God who gave it" (Ecc. 12:7). Here are two basic truths about physical death, and both must be believed:

1) **When we die, our flesh and blood returns to the dust of the earth.** Man has not faced this fact. We are made out of the same ingredients found in the soil: water, carbon, calcium, iron, phosphorous, etc. All living things, trees, grass, insects, animals, and humans, are designed that way for a purpose. So they will be biodegradable. If this were not so, if dead things were composed of a chemical or ingredient other than that found in the soil, pollution would occur. Grass, vegetables, and trees could not grow. Food suitable for human and animal consumption would disappear from the planet. But God did not make an earth that would pollute itself. It is man who pollutes the earth spiritually with his man-made inventions and literally with waste and chemicals. And so, as all living things do, the human body returns to the dust of the earth after death. This is acceptable, and we should not be frightened by this fact. Believe it.

2) **The spirit returns to the God who gave it.** The spirit returns. It returns to God! Now look into the grave. The body is dust to be added to the soil, and the spirit is with God—gone! What could possibly come out of the grave? Nothing! The grave is empty. Our ancestors are not in the ground waiting for that great resurrection morning when they will rise up out of the graves and be judged.

Our spirit returns to God. It is not possible to return to a place where you have never been; therefore, it is apparent that we begin our existence in the presence of God before we come to earth. The spirit was brought into existence in heaven and will return to heaven to live when it leaves the body at the point of physical death. Our bodies were conceived on earth and will return to the earth at the point of physical death, for our bodies do not live forever.

I attended a funeral of my husband's uncle whom I did not know very well. At the viewing of the body, I had visited with family members and went to sit down in a pew to let them continue their visiting. As I sat there the corner of the sanctuary, the ceiling and walls disappeared, and opened up a large opening in what appeared to be a gray sky. In the middle of the opening was the face of this uncle. No words were spoken, but by transfer of thought he said, "Don't worry about me, I am okay." Then he was gone and the room was normal again. For a moment I could see both parts of him, the body in the casket that will return to dust and evidence that the spirit had returned to God. He had already left his body and the part of him that will live forever was on its way to God.

We existed before our mortal body was birthed. And we will continue to exist after we leave our bodies here on earth when we die a physical death. It is at death, that both halves of us return to the place they originated from, the spirit to heaven and the body to the soil—dust.

Most believe in life after death, but it is just as important to believe in life before birth. Humans reproduce humans, and the temporal body is a dwelling place for a spirit. Humans are the only life forms designed to house a spirit. God reproduces spirits. That is why He is our Mother and our Father. Spirits come to earth and live in a human temple.

Today's Christianity has been stubbornly opposed to the idea that a spirit can come to earth more than once—reincarnation. And they base their opposition on the erroneous reasoning that our bodies will be resurrected from the grave after physical death and reunited with our spirit.

But if we believe God, the body decomposes and eventually becomes part of the soil again, dust. We begin our existence with God, come to earth, live in a human body, and then return to God when that body can no longer sustain life. Logically, it is possible for the spirit to come to earth more than once. In fact, it is very logical. The body of the infant who lived for three hours will return to the dust, the spirit will return to God, and then it will come to earth again. The body of the young sinner who died at the age of twenty-five will return to the dust, and his spirit will return to God and then come to earth again. There is no reason to oppose the idea of the spirit returning to earth more than once, and being housed in a different human being, through reincarnation. From heaven's point of view it would only be fair for each spirit to spend the same amount of time on earth and to also experience heaven on earth.

If this wicked generation is the chosen generation to see the light and move out of the wilderness and experience an end to evil on earth, is that fair to all who have died before this generation? No! Wouldn't it be wonderful if all our relatives were alive to experience the light, forgiveness, deliverance, and a full pardon from God, for certainly most of them were no worse than most of us. Is it fair for only one generation to have such favor with God? No!

God will conclude the world in wickedness, for all are dead in sin and sins, and so it will be a perverse generation that will be the chosen ones to see the light. A generation in its entirety will return to God and obey His laws creating a paradise on earth. All the spirits who began with the Father in heaven will be on earth in this last generation and will see a new heaven and a new earth. Yes, all our ancestors will be here. This is fair to everyone.

Glossary

Adultery: 1) Between two humans: all sexual activity outside of the marriage commitment. 2) Between God and a human: leaving God to follow Satan by committing oral sex. This can be done with your spouse.

Antichrist: Against or instead of God. The unjust (the sexually perverse) are unlike Christ and stand against a just Jesus. Collectively the unjust make up the body of the antichrist.

Babylon: Confusion. A spiritual city of whoring which includes all those who have committed original sin. Another word for Sodom and Gomorrah and the world.

Baptism: Openly and willingly confessing and repenting of sin and removing all sin from your life. Being washed clean by the word of God.

Blaspheme: To insult God to the degree He will leave you. Oral sex blasphemes God, and He leaves you. This sin also insults your own intelligence.

Born again: After Baptism (repenting and ending sin) you have returned to the spiritual state you were in when you were physically birthed, holy.

Bread: Truth from God is food for the mind.

Christian: A person who believes Jesus is sent from God, believes what He says, is baptized, and follows His teachings.

Clouds: People are likened to clouds; some have water (truth, the holy spirit) and some do not.

Commandment: When used in the singular is speaking of the one set given in the Garden of Eden.

Covenant, the new: Jesus will write this first law from Eden in your minds, (you will know it by heart), and you will learn to obey it. God will take the disobedient back, forgive, and forget the sin when the sinner repents and stops ignoring His law.

Covenant, the old: God gave one law in the Garden to man-kind and if we obey we remain His sons. But if we disobey He leaves and we are the children of Satan. No provision was made under the old covenant for a person to return to God.

Cross: Everyone has one. They are made of original sin and/or the sins each of us have committed. Everyone has died on a cross.

Darkness, spiritual: The law is light, so when it is missing from earth, the earth is in spiritual darkness.

Dead: Spiritual death occurs when the laws of God are disobeyed.

Dead, twice: The sexually perverse are twice dead. Their sin is more weighty.

Doctrine: A belief. Jesus comes to earth with the law from Eden. He will write it in your minds. It is the doctrine that all His teaching is based on.

Drunkenness: Fornication causes a spiritual drunkenness.

Eden, the Garden of: In the beginning when life on earth was perfect. No original sin.

Elements: The foundation on which a belief is based.

Evil: Oral sex is evil, evil in the sight of God, and those who commit it have been deceived by Satan and are evil.

Fable: When a spiritual truth is storied to us literally.

Fire: The law from Eden is a fire. When breaking the law a person dies in a fire. When keeping the law a person is refined by this same law of fire.

Foolish, the: Sodom and Gomorrah are the foolish. Adam and Eve were the first fools.

Fools: All those who were deceived by Satan and committed original sin are the fools of the Bible.

Forgiveness: To end the anger and resentment toward another.

Not having the desire to punish.

Fornication: Defines the sex of Sodom and Gomorrah.

Glory: Goodness.

God: The creator of all things. The author of all truth. The authority over us. Our heavenly Father.

Gods, false: The people of Sodom and Gomorrah who have exalted themselves above God and have made up their own truth, becoming gods of falsehoods.

Good: The opposite of evil. Good people do not believe in original sin. Evil people do.

Happiness: Comes from hating evil (original sin) and departing from it.

Heaven: Earth will be a new heaven when we return to living like we should live, without sin.

Hell: All those in Sodom and Gomorrah (Babylon, the world) are in a hell. They create a hell on earth.

Holiness: Living without original sin in your life.

Holy: The opposite of profane. Profane people commit oral sex. Holy people do not.

Holy Spirit: Truth. When the truth is in you, you have the holy spirit in you. When spoken it will go everywhere.

Hypocrite: Any person who practices original sin and then claims to be a Christian, to be like Christ.

Idolatry: Serving a god other than God. Following Satan is idolatry. The sexually perverse have made false gods of themselves and live in idolatry serving each other.

Image: We are created in the image of God. Original sin will change a person into an image of a beast, fish, bird, or creeping thing.

Imaginations: God gave Sodom and Gomorrah over to vain imaginations. Fantasies of evil.

Jerusalem, the New: In the last days we will have a new Christianity built by the just, and many beliefs will change. The new covenant goes out from this holy church.

Jerusalem, the Old: The Christianity on earth before Jesus, when the false Christs deceived so many people. It was built by the unjust and is vain.

Jesus: A just person. He comes with truth. He was sent from God to bring the unjust back to God.

Judge: A person qualified to settle controversy, to declare the law, and to decide the worth of anything. Jesus comes as a judge.

Judgment: The act of declaring the law and setting a standard for the purpose of correction. Jesus will explain the worth of sin, and settle the controversy man is having with God over evil.

Just: Just people are those who have not committed oral sex.

Justified: When those who have committed original sin return to being just, then they will be called the justified. They are just again.

Kill: Sin kills. You kill others when you ask them to commit original sin.

Kingdom of God: A time on earth when no one commits evil. There is no sexual perverseness in the Kingdom of God.

Law: When used in the singular, refers to the one law given in the Garden of Eden.

Laws: The Ten Commandments.

Leprosy: All who have committed original sin have spiritual leprosy. They have spots.

Light, spiritual: The law from Eden is spiritual light.

Literal: Not seeing the spiritual or symbolic meaning of the scriptures.

Lost: To be away from God and unable to find your way back. The sexually perverse are the lost.

Mark of the beast: Oral sex. It is the one sin that identifies Satan's followers.

Mediator: A person who settles a dispute between two parties. Jesus will settle the dispute man is having with God.

Mercy: Pity with a helping hand to lift the wicked up.

Overcome: To remove original sin from your life.

Parable: When an object or idea we know literally, such as a door, bread, or journey, is used in story form to explain a spiritual concept.

Pardon: No punishment for wrongdoing.

Profane: The opposite of holy. All those who have committed oral sex are profane. They are not holy.

Promised Land: Peace on earth. Life without sin.

Raised from the dead: 1) When the unjust return to God and have removed original sin from their lives, they can say they have been raised from the dead. 2) When the just repent of breaking one or more of the Ten Commandments they will be raised from the dead.

Redemption: To redeem or regain what once belonged to you. Jesus comes to redeem those who Satan stole from God.

Remnant: The few who are left at the end of this age who were not deceived by Satan and did not commit original sin.

Repent: Remorse over your disobedience to the point you end the wrongdoing.

Rudiments: The foundation of a subject learned. You had to learn original sin to join the world. Oral sex is the foundation Satan built "the world" on.

Salvation: When a person removes sin from his or her life as a result of following Jesus. The human race is saved from living forever in sin one person at a time.

Sanctification: Abstaining from fornication is how you get sanctified, made holy. You are holy again when original sin is no longer part of your life.

Sin: Breaking the Garden Law. When used in the singular, sin usually refers to the original sin of Adam and Eve.

Sin nature: Everything has a nature. Sin does also. It is the properties by which you identify it. We are not born with a sin nature. No Scripture tells us we have a sin nature.

Sin, original: Oral sex.

Spot: Always refers to original sin. The spots are a sign of spiritual leprosy.

Sodom and Gomorrah: All those who commit original sin, including husbands and wives who consent to commit oral sex within their marriage.

Stone: The commandments are written in stone. You can use these stones to slay the wicked.

Ten Commandments: Ten laws from God everyone should obey for the good of mankind. The commandments were written twice. One set, all ten, is broken when original sin is committed. The other set can be disobeyed one at a time.

Thorns: All humans who commit original sin are likened to thorns. They are people who hurt people.

Truth: The words of God and of Jesus, for they agree on truth.

Unjust: All humans who commit original sin are the unjust.

Vain: Empty, of no value, having no effect.

Victory: Refers to having victory over sin, original sin. Defined as victory over the mark of the beast.

Virgin: 1) In regards to God, a man or a woman who have never engaged in sexual perverseness, oral and anal sex. You can be married with children and still be a virgin. 2) In regards to mankind, a man or a woman who have engaged neither in intercourse nor sexual perverseness.

Water: Truth is spiritual water. Symbolic of the Holy Ghost.

Whore: All people, males and females, who commit oral sex.

Whoredoms: The practice of being a whore.

Wilderness of sin: A time of sinning. The time between the two lands when humans lived and will live again without sinning, Eden and peace on earth. We are presently living in the wilderness of sin.

Wine of fornication: The sex of Sodom and Gomorrah is likened to wine and causes a spiritual drunkenness on earth.

Wisdom: Living in obedience to the Garden Law is the beginning of wisdom.

Witness: Everyone is a witness. Your life, not your words, will testify if you serve God or Satan.

World, the: This is the world of fornication, whoring. All those who commit oral sex live in "the world."

Wrinkles: They are a result of breaking one of the Ten Commandments we are so familiar with.

Index

ORDER INFORMATION

Telephone orders:
>Bookmasters 1-(800)-247-6553 toll free
>*Please have your credit card ready*

E-mail your request to:
>order@Bookmaster.com
>*OR*
>http://www.atlasbooks.com/marktplc/00541.htm

Postal orders:
>Bookmasters
>P.O. Box 388
>Ashland, OH 44805
>*Please enclose check, money order, or credit card information*

Please send the following number of books: _____
I may return any of them for a full refund—for any reason, no questions asked.

Name: _____

Address: _____

City: _____ State: _____ Zip: _____

Telephone: _____

Sales tax: WA and OH residents include applicable sales tax.
Shipping: within the United States $4.00 per single book
Inquire about quantity discounts for large orders.

Payment: ❏ Check ❏ Credit card:

❏ Visa ❏ Master Card ❏ AMEX ❏ Discover

Card number: _____

Name on Card: _____ Exp.Date ___ / ___